Happy Birthday Son

THE HUMAN ENIGMA

AHMED HULUSI
www.ahmedhulusi.org/en/

As with all my works, this book is not copyrighted.
As long as it remains faithful to the original,
it may be freely printed, reproduced, published and translated.
For the knowledge of ALLAH, there is no recompense.

THE HUMAN ENIGMA

AHMED HULUSI

www.ahmedhulusi.org/en/

Translated by ALIYA ATALAY

I dedicate this book to all my enlightened brothers and sisters around the world who have reached the Reality and are experiencing the One.

Ahmed HULUSI

Inquisition is half of knowledge.

Muhammad (saw)

"Say: My Rabb, increase my knowledge."

Quran 20:114

"Do you still not reflect?"

Quran 6:50

To Hadhrat Ali (r.a.):

"...Be close to Allah with your intellect!.."

(Hadith)

Be not of the creatures who live with their eyes, but of the wise ones who evaluate with insight!

Ahmed HULUSI

This book has been penned for those who reflect.

Ahmed HULUSI

TRANSLATOR'S PREFACE

The Human Enigma is probably the most comprehensive book, in all aspects, on the mysterious and profound make-up of man and his perpetual journey. From the formation of the brain and the illusory 'compositional' identity, to the zodiacal signs and their effects on mankind, from fate and purpose, to the stages and conditions of Doomsday and the infinite afterlife, from the science behind the pillars of Islam and the recommended practices, to the Absolute Oneness and Unity of existence, nothing is left unexplained.

Given the biggest cause of religious misunderstanding and divergence is the failure to correctly decode the metaphoric and symbolic language used in religious scriptures, Ahmed Hulusi sheds invaluable light to this ambiguity with the lamp of science, bringing immense clarity to the confused intellectual, leaving no questions unanswered.

It's an enormous advantage to have access to this perspective as for many years the biggest fallout for the modern man has been the seemingly contradictory or unreasonable claims made by religious teachings. *The Human Enigma* deciphers and elucidates this vagueness and dubiety with so much depth and detail, that ultimately the enigma is transformed to plain truth.

This is a book on the human truth.

If you've been questioning, wondering and seeking the truth of your existence, and like Rumi 'wanting to know reasons' then you're at the right door:

"I have lived on the lip of insanity, wanting to know reasons, knocking on a door.

It opens...

I've been knocking from the inside."

(Rumi)

Enjoy the journey to your Self, from your self...

ALIYA ATALAY
14 July 2021
Istanbul

CONTENTS

INTRODUCTION

What is the purpose of religion?

What is the scientific basis of religion?

Why must we believe in the hereafter?

What exactly is this phenomenon called "human"?

How was it formed? Which effects and conditions is it subject to and what is it capable of creating?

What are the realities behind the recommended religious practices?

Where did humans come from? Why and how did they come and where are they going?

The universe, humans, life after death…

This book aims to provide answers to these and other such questions.

The brain is an invaluable and irreplaceable human treasure.

There are infinite qualities embedded in the brain of which we are unaware.

You will find different and perhaps even controversial perspectives in this book regarding such topics.

I aimed to focus on two main perspectives in this book:

1. The external (*zahir*) realities of religion.
2. The internal (*batin*) reality religion aims to disclose to man.

Most of the contents in this book are adapted from the recordings of conversations we had in the 1984. You may want to read some parts more than once, as the topics may be hard to understand. It's been prepared for those who contemplate!

I have nothing to say for those who follow the path of suffice themselves with imitation. My call is for the people of REALITY.

"Man's honor is in his intellect!"

As a result of all my 23 yearlong research I'm presenting the knowledge Allah has bestowed me in this book. The external aspect of the knowledge I share here is based on the Hadith Collections, such as the *Kutub-u Sitte*, and the teachings of eminent Sufi saints and scholars.

The internal aspect comprises my personal observations and insights as the blessings and endowment of Allah…

Nobody is perfect. I too may make mistakes. However, I would like to emphasize on the fact that all research and study done rests on the teachings of the Rasul of Allah (saw) in light of modern science.

If at any point you feel I'm saying something contrary or contradictory to the Quran or Hadith, please immediately disregard my words and live by the Quran and Hadith instead. For we are all liable to follow the Rasul of Allah (saw); we will all be called to account for this in the life after death.

I covered a great deal of astrology from a religious perspective, due to its close link to fate. Astrology is a crucial tool to know one's self. In regards to its predictions of future events and fortune telling however it is invalid. For there are so many countless factors to consider that even the most advanced computers can't compute it with accuracy.

In Ghazali's '*Ihya'u Ulumud'deen*' it is narrated from Ibn Abbas (r.a.): "*If I were to interpret the verse 'It is Allah who created the seven heavens, and of the earth, the like of them. His command continually manifests among them...*'" *indeed, you would stone me*", and in another narration, he says, "You would announce me a disbeliever!"

Another narration is from Abu Hurairah (r.a.), one of the closest of the Rasul's followers, who says, "*I received two vessels of knowledge from the Rasul of Allah (saw), I gave one of them away, as for the other one, if I were to dare to open its lid, you would behead me!*"

---

[1] Quran 65:12

What could these secrets be that cost the lives and reputation of even the most learned amongst the followers of the Rasul?

Let us know this for sure:

Religion is not a superficial list of rights and wrongs as most think it is.

There are such SECRETS in religion that can change entire lives in an instant. This knowledge is for brains with advanced contemplation capabilities.

So, let us abandon the limitations of the five-sense world and aspire to reach the most honorable station of vicegerency for which Allah has created us.

And let us never forget that there is never a chance to return to this world. Whatever we can gain right now is what we will have to suffice with for eternity!

May Allah give us the knowledge to enable the realization of the reality and the ability to live by it.

Ahmed Hulusi
17.10.1986
Istanbul

THE THIRD EDITION

I had covered topics in this book that are not generally discussed openly or easily found in books. Besides those who refused it based solely on their conditionings and with no proof of contrary claims, there was an enormous demand and interest in this book, which I based on the Quran and Hadith. All success is from Allah.

I want to take the opportunity in this third reprint to answer some frequently asked questions:

1. I'm not after any personal fame or success, this is why I don't write my surname but only my first name in my books.

   Allah willing, I will continue to share my knowledge via books in the future.

2. I don't approve using the knowledge of Allah for worldly material gain.

   This knowledge cannot be copyrighted in my opinion as it is universal knowledge. Also, according to an authentic Hadith in Bukhari, someone taught another person how to read the Quran and in return was given a bow as a gift. When the Rasul of Allah (saw) heard of this he said if you accept this gift it will be a bow of fire in the hereafter and be hung on your neck as a necklace."

   Based on this, I believe religious knowledge should be shared unrequitedly.

   Hence, as long as they remain loyal to its original, anyone can print, publish and sell any and all my books.

3. I don't have much to say to the grudging skeptical ones who refuse the truth that the Sun will engulf the earth and the earth will evaporate in its heat, simply because they've never heard this before, even though it is narrated in hadith.

   The verse that talks about the light of the sun becoming extinguished is in reference to a later stage when the sun will become a neutron star.

Let us remember these are not events that will transpire in a single day; it will take millions of years. According to Hadith, the "*sirat*" (bridge), the time when the spirits will escape the world alone is said to last a journey of three thousand years.

4. The most misunderstood and unfathomed truth is the reality of FATE! Here I present all the verses and Hadith, if after this you still can't comprehend the truth I have nothing further to say.

Ahmed Hulusi
20. 5. 1988
Antalya

THE 11th EDITION

Infinite gratitude to Allah after a great demand we've printed the 11th edition, I believe and hope that our success will grow even further...

No matter how much I thank my Rabb for blessing me with this book and allowing me to systematically share the truth of religion, from its most simple and superficial to its most in-depth level, it means nothing.

I hope the value of this book will be understood better in time. Unfortunately, the schools of religion are not giving adequate education to enable the understanding of such topics. My hope and wish are for Islam to be approached holistically, as it was during the times of the Rasul of Allah (saw), rather than like touching different parts of an elephant to decipher what it is!

I pray that Allah grants us all mercy, consideration and true discernment.

Ahmed Hulusi
20.2.1995
Antalya

1

THE PILLARS OF ISLAM

The religion of Islam begins with believing in Muhammad Mustapha (saw)! For we are bound to have faith in Allah, *as Muhammad (saw) informed us*, not the imaginary god we've created and formed in our heads and labeled "Allah."

If you were to conduct a little research in your circle you would see that everyone has a different understanding and conception of the word Allah. Despite the common points based on societal and cultural conditioning, there are still surprising differences.

This is why the first thing we must believe is Muhammad's (saw) claim, ***"I am the Rasul of Allah!"***

If and when we submit to and unconditionally believe in the Rasul of Allah (saw) whose teachings are applicable to all ages until doomsday, and who invited us to have faith in Allah the way he taught us to, we will have entered the circle of faith.

However, his teachings must be accepted wholly and unconditionally, without sparing anything. For if you accept some of his teachings and refuse others your faith will not be true, and its consequence will be detrimental.

The second thing is to understand the science behind the five mandatory pillars of Islam.

Have these pillars been established for the sake of "testing" people or do they actually have some scientific basis, involving the laws of physics and chemistry?

The being referred to as a human has the capacity to think and act on his thoughts. So, if he is to be asked to do something then obviously he will need to be presented with the reasons as to why he should do it, so that he may understand and make sense of it.

A human can't be asked to act on something about which he has no knowledge. First the knowledge is given then the request to act based on that knowledge.

In summary, Muhammad (saw) tells us the following regarding the application of the five pillars of Islam:

The earth and everything within it will be cast into hell during doomsday. The "tasting" or experience of death will not render you non-existent; you will continue to live forever. Once you experience death you will never have the chance to return to this world.

If you take heed of these teachings and prepare wisely for the life after death you will reach heaven with the grace of Allah. If on the other hand you don't prepare for the hereafter but spend all your time and energy for things you will inevitably have to leave behind with death, then your inescapable destination will be hell, with earth.

If you go to hell you will stay there forever and can never come out. Those who go to heaven on the other hand will never again fear going to hell. Those who don't heed this warning of Allah and work only for this world will most definitely feel deep regret in the future but it will be too late.

This world is the only abode of preparation for the life after death.

After death there is absolutely no way of coming back to this world to make up for anything. So, believe in Allah and this reality.

Based on this warning the minimal of what is asked of us is to:

Pray five times a day (total of 17 *rakahs*).

Fast one month a year during Ramadan.

Go to pilgrimage, at least once in your lifetime, if you have the financial means.

Give alms (*zakah*).

2

EARTH'S FINAL DESTINATION

We're living on a planet one million three hundred thousand times smaller than the sun with a diameter roughly around 12,500 km. Our known distance from the sun right now is approximately 150 million km.

We orbit around this massive scorching star at a speed of 108 thousand km/hour.

The solar flames emitted by the sun are known to reach heights of around 800 thousand km. In other words, you'd have to place 60 earths on top of another and place them on the Sun's surface to reach the height of a single solar flame!

The latest data tells us the heat of the sun's surface is around 6000-Celsius degrees!

What does 6000 degrees even mean?

Think of this as an example:

The most heat resistant element on earth is cadmium, as far as we know. It turns into liquid at 6000 degrees. So, if earth and everything on it were made of cadmium everything would liquidize at 6000 degrees and then eventually evaporate and disappear.

Let's remember what Muhammad (saw) says:

"The earth and everything within it will evaporate like a single water drop when it is thrown into hell!"

Indeed, the sun is 1,300,000 times bigger than the earth and the heat in in its core is 15 million degrees. Right now, it is our source of life.

But where did the sun come from and where is it going?

According to modern theory the solar system was a cloud of gas without a particular form. There was no real sun or nuclear energy. This gas was comprised of hydrogen, that is two thirds of what makes up a water molecule.

In time this cloud of gas started to assume form and its heat started to increase. But there was still no sun. As the pressure of the gas increased the part most prone to the pressure started to form a core. This central point, which started to give out radiation, was the crux of the sun.

As the light of the sun increased the homogenous make-up of the gas started to change and the pressure started to localize at particular points. These points then started drawing various elements from their surroundings to eventually form the planets. As the proto planets continued to grow their geomagnetic forces grew stronger and they drew more material from their vicinity. Meanwhile the suns radiant energy was also increasing but the solar system had not yet been completely formed.

As the main proto planets continued growing and strengthening their geomagnetic forces, drawing more and more material from their surroundings they began to form tangible shapes. Meanwhile thermonuclear reactions started taking place in the sun. After this very long process of proto-planet formation the solar system took its current shape and the sun stationed in its current orbit.

Every star has its own fate, that is, a destined time of birth, growth, and death.

The massive star we call the sun will also change; it'll burn its hydrogen fuel out and turn it into helium. Eventually its core will become so constricted that its surface will be forced to expand.

The Sun has already begun to turn into a red giant star. Its volume is continually increasing and this energy is already swallowing up the planets in its proximity.

As the heat in its core continues to rise the sun will eventually run out of its hydrogen fuel and begin to fuse helium. It'll grow to such a massive extent, both in heat and in size, that it'll engulf the earth with its heat and totally annihilate it.

At this point the sun will be a gigantic ball of fire 400 million times bigger than earth. This is beyond imagination!

Various reactions that take place within the Sun will cause the heat in its core to increase even further leading to the end of most planets in the solar system.

After all the nuclear energy is used up and the sun completely runs out of fuel it will suddenly begin to shrink and eventually become a dwarf star, though it will continue to shine for some time further.

Thus, is the predicted fate of the earth and the sun based on the latest science of the 80's.

3

"THE SUN WILL SWALLOW THE EARTH!"

There is an authentic Hadith (Muslim - Tirmidhi) regarding the heat of doomsday.

Miqdad bin Aswad (ra) narrates:

"The Rasul of Allah (saw) said:

'During doomsday the sun will be brought near to mankind until the distance between them is equal to a mile.

The heat of the sun will almost melt them and the people will begin to sweat according to their deeds. Some up to their hills, some up to their knees, some up to their waste and some will drown in their sweat!'

Soloman bin Amr (ra) who narrated this Hadith also added, 'I don't know if the word 'mile' was used in reference to the unit of distance or the stick used to apply kohl to the eyes (meel)'."

In truth, it does not really matter which was intended, the results remain the same.

This is a miracle!

Think of the level of knowledge of the people of Mecca 1400 years ago. While most of the people in the world at that time were thinking the earth is flat with no substantial knowledge about the sun and its nature, the Rasul of Allah claimed:

"The sun is going to envelop the earth such that there is only going to be a mile between them!"

Most people aren't even aware of this truth today!

Here is another Hadith from Bayhaki:

Ibn Masud (ra) narrates from the Rasul of Allah (saw):

"When the people are resurrected they will wait with their eyes fixed on the sky for forty years. Nothing will be said to them. The sun will be right above them and it will burn them. Everyone, good and bad, will wait in this state with sweat up to their heads."

Those who claim on doomsday the stars are going to fall from the heavens and the sun is going to black out are proven wrong with this Hadith. The sun will black out many years after it becomes a giant red star and shrinks to become a dwarf neutron star. This process occurs long after the period of doomsday.

This Hadith clearly verifies the science that the sun will eventually engulf the earth yet we are still looking for a hell in some imaginary faraway place!

4

WHAT IS HELL?

What is hell and how is it described?

Here's how Abdullah bin Masud (ra) narrates how hell will engulf and swallow the earth: "The Rasul of Allah (saw) said;

'On that day hell will be brought near. It will have seventy thousand bonds and seventy thousand angels pulling each one'."

Everyone without exception is going to pass through the fire, or radiation, of hell that's going to encircle and besiege the earth.

And there is none among you who He will not pass through (experience) **Hell! This is, by your Rabb, a definite decree.**

Then We will save those who protected themselves (who exhibit the forces that become manifest as a result of living ones' reality) **and leave the transgressors on their knees!**[2]

Indeed, Hell has become a place of passage (everyone will pass from it).[3]

It is then that Hell will be brought (to enclose the earth)!**[4]

---

[2] Quran 19:71-72
[3] Quran 78:21
[4] Quran 89:23

So, what exactly is this hell that's going to enclose the earth and through which everyone without exception is going to have to pass through doing now?

It's eating itself up!

No, I'm not kidding! I'm relaying the truth. Here's how the Rasul (saw) explained it in metaphoric language:

Narrated by Abu Hurairah (r.a.): "The Rasul of Allah (saw) said;

'Hell complained to Allah saying, 'O Rabb my parts have eaten each other up!' Upon this Allah gave it permission to take two breaths. Thus, the extreme cold (winter) is from its ZAMHAREER and the extreme hot (summer) is from its SAMUM!'"

Indeed, such a truth could only have been explained in this way 14 hundred years ago!

Those who go to heaven will pass through hell then converse among each other regarding the fire of hell, "Allah conferred favor upon us and protected us from the suffering of the (Hellfire; the state of burning) *samum* (an infusing microwave radiation)!"[5]

Let us first understand the expression "Hell has eaten itself up."

The sun is composed of a core made of hydrogen gas around 15 million degrees Celsius. Due to this heat there are constant nuclear reactions taking place and the hydrogen atoms are literally eating themselves up, i.e. burning out and turning into helium. The "left-overs" or the side products of this fusion are discarded whereby they reach earth. What are the leftovers of the sun, pardon me, of "hell"?

SAMUM!

What is *samum*?

The Arabic word *samum* has two meanings. The first is, a beam of light that infuses into pores, and the second is poisonous or toxic fire, in other words, radiation!

How else could the thermonuclear reactions of the sun and the radiation produced by them be explained 1400 years ago?

---

[5] Quran 52:27

The Rasul of Allah (saw) has disclosed religion, which is based totally on scientific truth, in the most perfect way. However, because people are accustomed to approaching religion in more conditioned ways rather than scientifically, their prejudice and predetermined beliefs deprive them from seeing this truth.

The destiny of earth and everything within it is quite conspicuously perceivable by those with a little insight and foresight. Yet this information wasn't compiled and arranged holistically and comprehensively in the past due to insufficient science. Today on the other hand it is divine grace and mercy that we have access to these truths. Thus, we must make the best of every cell in our brain to evaluate and discern the realities that were pointed out 1400 years ago.

The earth and everything on it are going to be engulfed by hell, or in other words, the sun is going to expand and become hell.

As for humans, depending on the level of energy of their spirit or holographic wave body they are either going to be able to flee from earth to higher dimensions of life within the dimensional depths of the numerous stars in space, or become stuck in earth and the magnetic pull of the sun, thus becoming stuck inside the sun or hell forever.

I say forever because if you can't flee from that magnetic field in the beginning then you can never escape it later as the density will only increase more and more with time.

This is why it is said both those who go to hell and heaven will remain therein forever.

Why wasn't it openly claimed that the sun is hell and instead only implied with a few hadith?

It wasn't accentuated because the people of that time were already deifying stones, objects, the moon and the sun! They were coming from a mentality that worshipped the sun and the moon.

If the Rasul (saw) said the sun is hell they would have started worshipping the sun again, praying and glorifying the sun to bestow its favors and mercy upon them and not burn them! Even today there are still people who worship the sun, who carry its symbol on their flags and pray to its "son"!

We should also consider the fact that even though rare superior brains have enabled humanity to experience technological leaps -we have travelled to the moon and sent satellites as far as Pluto- we are still living primitive lives centuries in the past! Mankind is living solely in pursuit of pleasure, to eat, drink, mate, flee from what he fears and run towards what he desires, unconsciously conditioned by the society! This has been the case for centuries, unfortunately still continuing.

The sublime being Jesus (pbuh) pointed to the reality of man and afterlife but alas, only a handful amongst the millions that have passed over the centuries have actually understood his message. May Allah help us to duly know his worth! The Christian population is said to be in the billions, yet how many of them have actually heard his message? How many of them have actually discerned his teachings?

As the Rasul of Allah (saw) informed us, he will return from the abode he is still living in, he will live amongst us for some time, and he will correct the misunderstood information among the people.

Who gives us this good news? Muhammad Mustapha (saw)!

The sublime being who has been created with an extraordinary brain capacity and was made to observe with divine grace all the future phases of mankind and the world. He experienced a dimensional leap with 'Ascension' (*miraj*) and observed the lives pertaining to heaven and hell. He spent his entire life trying to inform the people of the precautions they need to take against what is waiting for them ahead.

All of the Nabis and Rasuls of the past have tried to give the same following message:

Do not squander your lives by deifying and worshipping false imaginary idols and gods turn to Allah who is the creator of the earth, the heavens, all of the worlds, and the entire universe. Don't do wrong to anyone, try to be of beneficial service to humanity as much as you can. Get to know "Allah" so that you may be able to become aware of and evaluate the countless gems and jewels with which you, the vicegerent, have been embedded.

This theme has reached its climax with Jesus (pbuh) who claimed, "If you believe in the kingdom of heaven and want to be with me, leave everything behind and come with me!"

When Jesus spoke of the kingdom of heaven he was referring to the kingdom of the life after death. The Jews, who claim to be the superior chosen ones, and who prefer the kingdom of this world instead, did not accept him. He was put through countless torture after which he miraculously left this abode.

Muhammad (saw) gave us the glad tidings regarding his return!

Muhammad (saw), the noble being who offered humanity a most perfectly comprehensive book that leaves nothing out regarding this life and the life after death.

Muhammad (saw), who has explained all the details about the illusory nature of this world and the reality of the life after death...

This unmatched sublime being came to this world 1400 years ago with the mission of teaching the reality and had to address a bunch of nomads living in the middle of the desert! Imagine seeing and knowing everything regarding the future with all its details and possible dangers and having to explain this to people who are so far from having the insight and foresight to discern your message.

If you explain the truth openly they can't fathom it and hence refuse and defame you. So, you are forced to explain it using symbols and metaphors, which you do with utmost perfection, yet they still deny and refuse you! They call you a lunatic. They call you a sorcerer. They claim you have been possessed by the jinn and talk on behalf of them!

You can clearly see the scorching fire towards which humanity is approaching and you know if they don't take precaution they are going to suffer but you get mocked and ridiculed at the attempt of warning them.

Who can put up with such a situation?

Leave the people of that time aside, how about today? How about us? Have we been able to understand and duly appreciate him today at the brink of the 21st century? Despite all scientific discovery! Despite the clear warnings the Rasul of Allah (saw) gave 1400 years ago!

Humanity in my view stands at the door of the 21st century yet is still living in the Stone Age before the time of Muhammad (saw), unable to see the truth.

What is religion?

Why is religion necessary?

Why have certain rules and recommendations been made by the Rasul of Allah (saw)?

Is religion just about having beliefs?

Does it have scientific basis?

Why must humanity comply with religious regulations?

Let us now explore some of the scientific truths comprising the basis of the religion of Islam in attempt to answer the question "Why religion?"

5

THE SCIENCE BEHIND THE DESTINATION OF MANKIND

As I will cover in more detail in following chapters, man's spirit begins to form as of the 120th day after conception, as a holographic wave-body comprised of various waves produced by the brain.

During adolescence when the production levels of estrogen and androgen hormones are at their maximum the stage of responsibility begins. What does this mean? The brain, at the chemical effects of these hormones begins to upload and save incorrect mental activity as 'negative energy' to the spirit. In other words, as "sin", via the "two angels" on our shoulders. These brain activities at the same time produce either a positively or negatively charged electromagnetic field around the person.

If on the 120th day after conception while the essence of the brain is still forming, a special ray (angel) necessary to activate a specific circuitry hits the brain, the brain is able to upload anti-gravitational force to the spirit. With this, the spirit will be able to escape the magnetic field of the Earth, when it gets engulfed by the Sun (hell), and flee to heaven, or the dimensional depths amongst the countless stars in the universe.

On the contrary, if this circuitry isn't activated and the anti-gravitational force isn't uploaded to the spirit it will not have the strength to escape the magnetic pull of the Earth or the Sun and hence become stuck in hell forever.

How about the narrations regarding how the believers will burn in hell to the extent of their sins and then go to heaven? If those who go to hell will remain therein indefinitely how is it possible for them to go to heaven later?

This is about having too much negative energy or too little positive energy uploaded to their spirit bodies, i.e. the strength of the energy of their spirit. This will transpire before the Sun fully engulfs the Earth, that is, during the process of crossing the *Bridge of Sirat*.

"When hell comes and surrounds the earth from all around…"

As described above, during the phase referred to as "*mahshar*" everyone will be given the opportunity to gather together on Earth.

> **During that period the earth** (the body) **will be replaced by another earth** (another body)**, and the heavens as well** (individual consciousness will also be turned into another system of perception)![6]

As the verse affirms this will take place under different life conditions. At this stage the Earth will be like a huge plain on which the entire human race, including all people from the past, present and future, will be gathered.

The *Sirat* is a way out. It's not a bridge made of cement and concrete, it's a spacebridge, an escape route… its normal that none of this makes sense to us today for at that time a single day's length will be fifty thousand years:

> **The angels and the Spirit will return to their essence in a period** (which will seem to you like that) **of fifty thousand years** (the period of time to reach Allah in their essence).[7]

Clearly these are time spans that we can't fathom right now.

After tasting death all our concepts of time will be rendered invalid. Due to the dissolution of the biological-physical body and leaving the earth's day-night pattern the concept of time will be completely lifted.

It's not possible for us to discern the universal dimensions of time right now. According to our current understanding one sun year is 255 million earth years. Are we even aware of what this number means?

---

[6] Quran 14:48
[7] Quran 70:04

Billions of years have passed since the creation of Earth. The first appearance of man on Earth is said to be hundreds of millions of years ago.

When we read about the event of *mahshar*, the period of escaping through the *sirat*, it sounds like an event that's going to take place in a matter of a few hours but in reality, it's going to take 'thousands of years' in terms of our current understanding of time. Are we conscious of this?

The Jewish narration of man's history being 7000 years old is a fiction made up by a narrow-minded mentality, which we've all unquestionably accepted. It has nothing to do with the truth.

We must try to understand the concept of time in the life after death with the proportion of 1 day = 50 thousand years.

Various different hadith that refer to events pertaining to the life after death should also be considered in this light.

Expressions such as "six days" or the "seventh day" are days in the sight of Allah, days pertaining to universal dimensions; billions of years according to our current understanding of time.

It's difficult for those without sufficient education to comprehend these numbers so it's quite normal for them to deny and refuse. Imagine if these "billions of year long days" were openly talked about 1400 years ago!

Albeit he only slightly touched upon the real dimensions and the real events by way of symbols and metaphors they called Muhammad (saw) a lunatic, so think about what they would have done if they heard of the billions of years!

We don't have to go that far into the past. How many of us today can actually comprehend what billions of years mean? Yes maybe Doomsday will begin tomorrow, maybe a billion years later. But we must never forget that the reality of time is nothing like what we think it is.

For instance, you can never really understand the time you spend in your dream when you're asleep. Sometimes you can spend years in a single dream but we know that no dream lasts longer than 2 minutes. As for the time that passes in your sleep while you're not dreaming (in deep sleep) you have no consciousness of it at all. Some hours pass like seconds some minutes pass like days. Hence the famous phrase, "Ask the ill person the length of a single night…"

Tens of thousands of years of the life after death will seem like hours passing in respect to Earth time.

Thus, I want to reiterate that the dimension of time we will enter with death is not like our current concept of time. Especially for those who will be imprisoned in their graves, time will feel much different to them.

All of these have been explained in minimal basic metaphoric ways in the past to help people understand so that they may be able to prepare for their future.

Nevertheless, the phrase, "Talk to people according to their level of intellect" affirms why these truths have been reduced to basic and minimal symbolic expressions.

6

DHIKR: THE MOST IMPORTANT PRACTICE IN THE WORLD

If I were to list the verses and hadith regarding the importance of dhikr it would be a book of its own. Gratefully, I have already done that in *The Power of Prayer*.

Prayer and salat are forms of dhikr, just like reciting the Quran and bringing *salawat*.

Dhikr is said to be the highest form of worship in religion. Why?

In the following chapters where I will talk about astrology I will explain how only a tiny portion of the human brain comprised of 15 billion cells is activated via the rays it receives during birth and how further activation after this is not possible.

The brain can't recruit/activate new cell groups under the effects of the external rays it receives after the point of birth. But this does not mean that the inactivated potential will have to remain idle forever!

Cell groups can be activated via certain practices and new capacities and skills may well be attained.

Actually, the whole idea of religion is to activate these new parts and potentials within the brain to acquire and utilize new powers.

So why do we repetitively recite certain meanings that pertain to Allah by way of dhikr?

Let's say you're repeating the name *Allah*. Before you utter this name, your brain processes its meaning and via the electrical signals it sends to your tongue it allows you to assign and express a particular sound to it.

When this name is remembered (recited) in your brain a bioelectrical current is activated amongst the group of cells that are associated with the meaning of this name. In essence all functions in the brain are nothing other than bioelectrical activity among brain cells. Different meanings cause a flow of bioelectrical energy among different groups of cells in the brain. This flow then enables the activation of a myriad of meanings via the groups of cells that it triggers.

All functions of the brain are carried out via the chromosomes comprising these groups of neurons. Imagine the infinite number of activities carried out by 15 billion neurons where each neuron has connection to 16 thousand other neurons.

Fatabarakalllahu ahsan'ul khalikeen!

Hormones on the other hand, affect the chemical make-up of the cells thereby altering the speed and direction of the bioelectrical flow creating the various formations to which we assign meanings.

Various rays with different frequencies coming from the constellations and the different cosmic effects to which the brain is subject due to constantly changing planetary aspects also alter the bioelectrical flow in the brain, hence creating new meanings…

The brain never really sleeps; it constantly receives and outputs data. The differing moods people experience has nothing to do with the state of their souls; it is entirely related to their brains. The soul or spirit is just a backup copy (wave-body) of the brain.

Anyway, let us not digress…

When we engage in dhikr, that is when we repeat a word referencing a meaning pertaining to Allah, a bioelectrical current is activated in the relevant group of neurons in the brain and this energy flow is uploaded to the wave-body (spirit).

Additionally, when you keep repeating this word like a mantra, the bioelectrical energy that's produced gets stronger and stronger and starts to activate other cells, hence causing a capacity expansion.

Upon continuing even further, new meanings are formed in the brain via the newly activated cells and this leads to people saying things like, "Since I started doing dhikr my mind works differently, my understanding has enhanced, I can perceive things in a different light now…" etc.

Since the new meanings and the energy that is formed with dhikr are uploaded to your radial-wave body (spirit) the quality of your life after death is also increased.

> **"And whoever is blind** (unable to perceive the Truth) **in this life** (outer life) **will also be blind in the eternal life to come** (inner life)"[8]

I believe this verse points directly to this truth. For, the extent to which one's brain is activated and enhanced directly affects the state of their holographic radial body, as every bit of data in the brain is constantly uploaded to the spirit. Since no more data can be uploaded to the spirit after death, a brain that hasn't adequately developed in this world cannot in any way become activated in the life after death; it becomes indefinitely fixed with its capacity at the point of death.

Consider that! Millions and billions of years, an eternal life! And your only chance of preparing for this eternity is by developing your brain as much as you can in this limited, restricted worldly life.

If you can't see what the implications of this are then I have nothing more to say to you.

So, we talked about the bioelectrical energy produced as a byproduct of dhikr and how this is uploaded to their spirit body. Let us now address the second aspect of the benefits of dhikr.

There is a verse in the Quran regarding the creation of man, that says:

> **And when your Rabb said to the angels** (angels here are personifications of the qualities of the Names comprising one's body, hence the addressee here is you), **"I will make upon the earth** (the body) **a vicegerent** (conscious beings who will live with the awareness of the Names)."[9]

The word 'vicegerent' points to the fact that the human brain is created with the potential to manifest all of the meanings of the Names of Allah.

Based on the name of Allah you repeat in your dhikr an increase in capacity will take place in your brain in correlation with the meaning

---

[8] Quran 17:72
[9] Quran 2:30

referenced by that name. I will write more about this after I explain the technical aspect of dhikr.

Since existence is the plane in which the meanings of Allah become manifest, and since all forms and objects are basically the densified states of these various meanings, the rays coming from the innumerous constellations are carrying these infinite meanings to us at all times.

Let me explain this with an example:

There are numerous radio waves and TV waves inside the room you're sitting in right now, but let's say your radio's capacity to receive and convert these waves is limited and your TV only has a VHF band. Now imagine your next-door neighbor is able to view 100 different colored channels while you can only see one black and white channel. It's not that those waves aren't available to you, it's just that your TV doesn't have the capacity to receive and convert them. The good news is, unlike outdated radio and TV units, the capacity of a brain can be increased.

Essentially the brain is capable of processing the infinite stream of information coming from the 12 constellations and the innumerous stars. However, it's crucial for the person to expand this capacity. You've been given an invaluable capital with which you can invest in a prosperous life of eternity yet here you are playing with it as if it's some board game!?

It has been said, "The majority of the people of paradise comprise *Buhul* people". This word *Buhul* in Arabic means both "pure-naive" and "foolish-stupid".

The following words of Jesus (pbuh) further establishes this truth:

"Allah has created only one disease with no remedy and that is the state of being buhul" in other words foolishness!

Indeed, the majority of the people of paradise are going to be naive, but why?

As a result of divine grace these people are going to be able to activate the circuitry in their brain to produce the anti-gravitational force needed to be able to escape Earth's magnetic pull. However, due to not doing the necessary practices they will not have reached their highest potential to be able to evaluate the infinite blessings of that realm. Yet they will live an eternal life in paradise enjoying the countless pleasures with which they are familiar from this world.

The state of the *muqarriboon* in paradise on the other hand, those who have acquired divine closeness, no normal brain can even imagine let alone fathom!

But let me try to explain with a simple example:

Imagine someone spends an entire lifetime in pursuit of something, gives up everything for it, and in the end, he finally reaches it, can you imagine his joy! Now think of a brain that has reached its highest capacity, able to receive and process rays that activate countless new meanings, able to connect and resonate with the angels of brand-new starts at all times. Constantly receiving and processing new data, growing, developing and expanding.... I don't know if I'm able to explain...

Our brains are wired with the capacity to process, manifest and experience the infinite qualities and names of Allah. Depending on how much you repeat these names you will be able to get closer to Allah and understand and experience His meanings to that extent. Dhikr is the key for this! You can either use this key or throw it in the sea or amuse yourself with it like a toy!

All that you see around you, all actions that transpire through the people you see are different functions and processions of the brain.

Whatever quality you see on anyone, whether saintly or otherwise, know that you have the same potential quality within you, except that yours may not be activated.

The body has been designed solely to serve the brain; its purpose is to produce the necessary bioelectrical energy needed by the brain.

Additionally, certain organs have been installed into the body as a sample of the brain's innumerous receptive capacity, though it is great injustice to restrict the brains capacity to this.

The macrocosm is the universe...

The microcosm is the brain!

The universe is essentially a giant mass of countless magnetic waves where each wave carries a unique meaning. The brain, by origin, is an advanced receptor that can process these meanings in the form of waves and can also create new meanings. The brain uploads all of its products to the spirit, i.e. the holographic wave body that it produces!

One's after-life capacity, or in other words, the state and quality of his life after death is determined by the capacity of his brain at the moment of his death. After death, everyone without exception, will see how much they could have utilized the worldly life to develop themselves and feel deep regret at having lost the opportunity for good.

Now let us talk about the two types of dhikr.

Energy based dhikr.

Knowledge based dhikr.

Energy based dhikr is the common dhikr that we know of; it resonates with the spirit's attribute of power and allows the spirit to succeed in various tasks, enabling it to accumulate and store the necessary energy for transportation.

Repeating:

"Allah" ...

"La ilaha illallah..."

"La hawla walaa quwwata illah billah..." are all within the scope of common dhikr.

The positive energy that flows to you via the good deeds you do, or when others gossip about you, is also the same type of energy.

There is a second type of dhikr which we can call "Specific dhikr".

Specific dhikr is a list of Allah's names 'specific' to the person. As I will cover in more detail later, different names of Allah can be combined as a specific formula to produce different results and effects in one's brain according to the person's needs.

When you do the dhikrs in the common dhikr list the strength and effect of each name will be equal, thus resulting in equal degrees of activation and manifestation.

Whereas for example, if the name *MUREED* is inadequately activated in a person as opposed to the other names, this person will have a weak willpower and drive and hence be unable to put into practice his knowledge. Now if this person goes ahead and does the common dhikr, since all the qualities referenced by the names are going to develop at the same degree his willpower is still going to be inadequate relative to the others. On the other hand, if this person focuses on the name *Mureed* instead he will see big differences in terms of his willpower in a short span of time.

This can be applied to many other things like stinginess, crudeness, to increase knowledge, etc. However, the person who determines the specific list of dhikr must know this person and his brain very well. He must be aware of the astrological signs and the positions of the planets at the time of the person's birth in order to ascertain which areas of his brain are at the effects of which planet, what this person's potentials are etc…

Dhikr should not only be restricted to these either. All the verses and prayers we recite during salat are also considered to be dhikr.

Salat is the means of uploading various meanings to one's spirit by withdrawing from the external world into a deep meditative state.

Performing salat like doing gymnastics is nothing other than ignorance and a serious lack of insight.

Salat is a way to turn to one's essence, that is, to Allah. Those deprived of this are in so much loss in terms of what they can potentially manifest and experience that it is merely impossible to put into words.

Not performing salat is like ceasing your ties with Allah. It is accepting yourself to be only the physical body and life as only of this world therefore not feeling the need to prepare for life after death. Such a person doesn't even lift the lid of the treasure box called 'vicegerency' and will eventually die in misery and grave loss.

Think of someone who is deprived of using the tool that activates and develops all the infinite potential qualities that are dormant within him. Yet the only capital with which he can work in the afterlife is the treasure inside the treasure box of "vicegerency". Is it even possible to imagine or express the extent of his regret after death?

Let us know without doubt everything done within the scope of "prayer/worship" including dhikr, salat, fasting etc. is for the person's own good; these practices are crucial preparations for his life after death.

Your individual being is NOTHING in respect to *The Absolute Proprietor* of the infinite universe. If you were to spend your entire life in prostration do you think that signifies anything to that Infinity? What can you add to it?

Or if you were to spend your entire life in denial?

Your faith and denial bind you alone my friend.

7

IS ABLUTION ABOUT CLEANLINESS?

What is ablution and why is it necessary?

The popular answer is: "To be clean!"

Is it really?

If that were really the case why would we be advised to place our hands into soil and then rub our face and arms with it in the absence of water?

If it's really about being clean… would you tell someone to go and stick their hand into some dirt and then rub their face with it!?

Obviously not!

So, if it's not about cleanliness then what is it really about?

Hold your breath and look at your watch. How many seconds can you hold your breath for? Perhaps a minute or two… How about under the water? 15-25 seconds! Why the difference?

Because when your outside water all of the cells on the surface of your skin are constantly absorbing oxygen but when you're in water those pathways are closed and the only oxygen you have is whatever is inside your lungs!

Hence when you rub parts of your body with water the cells that come in contact with it supplement the body with a certain amount of electricity. That is, it's a short cut way for the brain to obtain quick energy without needing excessive water, a mere contact with the cells is sufficient.

So, if the purpose was to "wash" and to be "cleansed" then we would need a great deal of water but for ablution all that is necessary is to wet the surface cells.

How about *tayammum*, where you place your hands in soil and then rub your face, then place your hands in soil again, and then rub your arms (first the right arm then the left) with your palm...?

You guessed it, to obtain electrical charge from soil!

When you don't have access to water you can obtain the necessary electricity from soil and neutralize the static electricity of your body with earth, etc.

Indeed, the point of ablution has nothing to do with cleaning your body; as much as it is about giving the brain the electrical charge it needs. Hence the Rasul of Allah (saw) is said to have taken ablution with even a single cup of water.

Some claim, "I shower frequently and have sufficient electrical charge, I don't need to take ablution..."

Imagine you fill your gas tank up, start your car and leave it running like that...

Will you get anywhere?

Likewise, you load your brain with electricity, and then...?

What will you do with it? What purpose will this energy serve?

You can use it to produce energy for your spirit, crucial energy that you will need after death. Or, you can squander it in pursuit of transitory worldly pleasures and be left miserably with an empty tank when you will need it most!

How and for what purpose are you using your energy my friend?

8

THE SECRET OF FASTING

One of the mandatory practices of Islam is fasting.

What is fasting about? Having empathy for the hungry.

What is fasting about? Training the ego!

What is fasting about? Giving our stomachs a break and detoxing our bodies!

Fair enough, these are all true, but are these the only reasons why we are advised to fast?

The brain obtains all of the energy needed for itself and the other organs through the various drinks and food we consume.

The life of the cells within the body depends on the bioelectrical charge the brain sends out. So, while the brain emits a myriad of waves to its external environment, most of which are uploaded to form the spirit body, it also constantly supplies the necessary life force needed both for the survival of itself and the rest of the organs in the body.

However, in order to convert the food, we eat into energy and supply the body with what it needs, the brain constantly consumes energy! In other words, it costs vital energy to produce energy!

Whereas, this vital energy can be used by the brain in a more optimized manner to enrich the spirit, to raise one's level of consciousness through dhikr and/or other spiritual, meditative practices.

Hence, we are asked to fast for *at least one month of the year* so that we may pray more, engage in dhikr more, and hence strengthen and enrich our spirits, increase the capacity of the quality of our brains, and allow it be healthier and more productive.

9

WHO OR WHAT IS BEING 'WASTED'?

They say eating too much is "waste" or "squandering" …

It is important to understand that the concept of waste here is not in reference to the food that is eaten but the one who is doing the eating!

This is because the brain and other organs need a specific amount of energy to function. Excess energy is of no use to them at all; in fact, the brain has to work harder to convert this excess, which it doesn't even need. Plus, this stock of useless energy creates an extra 'cavity' in the brain, in terms of the energy the brain ends up wasting away.

Nobody can harm the brain of an overweight person more than the harm he causes to himself!

The dhikr that is done while one is fasting, on the other hand, produces a lot more energy than while not fasting. Hence the Rasul of Allah (saw) excessively praises the act of fasting and is known to have fasted very frequently.

Talking of the harm extra weight causes to the brain, we can't not cover the topic of alcohol and smoking!

10

THE DAMAGE CAUSED TO THE BRAIN BY THE CONSUMPTION OF TOBACCO AND ALCOHOL

I want to explain a few points regarding smoking and alcohol consumption...

We said the rank and quality of one's life after death is dependent on the capacity of his brain in this world. His capital in the afterlife will be to the extent to which he increases the capacity of his brain cells and stocks knowledge and energy to his spirit, or wave body, in this world.

But what are the effects of alcohol and tobacco to the brain?

They numb the brain cells!

They clog the connection points between the nerve cells (synapses) and prevent the bioelectrical flow between them...!

Imagine you're imprisoned in a cell and you're given the key but instead of using it to free yourself you habitually and tirelessly blunt the blade and damage the key to the point where it can't unlock the door anymore! Smoking and drinking alcohol are slow means of self-destruction!

Just when you're about to get the gist of the matter, just when you're about to come to that precious 'aha' moment and transform your life, lo and behold, you have a brain fog! You lose all mental clarity and there's nothing you can do about it! Because the chemicals in the cigarettes you've been smoking have clogged the site of transmission of electric nerve impulses between your nerve cells!

Or they've become dysfunctional from all the alcohol you've been drinking! And now you can't even renew them!

Why would you want to destroy your only key out to eternity, your only real capital in an eternal life, over meaningless transitory pleasures?

It's as absurd as someone throwing a bag of gold into the sea because he enjoys the sound it makes!?

If this sounds sane and profitable to you go ahead and continue! But don't forget that you will eventually suffer the consequences and will never be able to compensate the damage you've caused.

11

THE TWO BIG SECRETS REGARDING HAJJ (PILGRIMAGE)

The secrets behind pilgrimage are really quite unfathomable!

But before I explain the importance of this practice let us share some words from the Rasul of Allah (saw):

Narrated by Hadhrat Ali (ra) who said:

The Rasul of Allah (saw) said:

"Whoever possesses provisions and a mount that would enable him to reach the House of Allah, but does not do Hajj, it would not matter if he dies as a Jew or a Christian, because Allah says in His Book:

> **"Pilgrimage to the House** (Kaaba) **is the right of Allah** (the qualities of the Names in one's essence) **upon all people who have the means to undertake it."**[10] [Tirmidhi]

* * *

Ibn Omar (ra) narrates:

A man came and asked the Rasul of Allah (saw):

"What makes Hajj compulsory O Rasul of Allah?"

The Rasul answered:

---

[10] Quran 3:97

"Provision and mount (i.e. enough food for the trip and a means of transportation)." [Tirmidhi]

* * *

"An Umrah is expiation for the sins committed between it and the next, and a Hajj Mabrour that is accepted will receive no other reward than Paradise." [Muslim]

* * *

Abu Huraira reported Allah's Messenger (saw) as saying:

"He who visits this House (Ka'ba) (with the intention of performing Pilgrimage), abstains from intercourse, and neither speaks indecently nor acts wickedly will return (free from sin) as on the (very first day) his mother bore him!" [Muslim]

* * *

Narrated by 'Abdur-Rahman bin Ya'mar:

I was next to the Rasul of Allah (saw) while he was waiting at Mount Arafat when a few men from the people of Najd approached and asked, "O Rasul of Allah, what (how) is hajj (pilgrimage)?

The Rasul of Allah (saw) said:

"The Hajj is Arafat. Whoever sees (attends) the Arafat before the rising of Fajr, then he has performed the Hajj. The days of Mina are three. But whoever hastens to leave in two days, there is no sin on him, and whoever stays on, there is no sin on him either."

After this he sent a man to announce this to the people. [Ibn Maja, Tirmidhi, Abi Dawud, Nasa'i]

* * *

Narrated by ibn Mirdas as-Sulami (r.a.):

"The Rasul of Allah (saw) prayed for forgiveness for his ummah on the evening of the day at (Mount) Arafat. He was told, **"I have forgiven them all, except the oppressor, from whom I will indeed collect the due of the one whom he wronged."**

Rasulullah (saw) said;

"My Rabb, if you will you can grant (the due from) paradise to the wronged and forgive the oppressor..."

No response came that evening.

The next day at *Muzdalifah* he repeated the supplication, and this time his prayer was accepted."

Abbas ibn Mirdas said, "Upon this the Rasul of Allah (saw) laughed and Abu Bakr (r.a.) and Umar (r.a.) said to him, 'May my father and mother be ransomed for you! This is not a time when you usually laugh. What made you laugh? May Allah make your years filled with laughter.'

He said;

'The enemy of Allah, Iblis, when he heard that Allah answered my prayer and forgave my ummah, took some dust and started to scatter it on his head, uttering cries of woe and doom, and what I saw of his anguish made me laugh. '" [Sunan Ibn Majah]

As for the scientific aspect of hajj, the key lies in the phrase, **"Hajj is Arafat"**. For the House of Allah, Kaaba, can be visited at all times during the year, a practice that is called 'Umrah'. Even though the benefits of Umrah are extensive, it is not equal to hajj.

Why?

What is the great secret behind hajj that the Rasul of Allah (saw) felt the need to make the warning, *"He who has enough provision and a mount yet does not perform pilgrimage will die as a Jew or a Christian"*?

This totally renders invalid the popular convention that pilgrimage is best done after one buys a house, a car, raises their kids, becomes a grandparent and retires"!

Once you can afford the provision and the means of transportation, pilgrimage becomes a *fardh* (compulsory) upon you.

Otherwise you die as a Jew or a Christian.

This is profound.

12

THE SECRETS OF THE KAABA AND ARAFAT

According to my observation and understanding, and the knowledge bestowed to me by Allah...

Just like the bioelectrical energy that flows through the nervous system inside the human body, there are channels or streams of negative and positive radiation under the earth.

If for instance your house or workplace or farmland is located upon one of these negative radiation channels, you will constantly suffer from sickness, setbacks, and an endless loop of adversities. At home you'll deal with health issues, at work, financial delays and difficulties, on a farmland, trouble with crops and animals, etc...

If on the other hand they're located on a positive channel of radiation then your home will be peaceful and tranquil, your work will prosper, your farm will flourish and you will attract good health and fortune.

These energy channels are called lay lines. The negative ones are called black strains.

The most powerful point where these positive ley lines intersect each other as though forming a central station broadcasting this supreme positive energy is beneath the Kaaba at Mecca, the extension of which is Mount Arafat!

Abdulaziz ad-Dabbagh, one of the many who have observed this reality through personal revelation (discovery, unveiling, *kashf*) mentions in his book "*Al Ibriz*" that there is a stream of light (*nur*) emanating from the Kaaba up towards the sky.

Due to the extremely strong positive energy that radiates from this point the brains of the people who go there become stimulated and activated in ways I cannot explain.

Hence the Rasul of Allah (saw) says regarding the salat that is done around the Kaaba:

"The benefit of a two rakah salat that is performed at the Kaaba is one hundred thousand times greater than a salat performed in other masjids (prayer houses, mosques) around the world."

For, during every form of prayer and spiritual practice that is done in the vicinity of the Kaaba, the brain is constantly receiving the *Light of Jalal* (extremely high frequency waves) radiating from beneath the earth, thus producing extra potent brain waves, both to upload to the spirit body and to emit to its environment.

In another powerful hadith the Rasulullah (saw) says:

"Everywhere else you're responsible only for your actions, but at the Kaaba, you are also responsible for your thoughts."

This is because the immense strength of the energy the brain receives at the Kaaba enables it to evaluate thoughts at the level of actions and hence even the energy of one's thoughts are uploaded to the spirit as though they are real experiences.

13

THE SECRET OF ZAMZAM

Now let us look at the secret of *zamzam* water.

Zamzam water flows through the source of positive radiation beneath the Kaaba, which acts like a generator, and eventually forms a reservoir.

Think about the Chernobyl disaster, the explosion at the Chernobyl Nuclear Power Station and how it contaminated the water. You'd never guess it's poisonous if you were to drink it yet its full of radioactive substances that can cause serious health issues. And water can carry radiation for years on end! This is why there was huge panic in the West after the Chernobyl disaster.

Well zamzam on the other hand is the opposite example of this. Since zamzam flows through the source of positive radiation beneath the Kaaba it gives countless benefits to one who drinks it. Those who go there and drink zamzam and take wudu with it will notice its effects.

Due to the power uploaded to the brains from this radiation beneath the Kaaba interesting metaphysical experiences may take place during tawaf (circumambulating around the Kaaba). So, if the Kaaba is such an amazing energy station, a source of Nur, why does (the purification of) Hajj occur at Arafat? What's the deal with Arafat?

We mentioned how the extension of the positive energy streams beneath the Kaaba reach the Arafat forming another important station. Now when all hundreds of thousands of people gather at Mount Arafat with the same intention, all receiving the same profound positive stream of energy directly from beneath the mountain, they naturally all start to broadcast the same meaning. The process of waiting on Mount Arafat for a period of time called *wakfah* is basically a collective way of tuning into the same frequency of energy with the same intention: "Forgive us Allah!"

Hundreds of thousands of brains collectively emitting the same frequency of energy carrying the same intention in the same location inevitably forms a huge magnetic cloud on and around the area of Mount Arafat!

What happens if you forget a VHS video tape on top of the VCR while it's running? The magnetic field of the VCR will erase the data on the tape. You can call it the work of invisible hands if you like!

My point is, when you make the supplication, "O Allah, forgive me for my mistakes" you not only start to produce and emit this wave but also open your brain to receiving waves of the same meaning. Through this opening that strong magnetic field will immediately affect the brain literally erasing from the spirit all the negative data uploaded by the brain thus far!

Hence you will return from Mount Arafat like a new born, free of all sins and negative records in your database.

The Rasul of Allah (saw) says:

"The greatest sinner is one who returns from Mount Arafat and asks with doubt, 'I wonder if my sins have been forgiven?'"

This is how definite and certain this phenomenon is!

Allah will allow whom He wishes to cleanse to go to pilgrimage, easing and enabling the way for true purification!

14

THE SECOND ASPECT OF HAJJ

So, the primary purpose of pilgrimage is to be cleansed from one's sins.

But is this all?

"The reward of *Hajj Mabrour* is paradise."

Ok so all of our sins have been forgiven and all the negative energy have been neutralized. But it is all so easy to commit new sins, to make new mistakes, in fact a lot more than before!? One can even end up indefinitely in hell despite going to hajj!

Here we come to the second aspect or purpose of hajj: To activate new circuits in your brain with the new levels of comprehension enabled by this high potential energy, where your entire lifestyle will shift in alignment with the realities and principles of the afterlife. After this, worldly pursuits won't appeal to you as they used to and you will no longer condone the necessities of the afterlife. You will live your life totally aligned with the realities of the life after death. Ambition, jealousy, gossiping, cheating, worldly desires and acquisitions that carry enormous negative energy will no longer appeal to you and you will naturally abstain from such sinful acts.

As such, you will be rewarded with paradise as a result of completing *hajj mabrour*.

A frequently asked question is, "why is it that after one goes to hajj and returns to their normal life, even though there is usually an increase in spiritual practices sometimes there is also a significant increase in sinful acts, in fact more so than before?"

The powerful source of positive energy beneath the Kaaba significantly increases one's overall level of energy and performance. Even though one becomes completely cleansed of their sins during performing hajj the brain receives power at the ratio of one to one hundred thousand, which naturally increases the brains general capacity to a much higher performance level.

This is the pivotal point. If the person's brain has been strongly conditioned toward worldly pursuits and bodily pleasures the effects he receives will reinforce and intensify these even more, hence leading the person to be more daring and insolent than before.

The contrapositive of this is *hajj mabrour*.

So, anyone and everyone who fulfills certain requirements at hajj is given total atonement of all past sins. But only some people also achieve *hajj mabrour*, the most essential goal of enabling and activating the brain with intense positive energy so that it becomes totally aligned with and able to comprehend the realities of the afterlife.

Let us not forget that Allah has tied everything to a cause. All things are subject to an order, a system; a divine law.

In fact, this system is so perfectly automated that it is understandable for some to claim, "the universe works like an automated machine, there is no administrator!"

All systems from the human body to the cosmos are connected to a central system, and it is this profound system of divine law and order that we call 'religion'.

You reap what you sow. Do whatever you like as long as you're ready to handle its consequence.

The word "*jaza*" in Arabic which is most commonly translated as punishment actually means "consequence" in the Quran, the direct or indirect result of an action, and hence good things have good consequences.

Religious rules and requirements are totally aligned with scientific truths and the essence of life, things that are necessary in terms of one's eternal life. They are not random laws that descended from the sky! So whatever practice you neglect you will most definitely pay the consequence of this negligence.

This being the case...

Does it make sense to live a life of sinful acts, immersed in negative energy that will weigh your spirit down to the world in the life after death, to not cleanse yourself from this burden and spend your eternal life in an agonizing dungeon of suffering?

When you have no knowledge of when you're going to leave this body... and you have the opportunity to totally rid yourself of all the negative energy that's burdening your spirit... and Allah has opened such an amazingly easy path... and the Rasul of Allah (saw) has made the warning, **"*Those who have the means to go to hajj and don't, will die as a Jew or a Christian!*"** encouraging you to fulfill the necessities of the reality...

If one still stubbornly refuses to use this opportunity then what more can anyone say or do?

Do as you will and live its consequences!

Let us remember that we are talking about a domain of eternal life to which we will go totally alone, leaving everything we own and everyone we love behind!

The only valid and valuable thing there is the preparation one does in this worldly life.

Nobody can cause the harm that we cause to ourselves by not living in congruence with the realities that we accept and comprehend.

The Rasul of Allah (saw) has taught us everything we need to know and all the precautions we need to take to not be in loss in the afterlife but if we don't heed these warnings then who will pay the price?

There is no compulsion in religion my friends. The truth is shared and the person is invited to this higher level of understanding and experience, but whether or not he takes the offer is up to the individual.

In any case, the consequence of one's decision binds the person alone.

So, are you conscious of the cost of what you have undertaken?

15

GOSSIPING AND ENERGETIC DEBTS

"One's rightful due" is a term we hear often among the people… "You impinged on my rightful due" or "You took my rightful share" etc.

What is this "rightful due"?

We also often hear the word "backbiting" or "gossiping" (*giybah*) and how such an appalling act it is; yet we always seem to have some form of justification to continue to engage in it.

The closest translation of the Arabic word "*giybah*" is "gossip". What exactly is denoted by this word, why is it so wrong, and why has the Rasul of Allah (saw) so strongly advised against it with his words:

"Gossiping is thirty-six times worse than adultery."

Jabir and Abu Said (ra) narrate from the Rasul of Allah (saw):

"Abstain from gossiping for it is much worse than adultery. An adulterer may repent for his mistake and Allah may forgive him but one who engages in gossip will not be forgiven until the person he gossiped about forgives him." [Ghazali – *Ihya-u Ulumiddeen*]

Why do you think the Quran employs such an abhorring example to describe backbiting?

"O you who have believed, avoid most assumptions (guesswork about things of which you have no certain knowledge). **Indeed, certain assumptions are an offence** (lead to or are an outcome of duality). **And do not spy on others** (do not inspect or inquire into the private matters of others out of curiosity), **and do not backbite.**

Would one of you like to eat the flesh of his dead brother? You would detest it! So, protect yourselves from Allah, the *Tawwab*, the *Rahim*.[11]

Consider the authentic hadith reported by hadhrat Aisha (ra):

"The Rasul of Allah (SAW) was looking into marrying Safiyyah (ra). So, when the Rasul asked me about her I said she was nice and everything but made a gesture with my hand to show that Safiyyah was short. In response to this the Rasul said *'just this gesture; if it were to be put it into an ocean it would stain the whole ocean'*.

Some other time I had again spoken about someone to the Rasul of Allah (saw) and he said *'even if many of the things of the world were given to me I would still not like to speak ill of anyone in their absence!'*" [Abu Dawud, 41:4857]

Abu Hurairah (ra) reported: The Rasul of Allah (saw) said, *"Do you know what backbiting is?"* They said, "Allah and his Rasul know best." The Rasul said, *"To mention your brother in his absence in a way he would dislike."* It was said, "What do you think if what I said about him is true?" The Rasul said, *"If what you say about him is true, it is backbiting. If it is not true, it is slander."* [Muslim]

'Amr ibn al-'As (ra) reported: The Rasul of Allah (saw) passed by the carcass of a dead mule and he said to his companions, *"That one of you eat from this until his belly is full is better than to eat the flesh of (gossip about) his Muslim brother."* [Ibn Hibban]

Indeed, as the Quran states the act of gossiping/backbiting is as atrocious as eating the flesh of one's dead brother!

But why? Let us look at what this means.

As I've been explaining thus far, engaging in certain spiritual practices; prayer, dhikr, fasting, giving alms, or even an act as simple as removing an obstacle from someone's path, allow you to collect the energy you will need to survive in the afterlife.

But as soon as you start to talk about someone in an unpleasing way in their absence a connection is formed between your brain and their brain

---

[11] Quran 49:12

and depending on the extent to which you spoke negatively about them that much positive energy is immediately transferred from your brain to theirs! Imagine that! All that positive energy you strived to achieve, all the hard work you put in and all the prayers and practices you engaged in to collect that energy is instantly gone, donated to the person you gossiped about! You could have used that energy for millions of years in the afterlife!

To make things worse, if you don't have enough positive energy to give, guess what happens? The same amount of negative energy from that person is transferred to you and immediately uploaded to your spirit! In effect you have just done them an amazing favor!

All because you were not able to hold your tongue for some fleeting momentary pleasure at the expense of misusing and harming your most valuable asset in this world, your brain. Nothing can be a greater self-punishment than this!

Many engage in good deeds, they pray five times a day, fast and give alms and think they will go the hereafter with "full stock" whereas they have accrued so much energetic debt that they will go as totally "bankrupt" and they have no idea…

"Sufficient for one is his tongue as a sin!" (Hadith)

Can you imagine the disappointment and utter misery when one realizes all his accumulated positive energy has been squandered away with gossiping, slandering, judging, and to top it off he has taken loads of negative energy from others without even being aware of it?

Let us contemplate on the following hadith:

Abu Huraira (ra) reported: The Rasul of Allah (saw) said, "Do you know who is bankrupt?" They said, "The one without money or goods is bankrupt." The Rasul said, *"Indeed, the bankrupt of my nation is those who come on the Day of Judgment with prayers, fasting, and charity, but also with insults, slander, consuming wealth, shedding blood, and beating others. The oppressed will each be given from his good deeds. If his good deeds run out before justice is fulfilled, then their sins will be cast upon him and he will be thrown into the hellfire."* [Tirmidhi]

Are debts paid off here or in the afterlife?

Allah is *Sari'ul hisab* (swift at reckoning)!

Allah settles all accounts instantly!

If one does not receive or pay others' due physically then the transferal happens energetically; one pays from his stored positive energy or takes the negative energy of the other.

Smaller debts are paid off and settled instantly yet some debts are so great that the transferal continues until the person dies and, in many cases, ends up in hell as a result of this unsettled debt.

Everything in the system is in a state of absolute balance. This is why in Islam we are advised to return even the smallest of gifts with something of equal value.

This was the practice of Rasulullah (saw).

16

THE WORTH OF KNOWLEDGE

What is your knowledge worth?

Knowledge you need to navigate and operate through your life after death?

What is the due of those who spread knowledge, the paramount capital with which people can save their eternal afterlife?

Hadhrat Ali (ra) enlightens us with his prodigious words:

"I will be a slave for forty years to one who teaches me a single word!"

The worth of any knowledge is determined by the benefit it gives. So, the worth of the knowledge pertaining to the life after is by definition, infinite, just as life after death is!

We can never pay the due of the Rasul of Allah (saw) who taught us about the reality of the afterlife and who informed us of what we need to heed and how we need to prepare for this eternal journey, even if we pray for him for the rest of our lives!

The Rasul (saw) warns us about learning and teaching this invaluable knowledge for worldly gains with the hadith:

Narrated by Ka'b bin Malek (ra): The Rasul of Allah (saw) said;

"Allah will send to hell the one who acquires knowledge for the sole purpose of competing with the learned, to dispute with the crowd, and to establish esteem over the people! For he has exchanged knowledge

of infinite value with a trivial worldly profit!"

How about those who simply retain knowledge to teach others? Or those who take this knowledge, decipher its meaning, make new connections and unveil new depths?

The Rasul of Allah (saw) says:

"May Allah enlighten the one who hears a hadith from me and holds it in his memory (to teach it to others). For sometimes he may not understand it himself but may teach it to someone with a greater level of discernment." [Tirmidhi]

There are many people who simply memorize knowledge and pass it on. They are clever! But it takes an intellect, not cleverness, to decipher and discern knowledge. There are more clever people in the world than there are intellectuals. Cleverness serves to resolve daily situations in one's best interest. The intellect, on the contrary, is far more comprehensive; it allows one to make deep contemplations and connections regarding a wider scope of topics, encompassing all times. Hence the hadith above refers to the intellect.

Let us ponder on a few more hadith about the importance of knowledge:

"When Allah wishes good for someone, He bestows upon him the understanding of Religion."

"He who is asked about knowledge (of religion) and conceals it, will be bridled with a bridle of fire on the Day of Judgment."

"The superiority of the learned scholar over the devout worshipper is like my superiority over the most inferior amongst you. Allah, His angels, the dwellers of the heaven and the earth, and even the ant in its hole and the fish (in water) supplicate in favor of those who teach knowledge."

"He who follows a path in quest of knowledge, Allah will make the path of Paradise easy to him. The angels lower their wings over the seeker of knowledge, being pleased with what he does. The inhabitants of the heavens and the earth and even the fish in the depth of the oceans seek forgiveness for him. The superiority of the learned man

over the devout worshipper is like the brightness of the full moon to the rest of the stars. The learned are the heirs of the Rasuls who bequeath neither dinar nor dirham but only knowledge; and he who acquires it, has in fact acquired an abundant portion."

"Envy is permitted only in two cases: A man to whom Allah gives wealth, and he disposes of it rightfully, and a man to whom Allah gives knowledge, that he applies and teaches." [Bukhari]

17

HOW MUCH OF THE TRUTH ARE WE ABLE TO COMPREHEND?

I tried to explain to the best of ability that far from being groundless, fancy stories, religious teachings are directly related to the mandatory laws and regulations that govern existence, which Allah has manifested from absolute nothingness.

I don't mean to say my explanations are all there is to it, I'm just saying these are also part of the underlying realities of these laws. There are so many different truths pertaining to a single law each would be a book on its own, and that's only with my knowledge!

So why is it important to explore the science behind all of this?

Because religion has been passed on to the new generation as though it's a set of hygiene and courtesy rules that came to a bunch of nomads in the middle of the desert, thereby doing a complete injustice to the universal realities.

Also, I want to stress the point that every law of Islam is based on physics, chemistry, and electromagnetic and cosmic truths. Whomsoever discerns and applies these will see its benefits in the afterlife and whomsoever chooses not to heed these realities and to not use their brain will also face its irremediable consequences.

As a matter of fact, I wrote this book for the new generation and western society, who opt to do their research rather than simply imitating and who seek the truth at all costs.

There are yet so many topics that I have not yet discussed in this book, all of which are Islamic and Sufi symbols that are totally based on scientific truths. My hope is that they are researched into, properly understood and duly applied so that they may elevate the reader to a higher level of consciousness and a better quality of life.

For those who are conditioned to accepting the symbolic, metaphoric language as literal, explicit denotations, may find it very difficult to accept and believe my construal. That's fine. Don't believe what you don't understand. As long as you are fulfilling the primary practices and that feels sufficient for you, then that is okay too. Surely you will see the benefits of your practices no matter its size and amount.

The knowledge bestowed to me by Allah is based solely on the Quran and the six volumes of authentic hadith collections, upon which essentially all of the religious laws are based.

If in any case there is a verse from the Quran or a hadith that invalidates my observations, then surely, I will abandon my view and accept this knowledge even if I do not yet understand it, for there are innumerous truths beneath every sign.

And if, against all my goodwill and sincere efforts of comprehensive research I have been mistaken in any way, may Allah notify me (and you) of the truth in this life.

Amen.

18

THE GRANDEUR OF ALLAH & OUR PLACE IN THE UNIVERSE

Before I briefly list what science has thus far unraveled about this amazingly and infinitely mysterious universe with our ridiculously limited tools of sensory perception (!) I would like to talk a little about the concept of distance.

If we know our speed of travel then we can calculate how long it will take to reach a particular destination, right?

For example, if you're in a vehicle travelling at 100 km per hour then it will take approximately 4-5 hours to reach a city, say Ankara, that is around 450km away from Istanbul. This allows us to have a sense of the distance of Ankara, according to the speed of our vehicle. Or we can take as example a city 1000 km away from Istanbul and say the equator of the world is forty times this distance, to make it easier to comprehend.

But if I show you the sun and tell you there is one and a half million km between the Earth and the Sun this would have no meaning for you as you have no reference to what the distance of one and a half million km feels like. And yet this enormous distance, which we have no way of understanding, is like talking about the distance between your nail and your skin, in contrast to the infinite vastness of the universe!

Ah the universe…

In a single galaxy there is said to be about 400 billion solar systems like ours! Yet our galaxy, the Milky Way, comprising of 400 billions solar systems, is hardly a medium sized galaxy in contrast to other much greater ones. Our solar system is approximately 32,000 light years away from the center of our galaxy.

The Milky Way, together with Andromeda, the Triangulum Galaxy and thirty other nearby galaxies, constitutes the Local Group.

The Virgo constellation is the most important constellation of stars after the Local Group. There are more than three thousand galaxies clustered in the center of the Virgo constellation. Considering there are billions of stars within each of these galaxies and each of these stars probably form the center of a system, each with their set of planets, it would be correct to say the enormity of the universe is not at all comprehendible to the human mind.

Within a section of the sky as big as the moon there are approximately 400 galaxies and so far about one billion of them have been photographed.

So, to sum it up:

The size of the sun is one million three hundred and three thousand times the size of the earth. There are around 400 billion stars, most of which are bigger than the Sun, in our galaxy, the Milky Way, alone.

And there are about one billion galaxies that we know of, like our galaxy. So where is Earth in all of this?

How much space does it even take up?

Perhaps like the size of a virus in comparison to the size of the Sun?

We're talking about the creator of a universe that comprises a billion Milky Ways, each composed of hundreds of billions of Suns!

Muhammad (saw) referred to this creator with the name "Allah".

But from Tao to Nirvana, it has been given many many other names...

19

THE SOLAR SYSTEM

If you put 1,303,800 Earths together it would amount to the size of the star we call the Sun.

The diameter of the Sun is 1,392,000 km. Its surface heat is 6000 degrees Celsius and towards its core the heat reaches 15 million degrees Celsius. The heights of the solar waves that flare from the surface of the Sun reach 800,000 km. That is, twenty times the size of the earth's equator.

Solar flares are sudden flashes of increased brightness on the sun. They are usually accompanied by a coronal mass ejection, a significant release of plasma and magnetic field, which effects the Earth causing things like magnetic storms or disruptions to radio frequencies and compasses.

The source of the Sun's energy is nuclear fusion.

At the core where temperature and pressure are very high hydrogen atoms fuse into helium atom and release energy, which constantly makes the Sun brighter yet cause the Sun to lose 4 million tons of mass every second.

The distance of the Sun from the center of the Milky Way is 32,000 light years. It completes its orbit around this center in 225 million years.

So, there you have the Sun... the ball of fire that circles around a flat earth(!)

Sadly, there are still many primitive beings, even today, who in the guise of humans, operate more like robots, unable to think and contemplate and to go beyond the literal meaning of whatever has been passed down to them. They think the earth was created 6000 years ago and the Sun and the planets and pretty much the whole universe revolves around our flat earth!

So how about the earth?

Could it really have been created 6000 years ago!?

Let's have a look…

Using radioactive dating, the age of planet Earth is calculated to be around 4.6 billion years. The core of the earth, which is very dense and contains significant amounts of iron, forms an important magnetic field. The atmosphere allows the formation of life and protects the earth from the harmful rays coming from space that can be fatal for the creatures of Earth. The other factor that contributes to the formation of life is the distance of the earth from the sun.

The Earth is 149,6 million km away from the Sun. Its diameter (the equator) is 12,756 km. It takes 23 hours and 56 minutes for it to rotate around itself. Its escape velocity is 11,2 km per second and completes its orbit around the Sun in 365,2 days.

How about the other planets in our solar system?

Mercury: 58 million km away from the Sun. Its diameter is 4,880 km and rotates around itself in 58,7 days. Its orbit around the sun takes 88 days. Its mass is 0,055 Earth's mass and its escape velocity is 4,2 km per second.

Venus: Venus is 108 million 200 thousand km away from the Sun. Its diameter is 12,700 km. Escape velocity is 10,36 km per second. It rotates around itself in 243 days and orbits around the Sun in 224,7 days. The surface gravity on Venus is about 91% of the surface gravity on Earth.

Mars: Distance from the Sun is 227,940 km. Its diameter is 6,790 km. It rotates around itself in 24 hours, 37 minutes and 23 seconds. It orbits around the Sun in 686,89 days. Its mass is 0,11 of Earth's.

Jupiter: Its distance from the Sun is 778 million km, a lot more than those mentioned above. Its diameter is 143,000 km and rotates around itself in 9 hours and 51 minutes. Its escape velocity is 60,22 km and rotates around the Sun in 11,86 years. Its mass is 318 times the mass of Earth.

Saturn: Distance from the Sun is 1,427 million km. Its mass is 95 times the mass of Earth and its diameter is 120,000 km. Its escape velocity is 36 km per second. It rotates around itself in 10 hours and 14 minutes and orbits around the Sun in 29,46 years.

Uranus: Distance from the sun is 2 billion 869 million 600 thousand km and completes its orbit around the Sun in 84 years.

Neptune: Distance from the Sun is 4,497 million km and orbits around the Sun in 164,8 years.

Pluto: The furthest planet from the Sun in our system. Its distance is 5,900 million km away and takes 248,5 years to orbit around the Sun.

20

A UNIVERSE OF RAYS & THE SIGNS OF THE ZODIAC

The constellations known as the star signs were discovered and classified by the ancient Babylonians. The birth of this ancient knowledge (astrology) is also known to be the miracle of Nabi Idris (Enoch) who is known to have lived in the same era.

Later this knowledge was passed on to the ancient Greeks, Egyptians and the Islamic world.

The twelve signs i.e. "the zodiac" that correlate to the twelve constellations are as follows:

Aries

Taurus

Gemini

Cancer

Leo

Virgo

Libra

Scorpio

Sagittarius

Capricorn

Aquarius

Pisces

The people of those ancient times believed the stars within these clusters called "signs" create the events that transpire on earth and the planets in our solar system play a significant role in human fate.

As they found certain evidences to back their beliefs up the age of "star worship' (astrolatry) began.

People used to believe that each of these star signs were celestial deities who ruled over humans, and this belief eventually led to the single deity-god belief.

In contrast Nabis and Rasuls came to help people understand that there is only one infinite supreme force (ALLAH) that reigns over the whole of existence and It is not an entity-god in space.

So, do the signs affect humans and their behaviors and if so, how and to what extent?

Could there really be a link between the zodiac signs and the fate of humans?

If the signs do affect humans is there any harm in a Muslim believing in astrology?

What kind of impact do the star signs have on humans?

What do the Quran and the Rasul of Allah (saw) say regarding the star signs?

Do religious scholars offer any views regarding astrology?

Let us now address these one by one...

21

IN THE SIGHT OF SCIENCE, THE WORLDS ARE AN ILLUSION!

One of the great philosophers of the early modern period, George Berkeley, said the following in 1750:

"All those bodies, which compose the mighty frame of the world, have not any substance without the mind. So long as they are not perceived by me, or do not exist in my mind, or that of any other created spirit, they must either have no existence at all, or subsist in the mind of some Eternal Spirit."

Research done after Berkeley, especially in the last century, has brought humanity to a position of having to accept very "controversial" ideas. To sum up what scientific research has concluded about the make-up of the universe in the last century:

Matter is made of molecules that are made up of atoms that are made up of electromagnetic waves...

Therefore, it is not incorrect to conclude that the world is a single field of electromagnetic waves. To be more precise, the entire existence is a unified field of energy in which there is nothing that is strictly and absolutely solid or "material".

In terms of humans, the human eye can only perceive between the long wavelength end of the spectrum that corresponds to light that is perceived to be red (0,0007 cm) and the short wavelength end of the spectrum that corresponds to light that is perceived to be violet (0,0004 cm).

Here is a list of what we know about the world of wavelengths:

1. Wavelengths perceived by dogs

2. Wavelengths perceived by humans

3. Wavelengths perceived by cats

4. Ultrasonic waves

5. Radio waves (long, medium, short, very short) perceived and converted by a radio according to our hearing range

6. Television waves (VHF, UHF, SHF, EHF) perceived and converted according to our visual spectrum.

7. Radar waves

8. Spark waves

9. Motion waves

10. Waves between visible red and violet light

11. Ultraviolet rays

12. X-rays

13. Other rays that have not yet been discovered

Man has been able to discover these waves with his five senses, intellect, and the tools he created.

How about all the waves and rays he has not yet been able to discover?

How about if the capacity of the tools he used were different?

How about if, for example, beyond the rays of red and violet, the human eye was also able to perceive x-rays? How would the world look like? Could his view of the world be the same? Can he continue to assert his conception of the world as the absolute truth?

Obviously not!

And how about if we were able to perceive even more than this? What if our senses were designed to perceive all of the various innumerous rays in the universe?

Perhaps then we were going to see the whole of existence as a single unified field…?

Who knows…

Anyway, back to local waves and radiation…

As far as we're aware the above list of waves (and as far as we're not aware, countless other waves) constantly impact our world, bringing about various changes to us and our planet.

At least we know for sure the effects the radiation coming from the Sun has on Earth and its inhabitants. Based on this, it is evident that other Suns in other systems must also have some form of impact. And just as there are obviously many other repercussions of the Sun that science has not yet discovered, it is only logical to deduce that there are countless other effects constantly coming from the innumerous stars in space.

Just as matter is bound by and operates according to certain laws and principles, so it is with the cosmic rays. The supreme creative force of the universe applies Its command, at every instance according to us, in one single instant according to Itself.

And just like from gas to matter, all forms of energy are motions of waves, everything that transpires on Earth is also the result of the activity of these waves.

Hence, we may infer that the center of wave conversion, i.e. the brain, far from being limited by the five senses, is in fact designed and wired with a much higher capacity, one that is beyond our current scope of comprehension.

22

THE REALITY OF "LIFE BEYOND TIME"

We are living in a world that is essentially free of time and space yet we are so unaware of it! Our conditioning is so stiffened that even though it isn't far from our cognition our hard-wired beliefs and conditioning prompt us to refuse this truth.

From a universal perspective, formation and transformation are constantly taking place. Observing these formations and transformations, man with his limited perception tools and five senses, in the ignorance of the time he was in, surmised that a period of darkness followed by a period brightness is one "day" and linked this to the rising and the setting of the Sun.

Of course, at this stage the earth was still presumed to be flat so the idea was that the Sun rose from one side of this flat tray-like earth and set from the other side, rotating from beneath it to rise again, etc.

Then as time passed, a new group emerged who, based on the appearance and the disappearance of the moon, claimed a month was 28 days, and a period of twelve months was a year.

Then another group emerged and said, based on the revolution of the Sun there are 360 days in a year, and divided that into twelve to calculate the months.

Hence the model became that of a Moon revolving around the people on earth and a concept of time based on the Sun.

However, when we look at this concept of time from a scientific, philosophical, and spiritual i.e. Sufi perspective, existence is an indivisible whole, therefore it is impossible to talk about fractions of time. In respect of this whole, there is only one single instance. Only in respect of the individual units of manifestations within this whole, the concept of relative time gains some validity. Hence, it becomes evident that what we call relative time is only a linear sequence of events.

Indeed, even though man in essentially free of time and space, due to his conditioning and his delusive assumption that he is the body, lives in a universe limited by his level of comprehension bound by time and space.

Why is it that even though through contemplation and meditation man can totally escape the limits of his known world, he tenaciously chooses to confine himself to the dungeon of his body inside a material world?

How was man and the universe created in the first place?

Before we go into all this, let us first have a look at what certain Muslim saints such as Muhyiddin Ibn al-Arabi, Ibrahim Hakki Erzurumi and Imam Aziz Nasafi have to say regarding the star signs and the planets in the solar system…

23

ASTROLOGY FROM A SUFI PERSPECTIVE

Let's start by compiling the thoughts of Ibn Arabi on the creation of existence and the cosmos from his work *Al-Futuhat Al-Makkiyya* (Revelations in Mecca); Ibn Arabi says:

Allah, while nothing was with him, became present with the attribute of existence. It can be said that Allah is existence itself.

The Rasul of Allah (saw) stated:

"There was Allah, and there was nothing else with him."

Allah is unknown from the perspective of His Absolute Self and Essence, and this state of the unknown and the unseen is called Knowledge (Ilm).

The original form of Allah was a cloud-like dust (could also be understood as the quantum potential). Here existence was present in its hidden (inner-inactive) form. It was impossible for the cosmos to become manifest from this hidden form.

It was this first cloud-like dust that enabled the RAHMAN to activate its name ZAHIR. Through a sort of transformation Allah chose a spiritual form in the reflection of His Self.

When Allah looked at His Self through His Absolute Essence (dhat) he saw his Self, filled with endless qualities and attributes. Knowledge (Ilm) was the first glance at this discovery.

And the endless attributes are an inherent part of this data. It is due to the observation of these attributes within Himself that Allah is referred to as 'The First Intellect' (Aql al-awwal). This intellect (consciousness) observes the existence of attributes within the quantum potential, as His

Self. Existence becomes manifest from this consciousness which is the quantum potential.

And this became known as the Preserved Tablet (al-lawh al-mahfuz), the natural requirement of His being. And with it, this all became known as Life, Knowledge, Will, and the power to manifest.

From the perspective of the Elements, fire-air-water-earth, the perspective of objects, heat, moisture, cold, dryness, the perspective of lifeforms, blood, yellow bile, black bile, phlegm.

Then the First Intellect began its observation of His Self from this dust (the quantum potential). But there was nothing other than these attributes... So, existence is none-other than the observation of the quantum potential, as is the manifestation of His command. As a natural result of this observation, the manifestation of attributes (qursi), the cosmos, the heavens, the skies, the elements, and their eventualities. The father of this existence is Intellect, the mother, the Self.

And know this, Allah has formed the universe of waves from the quantum potential and formed galactic structures within it. Here, twelve segments have been formed. These are called Astrological signs.

These signs can be split into worldly elements as earth, water, air, fire. (What is emphasized by these elements is not their material form, but the frequency that they are associated with)

Each sign represents a heavenly power and all events are initiated from these heavenly signs. All change and confusion is due to the changes and re-organizations emanating from these signs.

In reality, our world is shepherded by the twelve powers housed across the twelve signs. As the heavens are governed by four principles, so can these twelve signs be divided into four categories.

There are three stations, worldly life, purgatory, and the after-life. Each station has four categories, each having an effect on their station. If we multiply the three stations with the four categories, we find the twelve signs.

As this world that feels like heaven to us will turn to hell on doomsday (with the sun engulfing the earth), purgatory is also under the command of these four levels, as is heaven.

Among these, Aries, Leo, and Sagittarius are of similar rank and character,

Taurus, Virgo and Capricorn are of similar rank and character,

Gemini, Libra and Aquarius are of similar rank and character,

And finally, Cancer, Scorpio and Pisces are of similar rank and character.

These four govern each station they are in.

The sign of this world is cancer.

Purgatory is under the governance of Virgo. However, the day the world is engulfed by the sun, it will no longer be under the influence of Cancer, rather it will be under the influence of Libra. Once the suffering of those bound for hell is exhausted, the influence will switch to Gemini.

The heavenly power associated with each sign has thirty different data sets (or frequencies). These powers become manifest throughout creation, and their effects prevail between one and one hundred years.

Heaven and hell are also under the effects of these twelve signs. As such, heavenly commands are all triggered by these twelve signs.

From all that is manifest in the heavens, to eating, drinking, sex, marriage, behavior, and change are by the guidance of the signs and the permission of Allah. Paradise of Awareness aside (the state of being aware of one's essential reality), all the heavens are constructed by the guidance of these twelve signs.

The rebirth of man in the afterlife is similar to his rebirth in purgatory. The inner reality of man is an individual illusion.

Our solar system is the 'floor' of paradise its 'sky' is the galactic universe. Air is the source of life. 'Air' is warm, it is moist. When the components of air heat up, they become fire. When the temperature decreases and moisture increases, air turns to water. There is nothing that can transform as quickly as air.

Thus, the most effective signs are the air signs, Gemini, Libra and Aquarius.

From the perspective of the earth, the moon is within its first reach, the second closest planet is Mercury, the third Venus, the fourth the Sun, the fifth Mars, the sixth Jupiter and the seventh Saturn.

Following the period of their formation, the treasures contained in the twelve signs descend upon these planets and commence exerting their effects on them.

Time is a relative concept and does NOT exist in the absolute. The day commences with the appearance of the sun and ends when it sets, and from these relative reference points are born; the months, the seasons and the years.

Allah has created the spiritual realms and powers to form all existence.

Before creating humanity, Allah had created the Jinn out of fire.

Upon departing this earth, the concept of sleep will no longer exist, such is the day of reckoning.

When the sun and its flames expand to engulf our solar system, this endless fiery realm will be called Hell.

'Sirat' is the period during which Man is able to soar above the realm of the sun. (The word 'Hell' refers to the state of life within the domain of the sun and its flames. Once the sun expands and engulfs the planets closest to it (also affecting the planets further out), evolved 'quantum brains' will escape this system, and the realm to which they escape will be referred to as paradise).

Life on earth is but a dream, an illusion.

That which we call home today will turn into the home of Hell following doomsday.

This sums up all we want to share from Ibn Arabi, one of the greatest scholars of the religion of Islam brought to us by Hadhrat Muhammad (saw)...

Now let's take a look at what the Gaws al-Azam and Qutub-ul Aktab of his time, Ibrahim Hakki Erzurumi has to say about Astrology:

Saturn is rather cold and dry, it is male (the planets in their characteristics have been further divided into two, male and female) its frequency emits sorrow, loneliness and pressure. Whereas they say that Venus brings pleasure and relief.

Saturn leads to stupidity, ignorance, fear, stinginess, hatred, regret, laziness and slow comprehension. When its effects are witnessed at the time of birth, with the will of Allah, its characteristics form the 'character' of the newborn.

Saturn rules Wednesday night and Saturday (Saturn day).

Ibrahim Hakki Erzurumi goes through these explanations for each of the planets, and also makes the following comment:

All references made to distances that take 500 years to travel in Islam actually refer to the 'vastness' of the distances and do not infer an actual measure.

He goes on to explain that the 'events' on earth are caused by these planetary and astral effects, but that the creator of these causes in essence is Allah. Regarding the moon:

The main cause of tidal effects is the moon.

As there is more warmth and moisture during the first half of each new moon, blood circulates more fervently in the veins, leading to strength and health for all living creatures.

Whereas following the full moon, with the dropping of temperature and moisture, growth and development become slower, and bodies become weaker.

Thus, during the first half of lunar months, recovery from illness is rapid, whereas during the second half, recovery generally takes longer.

During the first half the mind (brain) works better than during the second half.

If you fall asleep or spend too much time facing the full moon, this can lead to fatigue, laziness, headaches and colds.

Exposing meat to the full moon for too long will lead to a change in smell and in taste.

During the first half of the lunar month, fish stay close to the surface and become fatty and strong, whereas during the second half, they swim deeper and become leaner.

During the first half there is an increase of insects thus increased feeding activity, while the opposite takes hold during the second half.

Trees planted during the first half of the lunar month grow faster and better, those planted during the second half tend to be weaker or wither away.

And here are some notes from Erzurumi from *Marifetname* (The Book of Gnosis) on the effects realized when the moon conjuncts with certain signs:

When the Moon travels through:

Aries, Good time to embark on new projects;

Taurus, get married, do business, build;

Gemini, buy real estate, read;

Cancer, communicate, travel, use laxatives;

Leo, pass on your requests for assistance, engage in agriculture and repair, cupping;

Virgo, wear new things, converse with friends, meditate and pray;

Libra, go shopping, converse, listen to the Quran, drink ailments;

Scorpio, wash, purify, prefer solitude, meditate and turn inward;

Sagittarius, give blood, preferred time for shaving and haircuts;

Capricorn, dig a well, work the land, trade;

Aquarius, Travel;

Pisces, sea travel and partnership.

In the fifth chapter of his book, The Book of Gnosis, Hadhrat Ibrahim Hakki states the following:

The stars obey the angels, and the angels obey the commands of Allah. Everything moves or remains still based on Allah's will and power.

The sun is hot, it is dry. The moon, cold and moist. The planets orbit the cosmos with their own characteristics. Astrologists are correct in this; however, it is incorrect to assume that all action is based on this alone. The planetary powers are so because Allah wills It so. Thus, astral objects exert their effects on the world of actions.

There are twelve angels (powers) for the twelve signs. The seven planets travel and serve the twelve signs without interruption.

Ibrahim Hakki explains further that existence cannot be explained through one science alone, and that it is imperative to analyze existence comprehensively:

To try and comprehend the Reality of existence with either medicine, natural sciences or astrology on their own is impossible. Reality can only be known through the knowledge of Allah coming from one's essential reality!

Stating that even the hours of the day are separated into various astrological signs and effects, Ibrahim Hakki continues as follows:

In thirty couplets I outlined the hours to prefer and the hours to avoid.

That which is referred to by the name Allah is the doer of all deeds regardless of dimension,

Creating cause and effect from the micro to the macro dimensions.

Depending on the hour in which you are in,

The planet that effects that hour will cause a positive or negative effect thereof.

He continues to provide further detail as follows:

Split the hours into seven planetary effects

Know that the planet that coincides the hour in which you are in is its ruler

The hours of Saturn are burdensome and uncomfortable

Its place is the seventh orbit, you can construct but don't start anything new

Jupiter is a welcome host and insinuates a pleasurable time

A good time to eat drink and be merry

When Mars rules an hour, avoid doing much

It's a difficult time, well suitable for medical operations and giving blood

During the hour of the sun, the fourth planet, you can visit elders and loved ones

Venus is a fortunate hour, good for gatherings and meetings, conversations and music

Mercury is good for gatherings, poetry and prose, reading and calculating

The moon hour is pleasurable, a good time to journey, trade and communicate

Thus, the seven planets rule the hours

Get to Know your essential reality, for there lies the ruler of all that exists.

On his work on the human body, Ibrahim Hakki explains the following:

As the planets exude their effects on objects and beings with the power of Allah, the characteristics of people are formed whilst still in their mothers' wombs.

The thoughts and states of the mother and the father at the time when the sperm reaches the egg will effectively format the development of the egg.

For instance, their inner-peace, their unhappiness, understanding, idiocy, stinginess, generosity, fear, love, enmity, greed, thoughtfulness, benevolence, poverty or wealth, comfort or discomfort, whatever the state, it will affect the newborn.

For that is the data (software) that forms the newborn, and that data mirrors all of the data in existence.

Thus, some are destined for eternal bliss, and some for eternal sorrow, but all of this takes place while still in the mother's womb.

Regarding this matter, Hadhrat Habib-i Ekrem has stated the following:

The blissful are those who have found bliss in their mother's wombs, and the tormented are those whose torment starts in their mother's wombs.

Everyone's fate has in one way or another been predetermined.

Due to all of these effects, everyone's mortality is also predetermined at this point.

To not beleaguer the point further, I won't refer to the works of Imam Aziz Ibn Muhammad al-Nasafi. In his work *Zubdat al-haqa'iq* (Quintessence of Realities), he discussed the effects of the planets on people in great detail. Those that wish can try and find English translations of his works.

For those that read Ibn Arabi's *Revelations in Mecca*, they will note that the work contains many references that have still not been fully understood to our day.

Now let's look at the science of Astrology... and to its effect on humankind.

24

THE EFFECTS OF THE ZODIACAL SIGNS (BURJ) ON THE BRAIN

The constellations referred to as "*burj*" in Sufi literature are comprised of stars similar to the Sun that have clustered together over a period of 500-600 million years. They permeate cosmic rays to the universe based on their make-up and structure.

The rays they spread constantly bombard the earth and its inhabitants along with all the other planets rotating around the Sun in our system.

The planets in the solar system, namely Pluto, Neptune, Uranus, Saturn, Jupiter, Mars, Earth, Venus and Mercury constantly receive, and like a reflector, transfer these effects to us, keeping the human brain constantly subject to cosmic rays.

There are three crucial times when the brain is especially prone to these cosmic effects:

1. The 120th day after conception
2. The time in the womb between the 7th - 9th months.
3. The time of birth

120th Day:

When the embryo reaches the 120th day after conception the brain is just beginning to form and is ready to process the first cosmic rays. This first cosmic effect modifies the genetic make-up of the embryo to activate the formation of the spirit via holographic rays.

On the other hand, the bioelectricity that travels through the nervous system that holds all the cells together like an electromagnet, the holographic wave-body or the spirit, is also connected to the body and develops simultaneously.

Besides creating the spirit, if the strength and angular effects of the cosmic rays received by the brain, that is the aspects the planets make to each other, on the 120th day are sufficient and admissible, a specific circuitry necessary to produce anti-gravitational force will also be activated, and the brain will begin to upload this force to the spirit as well. This force will enable the person to escape the magnetic field of the earth during the period of doomsday, as I have explained in previous chapters.

If this circuitry isn't activated on that specific day the brain will not be able to upload the anti-gravitational force necessary to resist the magnetic pull of the earth. This is what determines the state of the fortunate (*said*) and the unfortunate (*shaqi*) ones.

Additionally, the effects received on the 120th day determine the person's lifespan. Similar to a timer, a switch is turned on that starts a count down for a specific period of time, say 45 years. If an accident doesn't occur, at the end of that time, a hard aspect made by Pluto, the Moon and Mars to the point of death in that person's natal chart will turn the switch off and the brain will immediately shut down. This is why we often hear things like, "he was perfectly healthy" regarding sudden deaths. Hence this third effect determines the life span and it is unalterable.

Finally, a fourth effect received on the 120th day determines one's sustenance, which is the main circuit regarding one's expansion capacity and the expansion one will live in the afterlife.

This truth was expressed by the Rasul of Allah (saw) 1400 years ago as:

"The constituents of one of you are collected for forty days in his mother's womb in the form of blood, after which it becomes a clot of blood in another period of forty days (80 days). Then in another 40 days it becomes a lump of flesh and (at the end of the 120 days) Allah sends His angel to it with instructions concerning four things, so the angel writes down his sustenance, his death, his deeds, and whether he will be of the fortunate (said) or the unfortunate (shaqi) ones. And then his spirit will be blown into him. By Him, besides Whom there is none worthy of worship, one amongst you acts like the people deserving Paradise until between him and Paradise there remains but

the distance of a cubit, when suddenly the writing of destiny overcomes him and he begins to act like the denizens of Hell and thus enters Hell, and another one acts in the way of the denizens of Hell, until there remains between him and Hell a distance of a cubit, then the writing of destiny overcomes him and he begins to act like the people of Paradise and enters Paradise." [Bukhari]

To sum up, the cosmic effects received on the 120th day in the womb determine the above-mentioned factors and commence the process of uploading data to the spirit.

As for the brain…

There are 15 billion neurons in the brain according to latest scientific research. Each cell makes contact with 16,000 other neurons. A normal person uses only 5-7% of the brain capacity formed by these 15 billion cells. Scientists and philosophers who exercise their brains more use up to 10-12%.

The bioelectric energy within these neurons connect to other cells and the activity of the brain increases to the extent of the brains bioelectric power and the group of cells that are related to it.

The first cosmic effects received by the essence of the brain on the 120th day forms the persons *"al-A'yan al-Thabitah"* (the immutable archetypal realities) in religious terms. That is, their unalterable fixed archetypal program or constitution.

7th to 9th months

The brain that rapidly develops as of the 7th month begins to process the effects it receives from the constellations. The closer to the point of birth the stronger the impact these cosmic effects have on the brain. These effects determine the person's intellectual capacity.

In the 9th month, especially the few days before birth the cosmic rays have even a stronger impact on shaping the person's intellectual capacity.

The moment of birth

The most powerful rays received by the brain after the above process is at the point of birth. These effects determine the person's ascendant or rising sign and when the baby leaves the mother's protective magnetic field he becomes fully subject to these energies, which determine the person's character, temperament, ability to form relationships and deal with situations etc.

You may wonder the role of genes at this point. Genes are only activated and hence the information they carry only have relevance if and when they find suitable outlets to express themselves in the person's brain. If they haven't received the specific coding from the constellations to make space for these expressions they remain preserved in an inactive mode until transferred to their offspring. And thus, it goes until they find the right conditions for expression.

I don't want to bore my readers with too much detail so I will try to keep things short and simple as I try my best to explain the divine order and its mechanics.

After this point, just like a plaster that has dried in its mold, the brain will no longer change its form. Its primary capacity and function, i.e. the persons capability and style of thought, emotion, imagination, illusion, assumption etc. are determined at this point and will remain as such until the person dies.

Hence, we often hear things about how people's temperaments or make-up won't ever change as it their ingrained dispositions, or that astrologically, one's natal chart reveals one's unalterable fixed constitution.

Is this really so?

Is astrology really this valid and determinative?

25

YOU AS THE LIVING PROOF OF ASTROLOGY

Is astrology fortune telling or is it a science?

If you ask me...

The mysteries regarding the creation and inner mechanism of man is contained within the science of astrology.

Hence Muhyiddin Ibn al-Arabi says, "*Everything that transpires on earth and within the heavens is subject to the effects of the constellations (burj)*".

Those who were aware of these energetic effects but were not able to see their place and role within the divine order, from a comprehensive and holistic perspective, deified the moon, the sun and other stars in the past. Thus, in time it was classified blasphemous and discouraged.

Whatever the role of rain, wind and food has within the divine order, it is the same with the constellations and the rays they permeate. They too fulfill the purpose for which they have been created; therefore, the energies they diffuse are also a part of and subject to the divine law and order, formed by divine power.

Just like we don't deify and worship food or water for nourishing our bodies, so too the stars and planets can't be deified for supplementing our brains with certain energies by order of the divine. Yet there are many today who are still deifying and worshipping the son of the Sun and even carrying its flag!

I challenge you to try it on yourself!

If you want proof of the validity of astrology, apply it on yourself.

For this you need to know three things:

1.   Your full date of birth
2.   Your exact time of birth
3.   Your place of birth

Once you have this information you can generate your personalized astrology (natal) chart or simply find your ascendant from just about any astrology book or site. You will see that 40-50% of your characteristics are represented by your sun sign and about 50-60% by your rising sign. As for your emotional make-up read about your Moon sign.

If you don't know your birth information try it on a friend. You will see how accurate the information is.

I personally have applied it on many people to verify its accuracy over and over again. I hope that you will also test it and see how perfectly the divine order works.

In following chapters, you will see how closely related this topic is to how the brain works. So, I urge you to understand this part really well. It is possible to identify about 90% of a person's characteristics by experienced proficient astrologers just by examining their natal chart.

In the past they used a reference book called the "Ephemeris" (precise information of the degrees and signs of each planet at a given point in time) and "Dalton's tables of houses" (the degrees or aspects the planets make to your brain at a given point in time) to determine one's natal chart. Today you don't need to manually calculate your chart as many astrology software and sites automatically generate it.

Consequently, once you have this information, you essentially have the map of your fate.

Whether this fate is alterable or not and if so, how - all of this I will explain in the chapter about fate.

So, once you have a natal astrology chart, the chart of the brain, you can see which planet falls into which sign and house and the aspects they make with each other to determine a significant amount of information regarding that person, such as their skills, potentials, temperament, characteristic, motivation etc. without even seeing them. However, I'd like to stress the importance of the accuracy of the birth information for this chart to be correct.

You may wonder if this is an assertion of knowing the "unknown"?

Let's say you read about the technical specifications of a particular car, its engine rpm, horsepower, cylinders, torque, etc. and you came across someone who owned that car and told them about its specs, is this knowing the "unknown"? Obviously not.

What I mean is, if you know which characteristics and attributes are formed when a particular planet is in a particular sign and house, then you can pretty much know the attributes of a person who was born when that planet was in that sign. This is not knowing the 'unknown', it is a branch of science among the many sciences of the divine system.

So, what can this science contribute to us?

Is it necessary to be acquainted with it?

What kind of benefits can it provide us?

Let me put it this way…

Once you see the validity of astrology based on your own experiences you will inevitably want to know the answers to certain questions, if you are of those who contemplate!

If all of your innumerous qualities and attributes have already been predetermined at birth without you having any say, then who is the 'self'? What *do* you have a say in? What and how much of anything is under your control? Why do you exist? Can you change your 'self'? How much? How?

Let us now explore astrology a little further before we come back to our main topic.

26

THE 16 GROUPS OF THE ZODIACAL SIGNS

There are four elemental energies of the signs:

Fire: Aries – Leo – Sagittarius

Air: Gemini – Libra – Aquarius

Water: Cancer – Scorpio – Pisces

Earth: Taurus – Virgo – Capricorn

Those who belong to the fire group are likely to be self-important, proud, and dominant. They like to be in control of their environment and always strive to be at the peak.

Those whose element is predominantly air are likely to be 'airy' and not very steadfast and persevering. They are open to all ideas but generally jump from one area of interest to another. They are unselfish and empathetic.

The water group is known mostly for their emotional make-up.

The earth group is known to be fixed in their ways and generally materialistic.

However, it is very important to note that everyone has two main signs:

    1. Internal (sun) sign
    2. External (rising/ascendant) sign.

Our first impressions of someone are always to do with their rising sign. People's lives are mostly driven by the qualities of their external sign. Most people have different internal and external signs, hence if you only know of someone's sun sign you probably won't see much of these qualities on them as the person's observable behavior and temperament is under the influence of their rising sign.

This is generally the reason why a lot of people discredit astrology and don't have much faith in it, as they are unaware of this distinction.

Based on the knowledge that has been bestowed to me I have become assured that around and after the ages 35-40 a person becomes more and more subject to and aligned with the effects of his/her rising sign.

Thus, it is imperative to know one's external sign based on their hour of birth rather than their internal sun sign based on their date of birth.

Let's have a look at the different categories of elements now:

Sun sign	Rising Sign
Fire	Fire
Fire	Air
Fire	Water
Fire	Earth

A person whose both internal and external sign is fire is selfish, self-centered. They want things to be in their favor. If the internal sign is fire and the external is air they will rebel against convention and act in favor of their environment. If the external is water while the internal is fire, like if the sun sign is Aries, Leo or Sagittarius but the external sign is Cancer, Scorpio or Pisces, their life will be restless and problematic as the outer water will suppress the inner fire causing internal distress to the person, at times it will increase and other times settle.

If the rising sign is an earth sign then it is similar to the example above except a little less problematic. They will be very generous 'mentally' but in practice they will find it difficult to spend money. Most of the wealthy people have the earth rising signs Taurus or Capricorn. Or they will have strong planets in earth signs, or in their second house.

Internal	**External**
Air	Fire
Air	Air
Air	Water
Air	Earth

Those who have strong air element in their chart will aim to be of benefit to the greater community. They are generally objective and tolerant. But if the rising sign is fire then they can easily become very arrogant and proud.

If the inner sign is Aquarius they will be intellectual but pompous. If the sun sign is Gemini they will be intelligent and proud, if the sun sign is Libra they will be frank and blunt. A general characteristic of those with an internal air sign is that sometimes they feel they don't really belong to this world.

An internal air with external water is an interesting combination. A free mind inside but restricted by emotional and addictive behavior on the outside.

If the free mind has a Cancer rising he will forsake himself for his family and home. If it's a Scorpio rising then you have someone who seemingly acts freely but not totally free of emotional ties, someone with a strong willpower albeit controlling. If he has a Gemini sun then he will be indecisive. If his ascendant is Pisces then he will become someone who eagerly indulges in pleasures.

Amongst the air signs the most intellectual sign is Aquarius, the most intelligent is Gemini and the most loving one is Libra.

As for earth rising, if it's a Taurus then you have someone who loves to eat and enjoy the pleasures of life, enthusiastic about earning money. A Virgo rising is ambitious, active, always looking for ways to make a steady regular income though never as lucky as the Taurus, he will acquire large amounts of money only to lose greater amounts. A Capricorn will be decisive, mature, tolerant and helpful but very attached to his monetary possessions. If the Capricorn rising doesn't have an Aquarius sun sign the Capricorn qualities will dominate over all other signs.

Internal	External
Water	Fire
Water	Air
Water	Water
Water	Earth

The most prominent characteristic of the water element is its emotional make-up. If this emotional nature combines with a fire ascendant it can lead to extreme behavior. 90% of those whom we call delirious have an internal water sign and external fire sign. Those who feel the most remorse are usually from this group. They frequently end up doing things they later regret because of their inability to control their emotions. They are exuberant people yet very compassionate and kind.

If the inner water is combined with an external air sign then you generally have a philanthropist as the air makes one generous and the water compassionate. If earth is the rising sign then this person will still be emotional but self-seeking and modest in general. If, however they feel threatened in any way then suddenly a lion will come roaring out of them. They are not very flexible and can find it difficult to adapt to change.

Internal	External
Earth	Fire
Earth	Air
Earth	Water
Earth	Earth

An external fire element combined with an internal earth usually makes a boisterous person but not as out of control as the water group. Also, whereas the water person is driven by his emotions the earth person is driven by his benefit and gain.

An external air makes one materialist in spirit but not so much in action. You will think they are generous people but in their minds, they are highly materialistic.

If the exterior element is water then they will be merciful but their charity/help will usually be of small amounts.

An earth exterior combined with an earth interior is usually a very modest person but acquisitive to the point of being stingy and almost always quite wealthy.

I'm aware that this information is extremely general and limited but given that this book is not a book of astrology it should be understandable that I cannot go into further detail.

Now four external elements combined with four internal elements yields 16 different groups of people. Upon further categorization we end up with 144 primary groups, and every person belongs to one of these groups.

For example, sun sign Aries with a rising sign Leo is fire on fire, or sun in Aquarius combined with Sagittarius rising is fire on air, or a Cancer sun sign with a Capricorn ascendant is earth on water etc…

As I said earlier everyone has two primary signs.

The sun (internal) sign shows their capability and aptitude.

The ascendant or rising sign (external) shows their skills and talents.

The brain is the person's *"Lawh-i Mahfuz"* (Preserved Tablet)!

The effects the essence of the brain receives on the 120th day after conception is the person's *"al-A'yan al-Thabitah"* (the immutable archetypal realities).

The worldly life and all humans are, by divine determination and precaution, under the governance of the zodiacal signs and the angels that transit their force (rays). Additionally, the intermediary realm (*barzakh*), that is all those who have left their physical bodies but continue to live until doomsday, and all of the heavens and hell are also subject to these effects.

Ibn Arabi's insights (*kashf*) are very accurate in this area.

This being the case, some people will be drawn to each other and some will repel each other.

If two people have the same internal and external elements they will have sympathy for one another. If their internal elements are the same but their external elements are different, where one is fire and the other is air or one is earth and the other is water then they will be attracted to each other.

If the internal element of one is fire and the other is earth they will not easily get along, especially if their external elements are fire against water then they will definitely repel each other.

If their internal elements are compatible but their external elements are incompatible then it's a difficult relationship. For example, internal air-water against external fire-water combination. Or, internal air–fire against external fire-earth or fire-water…

There is also the crosswise combination, for example you "think" you are fond of someone by looking at their appearance and external qualities but in effect your mindsets are very different. Why? Because your inner and outer realities are in conflict. Let's say your inner make-up is air and outer element is water, your partner's outer element is fire and internal element is earth. Your airy mind set is going to be drawn to their fiery appearance but when it comes to sitting down and actually communicating your values, you're going to conflict with each other; you're always going to have different perspectives.

So, then the success of all relationships, whether friendship, business or romantic, depends heavily on the compatibility of these signs and elements, and hence the attraction or repulsion of their brain frequencies. Those who have no attracting elements in their inner or outer make-up can't form a relationship.

The mystery behind "whomever you're with in this world you will long to be with in the life after death" is partly based on this truth.

The relationships between people, the sympathy or the antipathy that they feel are all driven by these energies. If you are drawn to someone and you like them, your signs and elements are compatible in some way, and it's generally an attraction between the external signs and elements.

One's make-up and relationships depend on how their brain has been programmed by these cosmic energies.

What about our emotions and reactions?

The sign the moon is in at the time of our birth represents our emotional sensitivity. The area in which we are most emotional is represented by the 'house' the moon is placed in our natal charts, at the exact time of our birth.

Again, I want to underline the importance of the ascendant sign. All astrological events transpire according to the effects you receive from your ascendant. If you don't know your rising sign, that is if you don't know your exact time of birth and hence don't have access to your natal chart you cannot conceive how you will be affected by certain events and situations.

Is there no way of understanding?

You can always pick up an astrology book and read up on the physical properties of all the rising signs to see which of them describe you best but of course this can't be an accurate guess. Sometimes a "stellium" occurs in a particular house, that is more than three planets are gathered in the same house creating a super strong force in that particular area, which can also affect your physical properties and be confused as the rising sign.

Here's a little summary of the different physical properties of the signs.

FIRE SIGNS

ARIES:

Long fingers but not thin, tips of the nails are square like. They have a strong build, usually of medium height to tall, a wide forehead that's protruding. Plump but not chubby.

LEO:

Leos can easily be recognized by their hair, hands and build. No matter how beautiful or handsome they may be, their hands always resemble a claw. The joints on their fingers are emphasized and bony, they have strong hands. As opposed to the fleshy chubby and soft hands of the water group, Leo hands are firm, stiff and bony. They have wide shoulders, effeminate, abundant and mane like hair. They have a strong and attractive appearance.

SAGITTARIUS:

They have a wide forehead, oval face but not so bony. A straight nose. Not very fleshy lips, they are usually sarcastic and tactless with their speech. Generally thin and tall until 35 but after the age of 35 they tend to gain a little weight around the waist area and have a slight belly. They are usually first to attract attention in a crowd.

AIR SIGNS

GEMINI:

Generally thin and skinny, of medium to tall height. Their hands are long and bony. Females have pointy, males have thin fingers. Their nails are long and sharp. Females usually have a pretty face, males have a bony, large nose. They generally have stomach problems. Their nervous system is sensitive. They are generous, very energetic and change their minds very often.

LIBRA:

All Librans whether male or female almost always have a beautiful face. Their hands are not bony but not chubby either, their heights are medium to tall. They have a proportionate body. They usually have a beauty spot on their face. They are talkative, sympathetic, warm and dynamic.

AQUARIUS:

They have a thickset, medium height, not pretty but cute, warm, they love anything to do technology and are generally big headed. Their hands are slightly fleshy, long and thin, with long sharp nails.

WATER SIGNS

CANCER:

Cancer ascendants can be easily recognized whether female or male. They are of short to medium height. Fleshy body, round head, their nose is bony at the top protruding towards the tip. They have a small chin. Females have distinct breasts, generally large. Their hands are chubby, short fingers, fleshy and sharp pointed nails. They tend to have major mood swings and can suddenly feel down and pessimistic.

SCORPIO:

Scorpio ascendants are also easy to recognize. Medium to tall height. Distinct bony chin that is v-shaped. Short legs. Generally, a charming face. Their skin is usually pinkish white. If females haven't received other effects their breasts and buttocks are distinct. They are usually highly energetic and like to dominate their environment. They have an administrative and cynical style.

PISCES

Pisceans are stout, large and round or slightly oval faced, they have a large nose, large ears but not as flat as with the Scorpios. Round fleshy chin and jowl.

These descriptions can be used as a very general guideline for those who don't know their rising sign but definitely nowhere near an accurate measure, for there are such countless formations created by the One that we can only try and surmise and study them in very general groups.

Now let's have a look at how astrology affects humans...

The first type of astrological influences: The position of the planets in the solar system at the time of your birth and the outer planets make 30-60-90-120-150-180 degree aspects to each other which stimulates the topics represented by the houses they are located in.

The second type: If transiting planets make any of the above listed aspects to any of the planets in your personal chart then the astrological influences become stronger. For example, transiting Sun or Saturn or Uranus making a 90 or a 120-degree aspect to your natal Venus or Mars.

The third type: The third type is through the Moon. The Moon very closely resembles our emotions. When it passes through our ascendant or the other signs that are of the same element of our ascendant it can make us very sensitive and reactive. If we can't keep our feelings and emotions under control at such times with our intellect we will most probably do or say things that we will later regret.

Let us remember the hadith narrated by Anas (r.a.):

The Rasul of Allah (saw) said,

"When Allah wills to fulfill the fate of his servant he takes his mind away and the person commits a sin in this state and then Allah gives his mind back *(brings him back to his senses)* **and the person feels deep regret saying, 'how did I engage in such an act?'"** (Dailami)

So how is fate fulfilled?

A perfectly sane person can do strange things when under the influence of certain transits. For example, Mars is transiting over his natal sun and the moon is conjunct with one of his planets in his 1st house (rising sign) and suddenly he becomes super sensitive and reactive to another person and ends up in a massive argument which leads him to stab the other guy with a knife. When he's back to his senses he claims he wasn't himself and can't understand or explain why he did what he did.

Such things we often hear on the news are examples of how fate plays out, which is confirmed by the hadith above. So then can we blame anyone? This I shall answer in the chapter about having faith in fate.

For now, let's just see how it plays out...

How does Allah fulfill fate at every instance?

Our brains are under constant bombardment of cosmic rays coming from the constellations. These rays (the continuously changing aspects, degrees, transits) stimulate specific circuitries that were originally activated by the planets at the time of birth.

For example, Mars in your natal chart may be aspected by Jupiter for some time, and then it may be aspected by Saturn, and then the Sun. These aspects may have supportive or difficult effects, depending on their degrees. Or your natal Moon is constantly under the influence of all the transiting planets that trigger the relevant circuitry according to your personal chart.

Hence, we are constantly going from one state to another.

Some people have very difficult natal charts with hard aspects and they have a very sensitive makeup, they may become extremely emotional and reactive by the slightest external trigger.

And some are extremely thick-skinned and fixed in their ways; they are hardly affected by external circumstances by which others may fall apart.

Some others are extraverted, confident, social, and assertive while others are introverted and passive, always waiting for others to take initiative.

Some experience rich and expansive internal states, which they can't express outwardly. While others are very expressive, talkative, energetic and magnetic outwardly but internally they may be very shallow and may easily find themselves in remorseful situations.

In short, all human characteristics are defined and determined by their natal charts, the programming their brains received by the cosmic rays at the time of their birth.

Their lives are driven in the direction of this initial programming. However, this is not an absolutely fixed unalterable program, for with *dhikr* new circuitry can be activated in the brain leading to new skills and changes in behavior.

These changes are related more to the person's "aptitude" and affect the programming based on their date of birth, not their time of birth, as the latter is harder to alter and takes much longer.

As I mentioned before the influences received on the 120th day program the person's *al-A'yan al-Thabitah* (the immutable archetypal realities) and are thus unalterable! The fortunate one is defined as the fortunate and the unfortunate one is defined as the unfortunate in their mothers' womb!

That is, there is only one chance at activating the brains ability to produce the anti-gravitational force. It is either activated on the 120th after conception or can never be activated again.

Indeed, Allah does as Allah wills! And none can question or judge Allah's will and activity!

To reiterate, the brain can turn on new circuitry, rewire itself via certain "dhikr" practices and thus alter the person's worldly life and life after death in new and different ways.

Now you may ask about whether dhikr is the same as the mantras that are used in Buddhism during meditation, which usually lead to a state of trance.

To answer this, we must look at the topic from a wider perspective.

Is Islam, dhikr is done with the names of Allah. These names are references to certain comic meanings and since the brain is formed and organized according to these cosmic energies, by repeating these names you tune your brain to the frequency of the universe and hence connect and make contact to the universal meanings. You start interacting with angels.

Other mantras on the other hand randomly create sensitivities in the brain making the brain more receptive, which open entry pathways to the jinn – the smokeless magnetic beam bodied creatures. Even in the best-case scenario where negative energies aren't involved you are still missing out on a great deal of transformation.

In short, while the repetition of the names of Allah bring you closer to Allah and adorn you with His infinite qualities and attributes, repetition of other words and names cause an increase in the sensitivity of the brain's receptor sites allowing contact with the jinn. This in turn means you become a victim to their trickery and subject to their ruling over you.

So, if you connect with beings who are in a constant state of dhikr and who thus constantly manifest the meanings referenced by these names, then these energies are naturally going to reflect on you and manifest in your world too. These beings are the conscious stars.

All creatures in the universe are manifestations of the innumerous qualities and attributes of the Creator. In other words, all of the constellations, the stars, the galaxies, are densified materialized forms of the infinite qualities of the Absolute Being and the infinite cosmic rays they permeate are no other than the divine meanings that comprise their very existence.

It is such primitiveness and narrow-mindedness to look at man and claim he is nothing other than an animal made of flesh and bones, that there is no spirit, no eternal life-after, and that he simply deteriorates with death and becomes recycled.

It is such archaic narrow vision to look at the sky and claim the galaxies, the constellations, the planets within our solar system are just unconscious inanimate structures that randomly come to life and die, that don't serve a particular purpose and don't receive or give any effects...

> **The seven heavens** (all creation pertaining to the seven states of consciousness)**, the earth** (the body) **and everything within them exalts Him** (*tasbih*; fulfill their functions by constantly manifesting in different ways to express His Names)! **There is nothing that does not exalt** (*tasbih*) **Him with hamd** (evaluation of the corporeal worlds created with His Names, as He wills)! **But you do**

not perceive their functions! Indeed, He is the Halim, the Ghafur.[12]

It is evident by this verse that the stars and planets are conscious living entities with specific functions.

The enlightened ones in the past referred to the same truth as 'angels' that abide on the stars - in fact they are the same thing. Some tried to describe it as the spirit of the stars, which is again the same thing.

The verse says:

> **And much more signs! And He leads to the reality by the** (Names comprising the essence of the) **stars** (the people of the reality, the Hadith: 'My Companions are like the stars; whoever among them you follow, you will reach the truth') **...!**[13]

This is such an open and clear indication 'for those who think'. Yet because man is so eager to deify and worship, or to give power to external entities, this truth has been disguised and hidden. The verse "…**leads to the reality by the stars**" clearly points to this truth but those who are conditioned to take only its literal meaning will attempt to deny this.

The fact that cosmic rays permeated by the stars reach the brain and activate certain circuitry, which then enable what is commonly referred to as "enlightenment" should not be regarded as strange at all!

Just like when you say, "It is Allah who feeds me" you don't mean to deny that when you eat, the nutrition is absorbed into your body via certain biological processes and thus converted into energy. It is the same thing.

The most important thing to understand here is the effects that reach the brain from the stars are just like the effects that the food we eat, the water we drink, the air we breathe have on the body. Just as we don't deify food for nourishing us and would regard this to be primitiveness, deifying the stars is also, if not more, an extremely primitive and unevolved way of looking at this.

Allah is the Absolute Ruler and Administrator!

He brings everything into existence through a cause.

---

[12] Quran 17:44
[13] Quran 16:16

If we use our intellect and try to conceive the magnificent mechanism by which the universe operates, in a holistic way, we will be fulfilling our servitude to Allah much more comprehensively. And if we don't have the magnitude for this, then indeed nobody is responsible for which they do not have the capacity.

> **And He subjects for you the night, the day, the Sun** (source of energy) **and the Moon** (which stimulates your hormones and senses with its gravitational force) **... And the stars are subjected by and in service to His command** (the stars are also a manifestation of the meanings of the Names comprising their essence) **... Indeed, there is a sign in this for a people who can use their intellect!**[14]

Allah willed to create man as the vicegerent of earth. He willed to display his own qualities on him. And thus, He created the magnificent cosmic factory we call the universe. Then with His Power He created man and made him a mirror to Himself that man may display and reflect the countless qualities of Allah.

> *Allah created his creation in darkness then spread his light (Nur) upon them. Whoever is touched by this light is guided, and who ever is missed by it will remain in darkness (astray).* [Tirmidhi]

> **And He leads to the reality by the** (Names comprising the essence of the) **stars** (the people of the reality, the Hadith: 'My Companions are like the stars; whoever among them you follow, you will reach the truth') **...!**

If we search with this understanding there are many more verses that we can find in the Quran pointing to the reality of astrology.

Indeed, "He leads to the reality by the stars". Who does He lead? Everyone who seeks the truth!

There is no limiting rule or precept in this verse. Yet sadly, many take it extremely literal and even reduce its meaning to 'those who lose their way in the desert can find their way by looking at the stars' (!)

Yes, Allah is *al-Hadi* (The guide to the truth, the One who allows

---

[14] Quran 16:12

individuals to live according to their reality.)

He guides whom He wills and leads astray whom He wills. He makes His Light touch whom He wills and makes easier their enlightenment, and makes His Light miss whom He wills and leaves them in the darkness of ignorance.

The verse, **"And the stars are subjected by and in service to His command"** is also a clear indication that the stars exist with His command for a purpose and that they are not inanimate, pointless structures for the purpose of adorning the sky.

But one must be an intellectual to evaluate such things, to comprehend the topic comprehensively and discern the magnificence of the system to perhaps get a little closer to understanding the grandeur and greatness of Allah.

How can the intellectual get closer and share knowledge with one another?

How can all humans become closer to each other?

What attracts or repels the spirits?

Underlying all sympathy and antipathy people feel for one another is the phenomenon of the stars and their compatibility. This is why we often hear phrases like 'our stars are in tune" or "our signs aren't compatible" in reference to the compatibility or incompatibility of the zodiacal star signs.

Abu Huraira (ra) narrates this mystery with the following Muslim hadith:

The Rasul of Allah (saw) said;

"The spirits are like groups (categories) *gathered together* (in the hereafter). *Those who know each other are fond of each other and get along. Those who don't know each other are in conflict with one another and do not get along."*

So, let us now explore what this "spirit" means...

27

THE WORLDS ARE NO MORE THAN A DREAM

Essentially there is only a SINGLE SPIRIT in existence to which Sufism refers as "The Great Spirit". Everything in the universe is created from this Great Spirit.

The Great Spirit, or in modern terms the *power* within the essence of existence or the First Reflection of Allah!

Abu Hurairah (ra) in the Muslim book of Hadith narrates from the Rasul of Allah (saw):

"Allah says: Man curses time yet I am time, for in my hand are night and day."

And, *"Allah said: The son of Adam abuses me. He curses time yet I am time, for I turn the night into day."*

The word "*dahr*" (time) in Arabic means "instant". It should not be construed as the linear concept of earthly time to which we have been conditioned.

According to us one day equals the time it takes the Earth to rotate once around itself, one year equals the time it takes the Earth to rotate around the Sun, i.e. 365 days, and a century is 100 rotations around the sun hence 100 years. All of this is "relative" time. It is according to us earthlings.

In reality there is only ONE time.

Pre-eternity and post-eternity, in the sight of Allah, is a single "instant" (*dahr*).

Relative time is an illusion we have collectively come to accept. It changes according to the speed and plane, i.e. the dimension in which we live. As one moves from being less matter to more consciousness and spirit, the experience of relative time also changes and becomes more expansive.

Essentially the word "*dahr*" refers to the universal energy that composes existence, that is, the attribute of divine power.

It is an unfathomable concept for one who is conditioned to the daily linear concept of time.

This is why the Quran narrates many of the "future" events as things that have already transpired using past tense to explain them.

For pre and post eternity is a single existence in the sight of divine observation or the 'Knowledge of Allah'.

This is the intimates of the reality have claimed:

"Essentially there is only one reflection. It is the Single Reflection (Tajalli-i Wahid). There has never been a second reflection."

The whole of existence is only one single reflection, referred in Sufism as the 'One Theophany' or the **Divine Self-disclosure of Allah** (*Tajalli Wahid*). There has never been a second reflection thereon. Everything that is seen, felt, perceived, imagined and experienced is a depiction of this Single Reflection.

Sufism also refers to this as the "constant instant". Though for the truly enlightened and awakened ones this "constant instant" is quintessentially an "imagined instant" and is no other than the Knowledge of Allah.

The entire existence in the sight of Allah is nothing other than a principle of knowledge. That is, the universe doesn't even have an actual existence in the sight of Allah. This is why the Sufis have frequently claimed, "*The worlds are only a dream*"!

To discern this is to become familiar with this reality. And that my friend, is entirely a matter of experience and joy. Only one who is passionate and dedicated enough may eventually be given the insight to perceive the inner depths of this reality through the activation of *ilm-i ladun* (manifestation of a special angelic force from His grace) by Divine Grace.

So, in respect to its essence there is really only a single dimension of time in the universe. For those who can perceive! Within this single frame of time, countless dimensions have 'materialized' through divine order, spawning innumerable forms of existence.

There is also a general misconception that I would like to correct.

Due to misconstruing the fact that "all forms of existence exist in the Knowledge of Allah" some claim "knowledge is subject to the known." That is, because all known existence was in the pre-eternal knowledge of Allah and Allah knew what they were capable of doing He determined their fates according to their known capacity.

This fiction has been fabricated to endorse the fact that Allah does not do wrong by His servants, He does not oppress or torment, He simply does as their pre-eternal states necessitate. Hence Allah does not cast anyone to hell by force.

The hadith states; ***"Allah was, and besides Him nothing else existed. No air was under him, no air was above him"*** to which Hadhrat Ali (ra), the zenith of Sainthood, added, ***"And it is still so…"*** i.e. ***"It is still that moment."***

That 'instant' that the Rasul of Allah (saw) referred to is this 'instant'; the only instant there is. The entire existence is contained within this single 'instant'. There is only one Single Reflection.

All forms of existence with innumerable names within the Divine Knowledge have been brought into existence, i.e. "created" from nothingness for the purpose of "Self observation"!

The source of all names, the One who gives life to the Names and manifests them, the source of universal energy (*al-Hayy*) willed with his name "*al-Mureed*" to observe the infinite meanings with his attribute of Knowledge and thus used His attribute of Power to give individual forms to them, and according to the meanings he willed to manifest, gave them an intellect. Because he created from his knowledge he gave them the ability to observe and be observed and hence the names *as-Sami* and *al-Basir* were expressed. While their individual existence were still in the form of words (*kalaam*) with the attribute of *takwin* (Divine production, formation, bringing-into-being) life emerged and manifested as the world of acts.

Despite this, in the sight of the One denoted as Allah…

There is only one single instant "*dahr*"! Everything has transpired within this instant. The rest is no different than the perpetual ripples that formed after the stone hits the water. Infinite dimensions like the infinite ripples, one leading to another. What transpires in one dimension is no different than what has transpired in the previous dimension.

When the brain is able to work at higher levels of its potential it is able to accomplish a leap in consciousness, which enables the person to experience these higher dimensions of life.

The enlightened ones are endowed with the ability to leap into higher levels of consciousness to then observe, with divine grace, why things transpire the way they do in this realm and for what purpose.

Coming back to the formation of spirits…

An infinite surge of energy sourcing from the single Spirit has formed angels depicting infinite meanings. These meanings in the form of angels then densified and materialized into certain shapes and structures brining about the world we see and experience. Some became the stars some became conscious beings.

The angels, or the conscious masses of energy objectified as "stars" permeate infinite meanings/rays congruent to their purpose of creation.

Lastly, "man" was created with a brain capacity to evaluate these infinite meanings.

When a human is first created, that is the 120th day after conception, he is uniquely programmed via specific rays coming from these "angels" or the star signs (constellations; a group of angels). This programming is done according to the qualities and attributes Allah wills to observe on the person.

This is explained in the verse:

"Who created you (manifested you)**, formed you** (with a brain, an individual consciousness and a spirit) **and balanced you** (the work process of your brain, consciousness and spirit)**!**

Whatever form (manifestation of Names) **He willed for you, He configured your composition accordingly."**[15]

Hence individual spirits, that is, spirits with a personality whom will continue on to eternal abodes of life after death, are formed in this fashion, in this world, via the brain.

Those whose brains are programmed with the rays of compatible star signs and the spirits that are formed thereof will attract each other and get along. Even if they've never met before they will feel an instant spark when they see each other. Or, if they are of incompatible elemental compositions they will repel each other even without an apparent reason.

As I said this is not a book of astrology so I do not wish to go into further detail. My purpose is only to explain how the human make-up is formed and programmed, the role of the cosmic effects on humans, the system in which humans and their future is subject to, and the mechanism by which the entire existence operates.

If Allah wills I intend to write new books exploring these topics in much greater detail. But for now, let us take a closer look at "man".

28

THE DIFFERENT ASPECTS OF MAN

Let's talk about "man" ...

The meaning of the word "man" is first depicted as the "body" that appeals to certain "senses". The body with its five senses, eats, drinks, sleeps, mates, and acts in favor of the body's comfort and safety.

Then we come to a second group of attributes; those related to the "ego-self-identity" (*nafs*). Seven in total, these are, intellect, thought, comprehension, illusion, design, imagination and memory. The first group of attributes is related to the external and the second group is related to the internal make-up of man.

The word "nature" refers to the external aspect. The material composition of man's exterior "body" is described as his "nature". That is, all of the qualities comprising the formation of the body and the affairs and callings of this body. In other words, his nature is the natural functioning of his physical biological make-up. It is impossible for one's nature to become abolished until the body dies.

One's character is related to the second group of attributes, regarding the "identity".

The word "*nafs*" denotes the sense of "I". It is one's identity. How one sees and feels about himself. The attributes that shape the *nafs*; intellect, thought, comprehension, illusion, design, imagination and memory are formed with the effects received during the 9th month during pregnancy.

For instance, one's thought capacity, which is also related to their intelligence, is determined by the effects of Mercury. Their intellect is determined by the effects of Uranus and Saturn. Their comprehension and discernment are affected by the rays of the Sun. Mars reigns over illusion and misgiving. Venus rules design, and the Moon and Neptune rule the imagination.

The *nafs* to which we refer as "I" is formed by the effects of the Earth. The fact that the person sees himself as a separate existence is due to the effects of the Earth on the brain.

Moreover, the person is "conditioned" by his environment for a specific lifestyle. The extent to which the person is suggestible to the conditioning he receives depends entirely on the attributes listed above.

For example, if his comprehension and intellect is strong he may not be easily conditioned. On the other hand, if his illusion and misgiving predominate he will easily become conditioned and may not easily escape the effects of this.

All actions are sourced and driven by either the intellect or by illusion. Either the intellect is the prevalent force or illusion is. If illusion predominates then the action is driven by the belief "I am the body" and hence it is an "ego-centric" action, as the Sufis would call it. If on the other hand the intellect overweighs then the motive of the action is not the self but the greater good and is hence inward directed, i.e. driven by one's essential being.

Thought, comprehension, design, imagination… Either they are driven by illusion or by the intellect. For example, in any given situation the ego sees an advantage and acts towards gaining it. This is due to the sense of "I-ness" and the conditioning the person has that if he fails in attaining that gain he will either be deprived of the pleasure of obtaining it or that he will be looked down upon by his environment. The thing that makes him think and feel this way is his illusion. He is acting under the effect of his illusion.

If the intellect had prevailed instead he would have thought, "who cares what anyone thinks, so what if I don't obtain it" and would have gone on with his life. He wouldn't feel any pain, grief or agony for not obtaining it or any fear or worry about what others would think or say. He would be wise enough to totally disregard such baseless worry and move on with his life.

Memory pertains to the spirit, which is related to the interior make-up of man.

The function of memory essentially belongs to the spirit. The brain uploads all data to the spirit and when necessary retrieves it.

Therefore, memory loss due to malfunctioning in the brain is not possible. Memory loss is due to a malfunction in the center that allows communication between the brain and the spirit. Hence the brain is unable to access and retrieve the information uploaded to the spirit. No data uploaded to the spirit can ever be erased, other than through "forgiveness"!

During pilgrimage millions of people gather together with the same intention turned towards the same point. The radiation they give out is so powerful that it erases their sins like erasing data on a tape, and the pilgrim returns home with no sin. This is the phenomenon regarding erasing the magnetic data recorded on the spirit.

Pilgrimage is an enormous invocation involving millions of people including the saints. Even if they don't physically go, the saints attend pilgrimage energetically or send their representatives. What does this mean? Someone through whose brain they can operate and broadcast their energy!

29

CAN WE TALK ABOUT THE SPIRIT?

We spoke about the body and the *nafs* as we discussed man. I had talked about the meaning of the word spirit in previous writings. Due to the misunderstanding surrounding the claim, "the spirit cannot be known" some have forbidden the discussion of spirit. So, allow me to make this clarification with the following Muslim hadith.

Narrated by Abdullah ibn Masud (ra):

I was walking with the Rasul of Allah (saw) through Medina and he was reclining on a date-palm leaf stalk. Some Jews passed by and they were talking among each other. Some of them told the others, "Ask him about the spirit!" to which the others objected, claiming the answer may displease them. But they insisted, so one of them stood up and asked the Rasul (saw) about the spirit. The Rasul (saw) went into silence and I immediately understood that he was receiving revelation. I stood by him until the revelation was complete. Then the Rasul of Allah (saw) said:

> **"And they** (the Jews) **ask you,** (O Muhammad) **about the spirit. Say, "The spirit is from the command** (*amr*; the manifestation of the Names) **of my Rabb. And you** (the Jews) **have been given little of this knowledge."**[16]

As can be seen this verse directly addresses the Jews who asked the question. This is evident with the expression, "THEY ask you" and "Say" i.e. tell them, the Jews, that they have been given little of this knowledge.

---

[16] Quran 17:85

Essentially for the followers of Islam the "Mystery of Unity" is based on the proper discernment of the reality of the Spirit. Because of this, countless saints in Islam have reached this secret and experienced the supremacy of unity.

For the Jews, to whom the doors of mysticism and abstract realities have been closed, cannot comprehend the reality of the spirit. If and when they do, they can no longer be Jewish, they will inevitably have to accept the way of Islam.

So, let us continue our discussion on the spirit.

The brain forms the spirit of a person. So how then does the spirit densify and form the person's body after life?

In the past 'Spirit' was the name used to refer to the absolute energy and consciousness in the universe. This was how they referred to the universal energy in that age. Hence, they claimed everything is created with this spirit and from this spirit.

In the absolute sense the word spirit refers to the spirit of the universe. This Spirit encompasses all of the meanings denoted by the Divine Names. As a matter of fact, these Names are used to describe the meanings that comprise the Spirit. Sometimes it is called the Great Spirit, sometimes the Reality of Muhammad and other times The First Intellect.

In terms of constituting the essence of life, it the Spirit and/or the Great Spirit. In terms of comprising the meanings denoted by the Divine Names, it is the Reality of Muhammad. In respect of observing and witnessing these meanings it is the First Intellect.

In Sufi terms the reflections of the Spirit, or in modern terms 'energy' densified and formed the galaxies, stars, and planets. These stars permeate certain radiations, which express the meanings of the Divine Names.

Finally, the brain was formed, with the capacity to process these meanings and manifest them. And It was able to observe Itself either conditionally or unconditionally depending on the brain's capacity to process and manifest Its meanings.

In this light, the Absolute Spirit forms the brain and the brain forms the personal (individual) spirit!

The Great Spirit, at the lowest level forms the brain, and the brain at the lowest level, forms the human spirit. Based on the capacity of this individual human spirit the meanings comprising the Great Spirit are uploaded to it. (The Great Spirit constitutes the highest level).

Therefore, on an individual level a human becomes the mirror to the Existence referred to as the Great Spirit or the First Intellect or the Reality of Muhammad at the level of Oneness. However, the person who acts as the mirror is essentially no different and nothing other than the reflection itself!

Take a look at what Imam Ghazali says regarding the creation of the spirit with the body:

If it is asked: "If the spirit is created with the body then why does the Rasul of Allah (saw) say "Allah created the spirits two thousand years before he created their bodies" and "I am the first of the Rasuls to be created but the final of Nabis. When I was a Nabi, Adam was somewhere between water and clay"?"

The reality is this: There is no substantial evidence in these words to the precedence of the spirit. But according to the surface meaning of the hadith "I am the first of the Rasuls to be created" there may be a possible indication that he was created before his body was brought into existence. Its esoteric meaning however, is obvious and possible to explain... In this context the word creation (khalq) does not have its ordinary meaning of "bringing into existence" rather it refers to Allah's determining the Rasul's existence. Before the Rasul's mother gave birth to him he was not created and did not exist. In priority and determination in Allah's plan he was first, albeit his physical creation was later. For Allah determines all divine matters in the Lawh-i Mahfuz (Preserved Tablet) appropriate to his knowledge.

As for Allah creating the spirits two thousand years before their bodies, the word 'spirit' here refers to the spirits of the angels and the 'bodies' refers to the embodiment of the Throne (Arsh), the Footstool (Qursi) the heavens, the constellations, air, water and earth.

If you have understood the two types of existence then you would also have understood that the creation of the Rasul of Allah (saw) being before the creation of Adam is not in the physical sense but in respect of divine determination.

This is the last word regarding the spirit. Allah alone knows the truth of this topic. (Imam Ghazali, Hadhrat Rawzatut Talibeen)

30

THE HUMAN SPIRIT

As known, what enables the continuity of man after death is his spirit.

What is the human spirit? How is it different to the universal "SPIRIT"? How is it formed and what are its properties?

The act of blowing the spirit into the fetus on the 120th day is a very symbolic expression. Clearly this isn't about Allah literally blowing His Spirit into the fetus. Allah is beyond and far from such concepts.

Gaws al-Azam Abdulqadir al-Jilani wrote in his "*Qasida al-Ayniyyah*" some one thousand years ago:

"This is a metaphor! Is not the SPIRIT His very existence?"

This is of grave importance! It is imperative to contemplate on it without prejudice and judgment.

As Imam Ghazali says, *"the human spirit isn't something that comes from outside and enters into the human body."*[17]

On the 120th day after conception the brain of the fetus is developed enough to process its first stream of cosmic rays. This event of incoming cosmic rays instigating the production of waves we call the "personal/human spirit" is explained metaphorically as an angel blowing the spirit into the body.

This wave-body called the spirit can be examined at four levels.

1. Carrier waves (spirit) holographic wave body

---

[17] More information on this can be found in *Spirit, Man, Jinn.*

2. Anti-gravitational force
3. Positive energy waves (*Nur*)
4. Memory waves

1. CARRIER WAVES (SPIRIT)

The human spirit is comprised of carrier waves; this is what enables man to continue his life after death. It is holographic in appearance. Even if to some extent it becomes deformed for various reasons it has the ability to repair itself and return to its original state.

Essentially, it is the counterpart of the physical body. Its form and appearance are the same as the physical body at the point that it separates from it. If at the point of death, the body has a missing organ due to an accident, say for example a leg or an arm is missing, because it existed before and this data was uploaded to the spirit, the spirit body will not reflect this absence. The body of the jinn, commonly mistaken for aliens, is of the same make-up as the spirit-body.

2. ANTI-GRAVITATIONAL WAVES

This has commonly been discussed covertly. I will share further information from the Rasul of Allah (saw) regarding this in the section about fate.

The brain core of the fetus encounters critical information on the 120th day in the womb. In fact, I can easily say without doubt that this is *the* most critical moment in the life of a human being. For the cosmic rays that penetrate the brain on that day have one chance at activating the anti-gravitational force that will allow the person to escape the earth's magnetic pull during doomsday. These anti-gravitational waves, if activated, are uploaded to and hence constitute the spirit-body. In other words, in the case of anti-gravitational waves being activated and produced, the carrier waves that form the spirit-body are composed of anti-gravitational waves. Otherwise, the carrier waves are formed unaided by the anti-gravitational force and thus unable to resist and become independent of the magnetic pull of the Sun and Earth.

The other attribute of the anti-gravitational force is that it uploads positive energy to the spirit. That is, a third type of waves is uploaded to the second type of waves.

If the brain doesn't produce the second type of waves then the third type of waves cannot be uploaded; they will serve no purpose in the afterlife for the person.

The person has no say and plays no role in the activation of anti-gravitational waves.

Just as the cosmic effects received on the 120th day after conception commence the production of spirit-waves with no effort or will on behalf of the person, the activation of anti-gravitational waves also has nothing to do with the person – nobody can do anything to alter or affect this process. One either receives the necessary cosmic rays on that particular day, to activate that particular circuitry, and hence begins to produce its spirit-body interweaving it with anti-gravitational waves, or the circuitry isn't activated, and the spirit is formed without the anti-gravitational force.

The inevitable outcome of the latter case is eternal imprisonment in the Sun, i.e. "hell".

This truth can be found recorded amongst various hadith regarding fate where the Rasul of Allah (saw) says:

> *"Allah appoints an angel to every womb, and if Allah wishes to complete the child's creation, the angel will say. 'O Rabb! A male or a female? O Rabb! Fortunate or unfortunate (said or shaki)? What will his livelihood be? What will his age be?' The angel writes all this while the child is in the womb of its mother."* (Bukhari, Muslim)

Thus, is the matter of the *said* and *shaki* (the fortunate/unfortunate ones) mentioned in some of the hadith that I shared in the section on fate.

Brains that produce the anti-gravitational waves are referred to as the *said* or the fortunate ones, i.e. those who have reached true happiness and bliss. And those whose brains have not been activated to produce anti-gravitational waves are called the *shaki* or the unfortunate ones, i.e. those in a state of misdeed and wrong.

Neither the fortunate have earned this state through their deeds nor the unfortunate have been deprived because of their misdeeds.

This is based totally on what transpires on the 120th day in the womb.

Those whose spirits have been strengthened with anti-gravitational waves will most certainly reach the state of paradise. Those who have been deprived of the anti-gravitational waves will inescapably be stuck inside the Sun-Hell.

The fact that this has nothing to do with one's deeds is validated with the words of the Rasul (saw):

"Indeed, none of you will enter Paradise by his deeds alone." They asked, "Not even you, O Rasul of Allah?" The Rasul said, "Not even me, unless Allah grants me his mercy."

As can be seen going to paradise has nothing to do with one's deeds and everything to do with the grace and mercy of Allah, which is represented as the activation of the anti-gravitational waves in one's brain, based on "divine determination".

3. POSITIVELY CHARGED ENERGY

Positive energy waves, or "good deeds" in religious terms (*thawab*), are formed in the brain by altruistic, unselfish thoughts and actions. Negative energy on the contrary, or "sin" in religious terms, are produced by egoistical and selfish concerns and actions.

Positive energy is uploaded to the anti-gravitational waves. If the person does not have anti-gravitational waves then even if positive energy is produced it will be of no benefit to the person after death. Albeit he will experience the positive consequences of this energy in the worldly life.

Negative energy on the other hand doesn't need anti-gravitational waves to be uploaded; it is directly transferred to the carrier waves forming the spirit body.

Positive energy (*thawab*) is produced when the person starts becoming conscious of his actions, hence as of the ages 5-6 children should be advised to engage in constructive positive actions.

Negative energy is produced and uploaded as of adolescence, i.e. with the production of sex hormones, as negative energy is produced when the brains biochemistry is altered by sex hormones. This is why religious texts often metaphorically say *no sin is recorded and hence nobody is accountable for their actions before adolescence.*

I swear it was revealed to you and those before you, "Indeed, if you associate anything to Allah (if you live in a state of duality – shirq) **all your work will become worthless and you will surely be of the losers!"**[18]

Dying in a state of duality is the inevitable end of the unfortunate ones who are deprived of the anti-gravitational waves needed to carry positive energy. Thus, all of their good work is lost.

4. MEMORY WAVES

Memory waves encompass all data associated to the person's thoughts, emotions, desires, and all mental activity that differentiates him from others. Similar to television waves they are uploaded to the holographic body with sound and image.

The person continues to live indefinitely after death with the contents of this data package.

All mental activity in the brain, without exception, is uploaded to the spirit at every instance, regardless of whether the second or third type of waves is present.

Individual consciousness is the depiction of these memory waves. In other words, the memory waves comprise the body of the person's consciousness.

So, to sum up "man" or "human" also consists of the human spirit, or the holographic after-life wave body, which is comprised of these four different types of waves.

---

[18] Quran 39:65

31

THE HUMAN BODY

After examining the human spirit let us now continue our exploration of man by looking at his bodily and humanly attributes.

A human, based on his nature, is obviously bound to eat, drink, have sex, and sleep. These are common necessities for a normal healthy body. Some brain damages can lead to insomnia but these people get worn out quickly. Additionally, sleep for the brain is different to sleep for the body, but in any case, even insomniacs get some form of sleep. It is impossible to survive without it.

Sex is also unavoidable. Even if the person never gets married or has a relationship, he still produces sex hormones. Whether he secretes this discharge in his sleep or with his urine, in some way or another this production and secretion is going to take place.

Eating and drinking is indispensable. The material that forms the human body, or energy, is received, processed and outputted constantly. This is what upholds the body. By all means the body has to receive energy in the form of food, process it and output it. When this function stops the life of the body will come to an end.

But how should the nature of man be directed at the level of the body? This is the first aspect. The second aspect is regarding the use of intellect, thought, comprehension, illusion, design and imagination, which I previously covered.

Generally, these qualities are used by the faculty of *illusion*, in line with one's conditioning and nature, or natural disposition.

Driven by illusion, we strive in the direction of what the society imposes upon us as "important" in order to acquire it, in fear that if we don't, we will be deprived and in great loss.

The first function of illusion is to make someone believe that they are in fact someone, i.e. that they have a separate existence, i.e. their body.

Psychiatrically speaking, believing that you are the body is indeed a mental disorder! Surely a detailed diagnosis is needed. Some don't believe they are their body for example, they believe they are an animal or an object! This is a sickness! It is a condition of false perception.

But if someone is aware of the make-up of matter, that the body is composed of cells, which are made of acids, that are made of atoms, which are comprised of electromagnetic waves...

Of course, atoms can be broken down into electrons, neutrons, neutrinos, positrons, mesons, and so on... We have not yet been able to develop a microscope with the capacity to see an atom. It is still in process. If and when it is developed, we will see that existence is nothing other than a field of electromagnetic waves.

With this observation the *person's* existence and function is going to be seen to be nothing more than a point of consciousness within this infinite field.

Where is consciousness? This consciousness is a reflection of the absolute First Intellect, it reflects to the brain and forms in the spirit. Without a spirit a 'person' cannot be and hence the person's individual consciousness won't exist.

Now as a result of this sequence a spirit is formed and whether consciously, through awareness, or unconsciously, by means of conditioning, a personality or an "identity" is formed. The former is a consciousness-based personality the latter is a body-based personality. Can these personalities be eradicated?

The personal-individual consciousness, once formed, can never become inexistent. It is a special spirit formed by the brain. Essentially it is no different to the divine Spirit except that it can never observe itself.

It is possible to know the spirit in respect of consciousness but impossible to know the spirit itself. It can't be known. It can't be seen. Your spirit points to your self. Your intellect or individual consciousness, which is the counterpart of the First Intellect, is what enables you to know your essential self.

Even after you realize your essential self and that your very essence is indeed the summation of all of the meanings, that is, you encompass the whole and contain the reality within you, this does not invalidate or annihilate your "individual" existence. This is the first point.

As for the second point, yes, the spirit will live indefinitely after the body is abandoned and won't ever die again, but as long as you are in this body you cannot live indifferent to it, because the essence of the body is the brain, the brain commands and controls the body. The brain also creates the person's spirit.

> **"Indeed, We have created man from a line** (sperm; a genetic formation) **of wet clay** (a mixture of clay, water and minerals)."[19]

The word 'clay' in this verse refers to cells not to soil. Man is made of cells. This has been symbolically expressed as 'clay' in religious texts. Cells come together to ultimately form a human and its brain.

There are fifteen billion cells in the human body. Since we can't discredit that, the body *does* exist, and as long as it does so do the programs and proceedings of its nature, i.e. the natural impulses of its cellular structure.

But let us not confuse the impulses of the cellular structure, the nature of the body with its compositional make-up. These are two different things.

In order for one to know himself and his essential reality he must first free himself from the illusion that he is the body by taking under control the impulses of his physical body. If he can establish control over his bodily impulses and govern his body instead of being governed by it, then he will have the opportunity to gain insight into the reality of his self.

Now as for the compositional make-up I mentioned above, this has to do with the activation of certain circuitry in the brain via the cosmic rays. It is the composition of meanings or the Names. Certain cosmic rays activate certain circuits in the brain. This then activates certain Names, which are expressed at different levels. This is your predisposition. Also known as the "immutable archetypal realities" (*al-A'yan al-Thabitah*).

---

[19] Quran 23:12

When you say "I thought of…" or "I had this epiphany…" or "I'm feeling such and such", you're actually expressing these specific meanings. But if you were to take control over your 'natural/bodily impulses' and cleanse yourself of your conditioning you may then be able to venture into realities beyond the veils of your predisposition and physical nature.

Simply knowing these are the expressions of the Names doesn't save you from the hellfire. Only when you actually learn to govern your body and control its impulses, not give it what it wants whenever it wants it for example, then you may overcome the captivity of your body and the sufferings that result from it.

Hence when Abdulkareem al-Jili said, "*I saw Plato in hell, his status was so elevated that it was higher than that of many believers*" he was referring precisely to this reality. In other words, simply being enlightened with knowledge alone, without applying it, without fulfilling the practices to discipline and gain control over your body, is not enough to admit one into heaven.

32

THE HELL OF HUMAN NATURE

How do you take your 'nature' under control and go beyond your compositional make-up?

Taking your nature under control is taking your impulses to eat, drink, sleep, and have sex under control. Performing salat, fasting, engaging in dhikr etc. are all advised for this purpose.

For example, your nature will not be inclined to waking up at a really early time and taking ablution and praying. Or let's say you didn't perform your *isha* salat (the last salat of the day) it's late and you're really sleepy. Clearly it goes against the nature of your tired body to get up, take ablution and pray at that time.

One must resist his natural bodily impulses and overrule his nature to accomplish this. This includes all bodily pleasures from food and sex to shopping and dressing up in fancy clothes. When you can't rule over your body then your body rules over you. There's no other way around it!

The point is to gain the ability to resist these things when the body desires it or to give it up entirely until the addiction ends.

This is the aspect pertaining to the physical body. There is also the aspect regarding one's compositional make-up. That is, the Names that comprise one's being, and hence the natural pull in that direction.

Think of the things that have been eased for you. Things you naturally find easy to do. These are things that are facilitated by the Names that compose your being. For a time, you also have to omit these practices. Until you can fully control and govern your self you must do this.

Say for example, your compositional make-up is such that running for the aid of those in need of help has been made easy for you. You constantly find yourself in positions where you're helping others out, giving, teaching, etc... Such a holy act! Right? Well not really. Not until you can control the impulse that drives you to do this 'autonomously'! This is your programming! It's not such an exalted or sublime act when you're programmed to do it. So, you must omit it for a while. That would be a greater challenge! Until you can gain control over this impulse you must stop doing it.

For those who find this controversial and want evidence, think of the many saints, like Abdulqadir al-Jilani, who practiced silent retreats in seclusion for long periods of time, made no contact with anyone, stopped teaching and preaching and applied intensive, strenuous spiritual practices until they were able to take full control over themselves before going back into the public as guides and teachers.

Running around in service to others before fully comprehending and experiencing the reality and disciplining your body will only empower your ego, giving you no benefit at all. In fact, it'll only keep you from doing the things that you should be doing!

You may think abandoning such allegedly benevolent acts may have a discrediting effect and leave you in a disadvantageous and unrewarding position. Yes, this thought is totally valid. It is driven by your compositional make-up. But it is not true. For, as long as you 'the person-identity' is in charge, all of your benevolent and charitable acts will be the works of the ego, and hence futile.

Moreover, you must first rid yourself of the idea of a false god you've created in your imagination and named "Allah"!

In the previous chapter we spoke about the formation of the personality and faculties such as the intellect, thought, comprehensions, illusion etc. The effect of conditioning precipitates a deity-god conception. First you must purify yourself of this! For your deity-god is the very source of your delusion:

"Did you see the one who deified his baseless desires and thus who Allah led astray in line with his knowledge (assumption) **and sealed his ability to sense the**

reality and veiled his vision?"[20]

You've conjured up a deity in your head and named it Allah. You are worshipping nothing other than your own conjecture!

In respect to the human factor, the universe –that is the infinite existence including heaven and hell- *knowledge is determined by the creation*. However, in respect to the origin and quintessential reality of existence *creation is determined by precedent knowledge.*

What does this mean?

If we observe the essence and origin of creation we may deduce that creation is determined by knowledge. But if we look through the lens of our compositional make-up and observe the infinite universe and the oneness of existence we may arrive at the conclusion that knowledge is determined by creation.

At the level of consciousness where **creation is determined by knowledge** there is no room for any conjecture and wishful thinking such as, "Oh Allah is al-Ghafur He'll forgive… Allah is Rahim, surely He'll have mercy…"

"The Satan deceives you by telling you Allah is ar-Rahim and al-Karim (generous and bountiful)".

The Satan instigates your illusion and succumbs you to the delusion of a separate deity god in some far away galaxy who is All Merciful and who'll forgive you no matter what you do.

As a result, you deviate from the reality and start creating your own hell.

Do you want examples? Look around yourself my friend.

---

[20] Quran 45:23

33

MUHAMMAD (saw) FOREWARNED ABOUT THE DANGERS OF THE FUTURE

In terms of his compositional make-up the Rasul of Allah, Muhammad Mustafa (saw) was a human. What do I mean by a human?

A human being has been given the glad tidings of being composed with the divine names. Muhammad (saw) was able to observe 'Allah', the names that comprise his essence, and reached the station of sainthood (*wilayah*). He then discerned that there is *nothing other than* the expressed and unexpressed divine names in existence and hence observed the universe as an eloquent architecture of these various compositions. He saw that these compositions express various meanings by means of an absolutely unalterable mechanism to which the future of all humans is subject. Thus, he informed mankind of the laws of Allah and fulfilled the function of risalah. He notified us that as long as man can't overcome his human nature he cannot escape hell (suffering) and only those who can rule over their nature can enter paradise. As for those who want to unite with Allah, he explained, they must move beyond even the meanings they naturally manifest as the expression of their compositional make-up.

The ruling pertaining to risalah, religion, the world, *barzakh* (intermediary realm), heaven and hell are all based on the dictum "knowledge is determined by creation." That is, creation –all things that have transpired and will transpire- was observed and all necessary measures were taken accordingly.

Muhammad (saw) observed everything that will transpire and forewarned us of the coming dangers. In this respect we say, "knowledge is determined by creation".

However, in respect of the origin and essence of existence "creation is determined by precedent knowledge". But what concerns us more is for knowledge to be determined by creation, this is the only we way we can know ourselves, our essence, and fulfill the requisites of the reality.

You can claim that you have reached the station of unity all you like, that you are at the point of Oneness and your observation is that of non-duality. You can even *feel* this is true. But you will continue spending your days as a "person".

This 'feeling' is true and valid, it pertains to your quintessential make-up and there are some secrets regarding it but I will talk more about this later.

The point I want to underline here is that the Rasul of Allah (saw) observed everything that will take place in the future and advised us about what precautions we need to take based on this observation.

Hence, the truly enlightened ones who have become intimates of the reality, who have observed and experienced it, strived to overcome their 'nature' their bodily impulses and did not stop engaging in these practices until they died.

Practices done to overcome certain conditioning and emotional patterns must not be stopped until its purpose is reached, namely until the conditioning is lifted, until that pattern is eliminated!

Once the cleansing takes place the person then can go back to practicing that particular action, for this quality has been given precisely to serve a particular purpose within the mechanism. All divine laws are such. There is always a counterpart in the ethereal world (creation) for every divine law (*amr*).

That quality and the action driven by it was put there to prevent its ethereal counterpart from causing any harm. Its either that or there is a threshold level that must be reached and that action is required to reach that level.

34

THE BRAIN-SPIRIT RELATIONSHIP AND DEATH

Let's go back to the brain-spirit relationship…

The brain starts to form the holographic radial body or the "human spirit" with the electromagnetic ray it begins to produce as of the 120th after conception. I will refer to this as the holographic radial body to not confuse it with 'the Spirit', which we talked about earlier.

The Spirit, or the Grand Spirit, is what forms the whole of existence. The meaning of every single form, no matter how we may refer to it, is contained within the Grand Spirit. When this meaning densifies as a particular composition we give it a name. In other words, that object comes to exist as the materialization of a particular meaning. As a result of this materialization it becomes the means to produce or materialize other meanings hence bring other things into existence.

For example, the brain, it produces various radiations.

The **first** radiation it produces is the one that forms the holographic radial body – the human spirit. Simultaneously, all meanings of all the brain activity are uploaded to this magnetic body.

Just as a radio station radiates electric waves and we receive these waves through our antennas and decode them to sound, the magnetic body both converts the meanings carried by the mind activity in the brain and carries that meaning.

Because it carries this meaning the personal spirit has an intellect. This is the intellect of the personality. When does this intellect mature? First, when it recognizes itself as a person and secondly when, if it engages in certain practices, it understands its own reality.

The **second** radiation the brain produces is of two types, namely negative and positive. These energies create two types of beings, those who are pleasant and amiable and those who aren't.

When the brain produces waves that are aligned with the person's wants and wishes it creates beings that it likes but when it is aligned with the person's fears then it creates negative and harmful beings. These beings surround the person when the he dies making him feels either joy or suffering in the intermediary realm and the realm of the grave.

Thirdly, the brain waves disseminate the person's thoughts, ideas and comprehension on earth. Those whose receptors are aligned with these frequencies receive and convert these waves and experience sudden inspirations or epiphanies. For example, when someone claims, "I have an idea!" it may actually be the idea of a like-minded person whose brain waves they've picked up on.

The **fourth** is directed waves. Directed waves are when one person's brain waves are directed specifically to another person whereby a particular meaning is conveyed and a specific circuitry is activated in their brain. As opposed to the third type of waves, which are general, this type is directed specifically to a target.

The intellect component of the brain is reflected to the spirit via the memory waves. Thoughts, ideas, imagination, the illusory identity are all products of the brain and are also uploaded to the spirit.

The spirit strengthens itself with the brain, which preserves itself in the body via the electric signals that travels to every single cell in the body through the nervous system.

If and when the bioelectrical activity in the body stops the brain stops functioning and hence the electricity that travels to even the furthers cell in the body are cut off, and the electromagnet quality of the body to hold and preserve the spirit within itself is lost. That's when the holographic radial body we call the spirit separates from the physical body. This is the event we call death.

The process of the bioelectrical energy sent by the brain being pulled back from the body is described in religious texts as "the spirit leaving the body by being pulled up from the toes." In effect, when the electricity is cut off the person feels numbing in and around their head and the body begins to lose its magnetic pull. When this pull is lost the spirit automatically leaves the body. This takes place instantly.

35

WHY DOES MAN EXIST?

Suddenly you have an idea... It is either the product of your brain processing certain information it has received regarding a particular topic – something you've previously thought of - or it's something that you've never thought of before.

In the case of the latter, that is if it's a sudden epiphany about something that you've never thought of before it's probably the rays of Mercury impinging upon your brain.

An idea is strengthened through the faculty of imagination and shaped with the power of design (*musawwir*).

After this it is either processed through the intellect or the illusion. The latter leads to an egocentric self-centered result. Which then leads the person to see and accept himself as his body, or a separate being with a spirit.

A separate spirit means separate from the One, an existence besides the existence of the One. Because the spirit is formed by the brain, it is the output of the qualities of the brain and the divine spirit comprising its essence, which isn't separate from the Absolute Spirit. But because it is the product of the brain it is by definition separate, or different, from the "Absolute Spirit." For, the meanings composing the Absolute Spirit form the meanings in the brain in specific *compositions*, after which the brain produces the personal spirit and enables the continuation of these absolute meanings. Therefore, the meanings carried by one's personal spirit is no different to the absolute meanings, in terms of their essence they are the same, but in respect to their *composition* they are different.

Hence the concept of comparability and incomparability (or sameness and difference) stems from here.

Do the qualities of the personal spirit not form by the reflection of certain meanings from the brain to the spirit?

Do these meanings of the brain not form by the reflection of certain Names during its formation?

Is the brain then not a composition of the meanings of the Names?

Since the brain uploads and saves all its data to the spirit, the composition of the names forming the brain is the same as that of the spirit. That is in terms of the "sameness" the meaning of the spirit is nothing other than a composition of names. But it is in the form of a composition. In the Absolute Spirit these meanings are not in the form of compositions.

The personal spirit is created as a composition of these meanings. That is, the *composition is created*, not its essence. A human is the platform through which the meanings of the divine names are expressed and made manifest.

Unlike the rest of creation, humans are created with the capacity to openly manifest the meanings of all 99 Names. If divine will permit to use this capacity, the meanings of the 99 Names may be expressed in various ways and to various degrees. No other creature has the capacity to holistically express and manifest the meanings of the 99 Names. Humans were created precisely for this purpose.

The meaning of "man" or "human" is "one who can express and observe all of the Divine Names".

Albeit other creatures also express and manifest these meanings they have not been endowed with the capacity to comprehensively observe them as humans have been.

36

MAN IS A COMPOSITION OF MEANINGS!

Whatever form (manifestation of Names) **He willed for you, He configured your composition accordingly.**[21]

A deed is when a meaning manifests so that it addresses the five senses. In other words, anything that you can sense with your senses is a deed or an act. And this deed is given a name. This name is a reference to the deed and hence it is linked to it, therefore the name and the deed point to the same meaning.

The act of showing mercy to the poor and giving charity is described as the "act of giving alms". Yet mercy and giving alms are derived from the same point. As the emotion we call "mercy" or the meaning that is referenced by this word, is expressed physically as the act of giving; that's how it manifests. So, when a meaning turns into an action, i.e. when it becomes expressed so that we perceive it in the sensory world, the act takes place under a particular name so that it appears to be different from the meaning.

As for the divine names, all acts in existence stem from the group of meanings we call the ninety-nine names of Allah. In this light, the universe is nothing other than the manifestation of these divine names, from the level of meanings to the level of acts.

That is, whether we can perceive it with our senses or not, everything except one thing, is the expression of the divine names from potential force into acts and motion.

---

[21] Quran 82:8

Note that, this so-called expression does not in any way imply or suggest an inside or an outside to Allah. The name Allah eradicates this concept. When we say there is nothing outside of Allah what we mean is there is nothing in existence that does not derive its life force from Allah, as everything exists as the various compositions of His Names. Any conception that suggests a dimension, size, space, form, or measurement to Allah is absolutely baseless and obsolete, as this would spawn the notion of a god who is either outside or inside the universe, which goes against the "*tawhid*" (non-duality) teaching of Muhammad (saw).

The only real existence is the Absolute One.

The observable multitude of existence, that is what seems to be many separate forms of existence, is due to our limited tools of sensory perception.

While the perception capacity of our eyes makes us see a normal human figure, an x-ray reveals a skeletal structure and infrared rays allow us to observe radial beings.

Whereas in reality, existence is an indivisible, inseparable whole, with no beginning and no end.

All things we perceive with our senses are essentially different compositions of the divine names appearing as the multiple forms. The infinite meanings through which existence shows itself have been described as the divine names.

Note the term "shows itself" does not in any way imply a need as these meanings are also of Its Self yet It is not confined or limited by them. All formations seen as deeds and acts are meanings materialized enough to address our senses, however even our senses are made of these meanings, hence the entire existence is nothing other than meanings. In short, the worlds are simply densified materialized forms of meanings.

What we call emotions are the outward expressions of the meanings of the divine names, as and through the senses. Ultimately the nature and temperament seen on humans are various compositions of the meanings of the divine names.

Let's now take a further look what we mean by different compositions of names…

There is not a single iota of existence that is other than Allah in respect of His Absolute essence, Attributes, Names, and explicit manifestations as acts. Note however these are not separate and different things. An action is the same thing as the name, which is the same as the meaning, which is not different and separate from the one who carries that meaning. The only apparent difference is because the holder of the meaning expresses its innumerous meanings through infinitely different acts.

Since meanings come about from the essence of that Being in order to observe Its various qualities, they are not separate from It. They are nothing other than the forms It takes. That is, the divine names are not independent of the essence of the Divine Being. Hence the names we use to refer to these meanings are not the names of a "god" beyond and separate from existence. Yet He is not bound or restricted by them either. The Absolute One is free from all confinements and limitations. It can take the form of any meaning It pleases.

All meanings are derived from the Absolute Essence of the One. However, a meaning that is expressed through you cannot be descriptive of the Absolute One, any description pertaining to the One is aberrant and invalid. No description can ever explain the Absolute Essence of the One.

This being the case, there is nothing in existence other than the various expressions of the divine meanings of the Absolute Self-sufficient One. What we call the Ninety-nine Names is simply a list of names that refer to these meanings. Though they are ninety-nine in number they are infinite in their expressions.

Almost all of the qualities of these names may be observed through a single name, that is a single individual whose name is Ahmed for example.

To further exemplify, the name "*al-Hasib*" means one who diligently holds to account; One who evaluates things down to its finest details and gives their due accordingly. Many of us can find ourselves in similar situations where we explore something in detail before making a decision about it. This is nothing other than the expression of the name *al-Hasib* through us.

The name "*al-Halim*" for instance, means the One who refrains from giving sudden (impulsive) reactions to events, but rather evaluates all situations in respect of their purpose of manifestation in a gentle manner, calmly and tolerantly. Many times, in our own lives we too may react in a lenient and gentle manner in the face of cruelty.

The names *as-Sami* and *al-Basir* on the other hand are constantly expressed through our ability to hear and see. The name *al-Kalim* becomes manifest through our ability to communicate. We exist with the name *al-Hayy* and owe our knowledge to the name *al-Aleem*. The strength of our willpower depends on the degree of manifestation of the name *al-Mureed*. When we are forgiving we are manifesting the name *al-Gaffar*. When we are giving we are expressing the name *ar-Razzaq* and so on...

In short, we manifest all of the divine names to various degrees, some more than others, some more frequently and some constantly.

Each individual has a unique make-up; when we think of a particular person we think of the meanings in their composition, besides their physical properties. The unique composition of this particular person may be comprised 12% of one name, 30% of another name and say 17% of a third name etc... The various degrees of dominance of the names is what makes up this person. So, when we are in contact with this person we are in effects in contact with the expression of a unique composition of the divine names and thus their meanings.

No doubt, the essence and the boundless, unrestricted forms of these meanings pertain to Allah. The expression of the divine names through a particular form or a person is an embodiment of a unique configuration of a collection of names. So, when we think of the name *ar-Razzaq* we think only of the attribute of giving but when we think of someone we know by the name Ahmed for example, we think of a collection of meanings composed together in various degrees. Hence with all of creation, every form, every unit of existence, is nothing other than a unique configuration of the divine names. Whichever name you use you will always be eventually referring to the One.

Now let us delve into the meaning of the words of *"Gaybi Sun'ullah"*:

"What you perceive to be 'existence' is in reality only Allah..."

37

THERE IS NOTHING IN EXISTENCE OTHER THAN HIM!

Let us continue with the words of Niyazi Misri:

"Allah has openly shown me that besides Him, nothing has neither an external nor an internal existence. It is only assumed to exist. He has let it be known to me that the gnostic cannot directly observe the One unveiled, unless he has totally annihilated his existence.

Allah says;

"On that day some faces will look to their Rabb with joy"

*If he doesn't annihilate his existence he will not be paying the due of the trust he has taken aboard, the trust that Allah offered to the heavens and the earth and which they trembled and hesitated to accept, the trust of "existence" that only mankind has taken. He will never be freed of treachery and will not be likable to Allah based on the verse, **"Allah does not like the treacherous."***

How can the veil be lifted from his eyes and how can he see Allah when he takes ownership of the trust of existence, which belongs only to Allah! Whereas the faqr (poor) means one who is absent of existence, one who does not associate existence to anything other than Allah. For when the veil of a supposed existence is lifted from things the One is seen and this seeing is never lost! If you were to ask, "If the observable existence belongs only to Allah then who are the gnostic? Who is it that looks at and sees Him?" To this my answer will be: existence is one but its layers are many! At one level it appears as the lover at another the beloved; at one level it is the rose, at another the nightingale..."

In the *Al-Futuhat al-Makkiyya* Muhyiddin Ibn al-'Arabi writes:

"The Rabb is the One (the ultimate Reality), the servant is the One;

Oh if I only knew who is the amenable one?

If I say it is the servant, he is dead!

If I say it is the Rabb;

How can the Rabb be amenable?"

The servant is the One! The Rabb is the One! That which is referenced with the word servant and that which is referenced with the word Rabb are one and the same. So, from whence does this "amenability" is born?

That which we refer to as the One exists fully in every iota, that is, with its Absolute Essence (*dhat*), which encapsulates infinite meanings, some of which we know as the Ninety-nine Names, and their manifestations, which we call the Dimension of Acts (*af'al*). In short, every iota is nothing other than the existence of the One.

This being the case, whatever object we perceive and name, whether it is animate or inanimate, from the micro level to the macro levels of life, all of it is the existence of the One. There is nothing that exists independent of the One.

So, once we understand this, that the entire existence is a dance of manifestation of the divine names and their compositions, what's next?

The next step is to understand that our own existence, or what we believe to be our own, is an illusion.

That is, if a person is a unique composition of divine meanings and qualities then how can we talk of a "person" separate and independent of Allah?

Since the person's being is comprised of the divine names which are one and the same as the divine, one who reaches this level of awareness and comprehension can no longer be in a state of duality, they will observe the One in everyone and everything.

They will know that wherever and whenever the One is mentioned that it refers to their quintessential reality. More than knowing, they will feel and experience this. As a consequence of this observation they will be driven to prove their reality.

So, what is this quintessential reality?

38

DID HE NOT COMPOSE YOU AS HE WILLED?

When you become aware that your being and the qualities that comprise you are nothing other than the compositions of the divine names and meanings you will inadvertently want to know the reality of these meanings and manifest them in a way that is befitting the One.

You will find the meaning described by the Rasul of Allah (saw) 1400 years ago within your own essence and with this conquest you will bear witness that there is nothing other than Allah in the worlds – albeit free from any form of limitation pertaining to the worlds!

When you recite the *Ayat al-Qursi* for instance you will find the correlative meanings of the qualities that describe Allah, *al-Hayy* (the source of universal energy, the essence of life) and *al-Qayyum* (the One who renders Himself existent with His own attributes without the need of anything) etc. within your essence.

You will know that just as sitting or standing doesn't alter your existence, living or dying doesn't make any changes to your true Selfhood. All actions are driven either consciously based on the meanings you manifest, or subconsciously based on your natural programming.

Eventually these observations will deepen and you will begin to openly see the principle *"Allah gives guidance to whom He wills and leads astray whom He wills"* and experience the living meaning of the precept *"Allah increases the sustenance of whom He wills and decreases it for whom He wills."*

Thereafter, if the veil of the Names is lifted, you will observe your singularity (*witriyyah*), individuality (*fardiyyah*) and unity (*wahidiyyah*).

Whilst manifesting the meanings of the various names you carry you will no longer be veiled from your essential reality as the veil of your illusory identity will be lifted and therefore your name, which is a reference to this identity will also drop.

As a result of this observation the trust will be given back to its original owner.

That trust was the divine meanings given to your "name" as a loan! When the illusory identity referenced by your name is lifted the trust will be given back to its owner and the One who manifests all His names as the worlds will begin to observe the meanings of His names through you.

Although in essence all acts stem from the names of the divine it is due to our inability to observe this and hence our own veil that we fall into the state of ignorance. There is no veil in the outside world. The only veil is our illusory identity. Once this is lifted nothing remains other than the compositional manifestations of the divine names and meanings.

You will have died from your illusions, which was a construct anyway!

"All shall pass, only Allah is al-Baqi!"

The only way your existence can be annihilated is when you "die before death"!

This can only be achieved by removing your illusory constructed identity and observing that there is nothing in existence other than the meanings of the names of the One. One who sees himself as a 'person' at the level of acts is in a state of duality. One who sees himself only at the level of names is also in a state of duality. One who sees himself only at the level of attributes is also in a state of duality, albeit hidden. And so it is the same for the one who sees himself only at the level of the absolute essence.

Let us remember what the Rasul (saw) says about hidden duality narrated by Ibn Jarir (ra):

"O Abu Bakir, duality is as discrete as the sound of an ants footsteps. When someone says 'Allah willed and therefore I willed' it is duality! And when someone says, 'If it wasn't for such and such person that man was going to kill me' he is discretely associating a partner to Allah and hence he is in a state of duality... Here is a prayer by which Allah will remove both hidden and explicit duality from you:

Allahumma inni audhuBika an usrika bike shay'an ve ana agh'lamu wa astaghfiruka lima la aalem!.."

That is, when you don't see Allah in your being and instead of Allah you give power to your 'self', which is an illusion, this is discrete duality. For, whether at the level acts or meanings all existence pertains only to Allah.

Since it is impossible to find Allah in the external world which itself is lost amidst the billions of stars and galaxies how and where can you find Allah?

Ibn Omar (ra) narrates, the Rasul of Allah (saw) was asked, "Where is Allah? Is He on earth or in the heavens?" to which the Rasul (saw) said, ***"Allah is in the hearts of the believers"*** (Ghazali – Ihya)

So, find Allah in your essence, your heart, your consciousness, your knowledge and refrain from confining and limiting him to any meaning!

Essentially the Absolute Essence, the domain of Attributes, Names, and Acts are all the same dimension. One who finds himself in the Absolute Essence will find himself in all four of these dimensions.

One who finds himself only at one of these levels and disregards the others has not yet been cleansed from the veil of duality.

Let's say I found myself at the level of attributes and I'm experiencing my oneness but I have "surpassed the meanings of the names" … this is not possible! You see the acts and say I don't care about the acts. You are still in a state of duality; you still haven't found your true self! For an act is the same as a name which is no different than the meaning it references – the meaning of your essence.

Therefore, to exclude yourself in this manner makes evident that you still have not gone past the illusory conception of an external god.

We talked about how acts are the manifestations of the meanings of the names in the form of compositions. In other words, acts equal names.

Let us now look at their differences and why we call it the acts.

An act is a composition of names and their meanings. When we say 'Names' we mean pure meanings. Whatever name is used, we are always referring to a meaning. But when we talk of acts we are referring to compositions. So, when a few different meanings come together they form an act hence every act comprises various meanings composed together in different proportions. The domain of acts refers to the endless collection of such compositions.

The domain of names on the other hand does not consist of compositions. Each name refers to a specific meaning. For instance, a person is composed of a collection of divine names. The different compositions of the meanings of these names come together to form what we call a person. This is the level of acts.

The domain of attributes is the state of knowing the pure Self – not the illusory constructed self!

Hence, meanings form the names, and compositions of names form the acts. Therefore, the compositions that form the level of acts are existent with your being. If it wasn't for your essential being these meanings would never exist.

In short, the Absolute Essence is totally present at the level of acts.

Based on this what is observed at the level of acts, is the Absolute One, yet free from any form of limitation and restriction.

39

HOW CAN YOU REMOVE AN IDENTITY THAT DOESN'T EXIST?

How can one forego and be cleansed of his illusory identity when it doesn't exist in the first place?

Let's have a look at what we mean by an illusory identity.

A person named Ahmed is actually a unique composition of names and meanings. Let's say Ahmed is composed 23% of one name, 2% of another name, 7% of another name, 18% of another name and so on… All of these names have come together in the form of a body and we gave this body a name, Ahmed.

This composition can also be described in terms of particular characteristics and temperaments, which are basically the manifestations of the names that comprise him at the level of acts.

Now in order for one to know his essential self he must become conscious of and act from the point of his unity. If one is aware of his unity - his oneness- but fails to identify the meanings in his being, he is still in the illusion of conceiving an imaginary external god. If one does not enhance and develop his character and temperament with the morals and virtues of Allah, that is if one does not moralize himself with the morals of Allah, he can never get to know the reality of Allah. He will only assume he knows, but this will not go any further than an extremely limited conception of a god, perhaps only one aspect of Allah.

The Rasul of Allah (saw) says:

"Moralize yourselves with the morals of Allah!"

But if we look from the level of "oneness" and the "unity of existence" can we not argue that the morals of a given person are the very morals of Allah? Indeed, they are! However, the morals reflected on a person are a particular set of morals based on a particular composition of names. That is, when the morals and qualities of Allah which are unlimited, unrestricted, and infinite in essence, are observed at the compressed level of a person they become extremely limited, constricted, and conditioned to a very defined finite composition, and hence can no longer be solely attributed to Allah.

So how can you fulfill your duty to model the morals of Allah?

How can one actually moralize himself with the morals of Allah? What does this mean?

It is constantly "said" that Allah is free from time and space - that Allah is not a local being, that he is not a 'something' in some 'place' at some 'time'.

Yet in our daily lives this is never the case! We spend our days with the conception of a god who's sitting on a throne in outer space, managing Earth from afar, putting some of our affairs into order while leaving some up to us... A god who is sometimes kind and benevolent and sometimes a cruel dictator... A god who is the product of imagination to whom we unjustly and wrongly ascribe the name 'Allah'.

No matter what is written on one's ID as his religion, one who has this kind of mindset does not believe in Allah, he believes in a totem, a deity that he created in his head!

What and who is Allah then?

Let us look at the way Allah defines himself, for it is impossible for us to define him with our limited knowledge:

> **"HU is the *Awwal*** (the first and initial state of existence) **and the *Akhir*** (the infinitely subsequent One, to all manifestation)**, the *Zahir*** (the explicit, unequivocal and perceivable manifestation; the Absolute Reality beyond the illusion) **and the *Batin*** (the unperceivable reality within the perceivable manifestation, the source of the unknown; the Absolute Self beyond the illusory

selves)! **He is *Aleem* over all things** (the Knower of all things as their creator with His Names)!..."[22]

"There is nothing that resembles Him!.."[23]

"Say: Allah is *Ahad* (One). (Allah is the infinite, limitless and indivisible, non-dual ONENESS.)

Allah is Samad. (Absolute Self-Sufficient One beyond any need or defect, free from the concept of multiplicity, and far from conceptualization and limitation. The one into whom nothing can enter, and the One from whom no other form of existence can come out!)

He begets not. (No other form of existence has ever originated from Him, thus, there is no other) **Nor was He begotten** (There is no other god or form of existence from which He could have originated).

There is none like unto Him! (Nothing – no conception – in the micro or macro planes of existence is equivalent to or in resemblance of Him)"[24]

If we duly examine the above few verses and contemplate on their meaning we can see clearly that it is not talking about an external deity-god.

All of the qualities listed above, *Awwal, Akhir, Zahir and Batin* are all referring to the same reality and there is nothing that resembles it or can be likened to it in any way.

Allah cannot be divided or fragmented into parts nor is he a conjunction of different components. Allah is ONE. This is such a sole single oneness that it includes everything so that there is NOTHING in existence others than or besides this ONE.

Anyway, let us not delve any deeper or digress any further my friends…

---

[22] Quran (57:3)
[23] Quran (42:11)
[24] Quran (112:1-4)

In short, there is a single sovereign ONE who is reigning over existence and everything is a reflection of His perfection.

Now in this light if we ask again, what does it mean to moralize one's self with the morals of Allah if there is nothing besides Him and hence no other morals other than His?

Your morals are the morals of your 'Rabb'. But you are being asked to adopt the morals of 'Allah'.

Now we have come to a very important distinction.

What is the difference between ones Rabb and Allah?

What is *Rabb* and *Rububiyyah*?

How can one get to know his Rabb?

Let us now explore these concepts…

40

THE EXISTENCE OF ALLAH

Allah has created man!

"Has there not been a time, when man was not a thing even mentioned? (Man was not yet manifest; he was the unmanifest within the dimension of the Names)!"[25]

The primary purpose of man's creation is so Allah can observe Himself through the meanings of His names manifesting in the form of compositions.

It is impossible to talk about or discern Allah in terms of His Absolute Essence (*dhat*).

Yet this is a mandatory existence! His in-existence is inconceivable, in terms of His Absolute Essence. Why? Because of the 'Self'. Anything that has a sense of self, anything that can know its 'self', must have an essence. That essence makes-up the existence of that thing. It is its quintessential reality. If one does not have an essence, a core, a self, how can it know itself?

In this respect the existence of the Absolute Essence is imperative. But it is absurd and senseless to try and conceive or understand the essence of this mandatory existence.

For whatever example you take it has been created subsequently. Something that has come into existence 'later' cannot be a precedent to the Absolute Essence, nor can it take you closer to understanding It.

---

[25] Quran 76:1

The Domain of Attributes refers to the state of being aware of the Self. It is the state of knowing His existence and knowing the impossibility of His non-existence.

Knowing the existence of the Self takes us to the station of "Life". That is, when one reaches the consciousness of "I exist" and by this I don't mean the primitive state of knowing, for one never claims "I exist" to himself, he just *knows* he exists. This pure knowing of one's existence, being aware of the state of being "alive" and manifesting the quality of 'life' is what I mean by the station of "Life".

This state of knowing that one exists and knowing himself is described with the attribute of Knowledge.

The natural result of knowing that one exists is 'will'. When one knows he exists this knowing leads him to will and desire things and hence the name "*Mureed*" is expressed.

When will and desire drives him to act and attain his wants the attribute of "power" comes into play. For without power will cannot be actualized. A will that isn't realized is inadequate. Since inadequacy is unacceptable for the One, the natural product of will is the attribute of power.

When One begins to know Himself in detail, the attributes of *Sami* (hearing) and *Basir* (sight) emerges.

This in turn leads to the attribute of speech and expression (*Kaleem*). Eventually the attribute of "*takwin*" that is formation, i.e. forming the universe takes place.

Knowing Himself at the level of these qualities comprises the Domain of Attributes. The natural result of this domain – knowing thyself – allows Self-observation; observation of His various meanings.

A part of these meanings is observed through Self-observation and a part through observing the manifestations of His qualities and attributes.

When we refer to the meanings that He wills to observe on Himself we say the 'Names of the Divine' (*Haqq*) and when we talk about the qualities and meanings He wills to observe as compositions we say the 'Names of creation' (*halq*). The latter actually constitutes the meaning of the word 'creation'. For example, the name *ar-Razzaq* necessitates the existence of a creation, for without a creation that needs provision the point of a provider becomes redundant. Hence it makes creation mandatory.

The realm in which all the meanings of all the names are seen is the realm of acts.

Conceiving these four realms as four separate dimensions is a grave mistake and clearly the result of being veiled.

The 'universe' is nothing other than the Absolute Essence! There is nothing other than the Absolute Essence inside, outside, within or beyond the universe. He is the crux, the soul of the universe! The ipseity of the universe pertains to Him. His meanings take various different shapes and forms as different compositions to bring about what we call multiplicity, or the observable universe.

Multiplicity, or the corporeal word that we observe, is nothing more than the manifestation of the different compositions of the meanings of the divine names. In point of fact, it is the domain in which the compositions observe one another. In this respect, there is no separate domain of acts, for the very thing you call acts is merely the manifestation of the compositions. Call it whatever you want, they are all the same. *The compositional manifestations of the divine names.*

Now let us move on to the Domain of the Names, the source of the Domain of Acts, and examine the compatibility and incompatibility of the different Names.

41

DO THE DIVINE NAMES HAVE OPPOSITES?

Some meanings of some names may not seem to manifest as conspicuously as others; their expression may not be easily observable. So how are they expressed, how can we observe them?

Such divine names, manifest certain primary meanings in a way that is befitting to the Absolute One. Their opposite meanings (antonyms) for example the opposite of *Nur* which is darkness, or the opposite of Knowledge which is ignorance, do not actually exist, as they are by definition the **lack of** light or knowledge. But they are perceived to exist as reflections or compositions of the divine names, as per the divine will. And these meanings are also of divine wisdom.

Anything that is perceived as absent, is perceived as such in respect to the composition, for in respect to Allah, every act is in its state of perfection. Even what we call darkness, the absence of light, is of divine perfection. Every quality of divine perfection is expressed through its opposite quality, which is also of divine wisdom and perfection. For if what we call darkness, which is the absence of light, was not observable, the light and perfection of Nur couldn't be observable either.

If the name *al-Aleem* (The One who, with the quality of His knowledge, infinitely knows everything in every dimension with all its facets) wasn't expressed, we would never have known ignorance, the lack of knowledge, and hence the perfection and value of knowledge would never have been discerned.

The opposites of the meanings of all the divine names are expedient for the perfection of the divine names to be observed through them - through their not so conspicuous manifestation. And this too is based on divine wisdom; it is of divine perfection.

In point of fact, the meanings of such names cannot be 'not' expressed. Take for example the name *Nur*, its meaning is manifest from pre to post eternity, internally and externally, much prevalently. Observing its 'lack' thereof is due to the compositional weave of names pertaining to the observer.

Is it not a composition of names that form a 'person'? If the meaning of a particular name is relatively weak in that composition that 'person' will not be equipped to see the expression of that meaning in the outside world. So, it's not that the meaning isn't adequately expressed in the outside world, it's that the person who is observing it isn't adequately equipped to see it because his compositional structure has less of or a weaker transmission of that name. Hence, he cannot fully perceive the actual counterpart of that meaning externally.

42

CREATOR vs CREATION

Creation (*halq*) refers to the compositional state of existence. The Word '*halq*' comes from the name "*al-Haliq*" – the Creator – i.e. creation comes from the Creator as compositions are 'created'.

To create is to bring into existence that which does not exist. Creation in itself doesn't exist. Hence, He makes that which is non-existent existent! But with what does He bring it into existence? With His own meanings. Different proportions of divine meanings come together to form particular compositions and hence 'creation' comes about. So, in other words that which essentially referenced with the name 'creation' is no other than the Creator Itself. Albeit when we use the word Creator we refer to the Names and the One to whom the entirety of these Names belong.

When the meanings of these Names come together within a particular locality we call it 'creation'. Therefore, the compositional layer of existence is called **creation** even though it is essentially nothing other than the meanings of the **Creator**. We use the word 'Creator' exclusively to refer to the owner of these Names, and the word 'creation' to refer to the compositions.

When we say 'creature' and 'creation' it is in respect to an observation made from the point of the *created*. If and when the essence of that particular thing is observed, not its compositional structure but the essence of that name and its meaning, then you can call it the Creator.

This is like looking at an aquarium, seeing the fish swimming in the water, and saying, "The fish are living in the aquarium" even though they are essentially living in the water inside the aquarium. We know they are living in water, for without it they cannot survive, but to cut it short we simply say the fish are living in the aquarium.

If you can look at that water inside the aquarium and see that it isn't different to the water in the ocean or the lake and that in point of fact it is the same water, then you can look at any composition and see the owner of the meanings it comprises and call it the 'Creator'!

But when you look at a composition and see that it is composed of different degrees and ratios of the Names, whereby some are less or more than others, then you must call this 'creation' and relate the lack thereof to the creation and not the Creator.

What we call a 'lack' is unavoidable and actually a mandatory part of creation. For without lack, wholeness and perfection cannot be observed and appreciated. Every lack is a means to manifesting perfection. The Divine Names must be observed in this way, that is as compositions with seeming inadequacies so that their ultimate states of perfection may also be seen and observed!

Limited observation done through a locality, i.e. something that is bound to space and time, is called creation. Unlimited observation pertains to the Creator. It is impossible to see the creator explicitly with external eyes. For physical external eyes are by definition limited tools of perception. Hence you can't call anything you observe with your physical eyes the creator. You must call it creation. As everything that is limited or observed through limited tools is a composition and hence it is referred to as creation.

Allah may only be observed implicitly, through internal eyes. But what does this mean?

Both the names *Zahir* (the external) and *Batin* (the internal) belong to Allah! But you can't say I see Allah externally! Because the external world is the realm of limitation.

According to who and what? According to your tools of perception, your sight. And your sight is linked to your eyes and hence to your brain.

Therefore, even though these localities are the Creator in respect to the name *Zahir* they are still confined to a certain composition and hence limited. **A limited being cannot see the Unlimited Being!** A limited being can only see limited beings!

Since limited beings can only observe other limited beings, nobody has the discretion to claim, "I see Allah"! One can only claim, "I observe the world comprised of the names and meanings of Allah"!

With what can you observe Allah? How can you see Allah?

What does it even mean to see Allah?

Seeing Allah does not entail the act of seeing as you and I are conditioned to conceive. It has nothing to do with the sense of sight!

As I had explained previously, the name Allah encompasses the Absolute Essence (*dhat*), the Divine Attributes, the Names, and the Acts, i.e. the entirety of existence -perceivable and imperceivable.

This grand infinite existence! So, when you say "I see Allah" if we eliminate the "eyes" at the level of acts, then seeing is merely a perception, a comprehension. So then?

Can perception perceive Allah?

> **Vision** (sense   perception) **perceives   Him   not   but   He perceives** (evaluates) **all   that   is   visible.** *HU is al-Latif, al-Habir.*[26]

Perception, my friends, can never perceive the Absolute Essence of Allah, for perception is an expression of a meaning at the level of acts, that is originally formed at the level of Names.

Perception is related to cognizance and cognitive ability.

Cognitive power is determined at the level of Names. The meaning of the attribute of knowledge at the level of Names is expressed at the level of acts to form cognizance and perception. Knowledge is existence at the level of Attributes.

So whichever angle you look at it, it is absolutely impossible for you to see the meaning of the name **Allah**!

However, claiming to see anything *other than* Allah is also unacceptable and unforgiving, it is an outright lie and slander!

---

[26] Quran 6:103

43

WHAT DOES "RABB" MEAN?

The One who administers at the level of acts, is the One who forms the level of acts; Allah, the Absolute Being! Because He forms the level of Acts and is the Absolute Administrator of it, He takes the name Rabb.

Rabb means the administrator, trainer, discipliner. But this is nothing like a mother disciplining her child, or a teacher training his student - this line of thought is like a quicksand. It will only bog you down further into the pit of duality – the dualistic conception of "me and the one who trains and disciplines me… me and a god outside of me…" etc.

So how are we to understand the disciplinary role of the word Rabb?

RABB means the owner of the station of *Rububiyyah*, which is the compositional qualities denoted by the Names comprising existence and the manifestation of their effects.

When we look at it from this point of view, we will see that your Rabb is no other than the Name composition/divine qualities comprising your essence. However, these divine names express themselves through you in the form of compositions, and this compositional structure is your unique constitution as an individual.

Indeed, in respect to your compositional constitution, the names comprising your essence and their specific proportions, you are a servant of your Rabb. In respect of the attributes of your being and your absolute essence you are not different to or separate from Allah.

Once you get to know your essence and your attributes, you will see that all of the meanings that manifest through you are the results of the divine names, and that's when the path to knowing thyself will be opened to you.

Then you will begin to know yourself in terms of your essential being and as the various forms and meanings in existence.

Knowing one's Rabb is knowing 'man' in terms of his compositional constitution.

It is the administration and ruling of Allah that is in full effect behind the seeming form of every human being.

Your Rabb is your unique composition of the Names and meanings of Allah!

Your Rabb and my Rabb are both different and the same! They are different in regard to their compositional constitution, but they are the same in respect to their essence, the essential reality of their compositions.

He who knows his Rabb knows Allah, in regard to His names and meanings. That is, he will know Allah at the level of the Names. However, the name Allah is the totality of all of the levels; Absolute Essence, Attributes, Names, Acts, etc. So, when you know your Rabb you know Allah at the level of the Names.

Even though the meanings of the Names belong to that Essence, you can observe that essence behind the curtain of the Names.

But how about knowing this Essence at the level of the Attributes rather than watching behind the curtain of the Names?

As long as you are confined to your compositional boundary and conditioning, even though you may know your essence at the level of the Attributes you will never go any further than just knowing.

Indeed, he who knows his Rabb knows Allah!

Knowing your Rabb doesn't free you from hell! You must go beyond just knowing; you must overcome the boundaries of your Rabb, i.e. your compositional make-up!

But this is only possible through first *knowing* your Rabb, then *knowing* the One denoted by the name Allah, and *escaping* the limits of your Rabb in compliance with the commands of Allah.

Thus, to become "moralized with the morals of Allah" is to observe and witness that within your constitution and essential reality, there is no other than Allah, and that all the divine names that are manifest in the domain of Acts are in perfect balance, perfect state, and everything is exactly the way it is intended to be.

This observation is only possible after foregoing your delusional individuality, your relative illusory identity, and your sense of "I".

You must **witness** that there is no other existence besides that of Allah... You must be freed of your delusive conception of 'others' spawned from your conditioned sensory perception, the limited five senses.

You must see that the entire existence is a single wholeness. When someone speaks of the One, the Absolute Reality, you must see that One within your own being. Only then you can experience the reality. Otherwise it is merely knowing, learning, accepting and imitating, no application and experience!

To experience this, to feel this, to observe this at the level of acts, the illusory identity, the 'person' must dissolve! There is no other way around it!

Once the 'inexistence' of the person is understood with certainty, all of the attributes, the temperament, the personal nature pertaining to that program also dissolves.

But without this liberty one cannot experience "unity". First **cleanse** yourself from your ego-identity, then the meanings of the Names will express themselves through you as actions.

What do we mean by cleansing?

Essentially there is nothing to cleanse, as it doesn't exist in the first place!

The purpose of cleansing yourself from your ego is to **balance** the meanings that you express. To strengthen the weak expressions and lessen the forceful ones. When the heavy forceful meanings are lessened, you make room for newer expressions to come through!

For example, stinginess is an attribute resulting from the weak expression of a particular meaning. So, when this weak expression is strengthened the resulting output, in this case 'stinginess' is *lifted*, the person is *cleansed* from this attribute. In fact, as it strengthens, the opposite quality is produced and the person becomes very benevolent, giving and philanthropic... This process is achieved with the practice of dhikr. Dhikr intercepts the automated brain program and re-programs it.

So how do we express our inactive dormant qualities, strengthen the weak ones, and balance the deficiencies to allow new expressions to take place?

How to become moralized with the morals of Allah?

There are two ways:

1. From the outside in
2. From the inside out

The first is relatively easier to achieve. The most effective way is to find someone, a master, who has already achieved this, and submit to him. Constantly following his orders, doing things that go against your comfort zone, conditionings and egoistic tendencies allows one to move to a higher more refined level. Consequently, new meanings will begin to reveal and express themselves.

"The hue of Allah! And what can be better than being colored with the hue of Allah?"[27]

The second way is much harder to achieve. One must have a very comprehensive and deep contemplative intellectual ability. So that through extensive research and study he can discover the meanings within his essence and take their hue and hence be colored with the hue of Allah.

In order to know thyself, one must first discover and understand the meanings of the known names of Allah and then the infinite unknown names within his own essence…

Any and every action done without consciously knowing why, how and for what purpose it is done, is the outcome of your 'nature', based on your 'program'. And every counter action of a behavior you put forth as your nature, will lead to suffering.

The individual Hell is nothing other than the state of being stuck within the stifling boundaries of one's nature, temperament, conditioning, personality, ego-identity! These constitute the fuel of hellfire. When you act according to someone's make up and temperament you are only fueling their hellfire. Yet due to their programming, they will actually take pleasure in it!

---

[27] Quran 2:138

On the other hand, when you invite them to an area that is outside their comfort zone - their deeply ingrained identity program- and ask them to accept certain things that go against their set ways, even though they may at first be extremely discomforted by this, eventually when they start accepting it with tolerance and grace they will have entered the state of paradise. For when one reaches the station of acceptance all suffering will end.

Anything that gives one a sense of internal burning, leads them into a state of suffering or depression is undoubtedly conflicting with their ego-identity and nature, that is, the essential reality of the person is overshadowed by and repressed by these programs.

If and when he can overcome these limitations, he will be free from all suffering and classify as one of "those who are freed from hell while in this world". Otherwise his suffering will not end for a very very long time, neither in this world nor in the hereafter.

The grace and blessings of Allah and the intervention of the Rasul of Allah (saw) is the progression from the state of being the "servant of one's Rabb" to being the "servant of Allah". That is the evolution from the dependency on one's compositional limitations, the restriction of his personality and programming, to reaching and experiencing his infinite limitless Self. It is the divine invitation to be freed of one's illusory restraints and experience his authentic reality.

If Allah wills for his servant to taste the grace of infinity, He will allow him to be freed of his captivity to his ego-identity conditioned self, i.e. annihilate his illusory personality ("die before death") and allow him to unite with his essential Self! Thence the servant will unite with Allah!

44

AN IMPERATIVE & MANDATORY WARNING

There is a great danger and pitfall encountered by those who see the illusory nature of their identity and realize it is actually the Absolute Self.

One who comes to this realization inevitably begins to think there is only one self in existence and that is his self, not the individual self of course!

This self comes from the absolute essence of *Rububiyyah*[28]... And thus, *It does as It wills!*

However, one must be very cautious at this point and remember that:

The acts that form the conditioning to which we are all necessarily subject are the very veils that prevent us from experiencing our absolute Self. The incomparability (*tanzih*) and the impeccability (*taqdis*) of the Absolute One, necessitates abstinence from all actions and rituals that form the illusory identity and cause one to become conditioned and confined by it, if not lost and stuck in it. No matter what the action may be, even if it pertains to the reality of *Rububiyyah*!

As a matter of fact, those who reach the secret of *Rububiyyah* and stop engaging in religious practices or start trespassing certain religious rules and regulations, have not really understood the reality of their Essence. Or, their companions are not at the level of warning and rightly guiding them.

Whereas those who truly find their *Real Selves*, that is after unveiling the secret of *Rububiyyah*, those who also reach the stations of Oneness and

---

[28] Compositional qualities denoted by the Names comprising existence.

Uluhiyyah[29] and observe their essential reality from the level of the Names, Attributes, and the Absolute Essence, become free from establishing or proving their *Rububiyyah* at the level of acts. They reach a perfect state which allows them to give the due of every level of consciousness, properly and befittingly.

---

[29] *Uluhiyyah* encompasses two realities. HU which denotes **Absolute Essence** (*dhat*) and the realm of infinite points in which every single point is formed by the act of **observing knowledge through knowledge**. This act of observing is such that each point signifies an individual composition of Names. (*The Beautiful Names* – Ahmed Hulusi)

45

THE ESSENCE OF EXISTENCE

Let's now review the previous chapter from another angle...

In terms of its compositional make-up the brain is comprised of atoms. It's made of cells, which are made of molecules, that are made of atoms – the smallest unit of life that we can conceive.

Since every atom with its essence, attribute, name and action isn't anything other than the One, **the brain is also, with its essence, attributes, names and actions, nothing other than the One.**

The activation of the various circuits in the brain that correspond to certain divine names is a process that takes place only during the initial stages of brain formation.

Since essentially a stone, a star, an animal isn't anything other than the One, then a constellation of stars or what we call the star-signs are also nothing other than densified grand masses of divine meanings.

This being the case, when a colossal mass of a specific meaning emanates its mighty radiation, a newly forming brain receives this beam and is shaped by it. The beam activates in the brain the circuitry that is equivalent to the meaning it carries and this activity is then observed as thoughts and actions through the person.

The meanings that are prevalent in the brain during its formation become the characteristics that we see most on that person, this is what "something being *eased* for a person" means.

Until the time of birth and specifically at the time of birth the brain receives these cosmic effects and develops the ability to express their meanings.

In essence all brains of all humans are the same. Their only difference is due to the effects they receive and hence the circuitry that is activated. This is what causes all the infinite intellectual and behavioral diversities between all humans.

Simply put "fate" or "destiny" is this very transmission of the cosmic effects. Hence the brain, the predisposition and capacity of which is thusly pre-determined, is the *Lawh-i Mahfuz* (Preserved Tablet) of the person.

Everything that is formed in the universe is the result of the cause-and-effect procession that I try to define as these "physical-chemical-cosmic" effects.

"You will never find an alteration in the sunnatullah!"[30] is a clear validation of this truth.

The phenomenon we call "miracles" is also a product of Allah's immaculate order and system. In short, there is no magic wand in the universe! Just because we may be unaware of the causes that lead to that effect does not mean something magical is happening!

Since the brain is nothing other than the One in its essence, it's wired to manifest the meanings of all ninety-nine names. The difference of the strengths and ratios of these manifestations generates the differences between individuals. When we hear someone manifests ten, twenty, or thirty names it is simply for arguments sake and allegorical.

Essentially every brain manifests all ninety-nine names. However, these manifestations differ in their compositional make-up and distribution, resulting in infinite variations in humans.

All of this happens through the cosmic radiation received by the brain and the genes the person inherits from his lineage.

Talking of genes, even though the genetic information received by the parents and the forefathers are transferred to the brain via the genes, they are only expressed if the person has the specific circuitry suitable for their expression.

For example, if the mother is an Aries and the father is an Aquarius, the child will express the qualities that are most aligned with his own constitution. So, if he has strong Aries qualities, he will express the qualities of his mother more. If he has a strong Aquarius energy, then he

---

[30] Quran 35:43

will express his father's qualities. Let's say the child is neither; he's a Capricorn. In this case he will express the qualities of his Capricorn grandparents or aunts etc.

This shows that not all genetic information inherited is directly expressed through the person, but rather, those that are aligned with the person's individual constitution. There is a lot more to be said about this topic but I'm afraid I can't share more in this book.

The constitutional meanings that are felt by the person form some of the primary emotions. Anger, sadness, possessiveness, sympathy, attraction, etc. Emotions are expressed based on the person's conditionings, which are shaped by the cosmic and environmental effects that are received.

The Rasul of Allah (saw) said;

"When Allah wills to fulfill the fate of his servant he takes his mind away and the person commits a sin in this state and then Allah gives his mind back *(brings him to his senses)* ***and the person feels deep regret saying, 'how did I engage in such an act?'"*** (Dailami)

The expression "takes his mind away" in this hadith refers to the restriction of intellectual functions via astrological effects leading the person to act with his emotions and instincts then regretting his actions after the effect passes.

Such situations generally occur when Mars makes a hard aspect to the ascendant or the transits of the Moon. Usually it's over and done with in 24 hours.

With the cosmic effects received by the brain certain activities start taking place in the brain. As a result, a meaning is transformed into an action. The cosmic effect activates specific circuitries in the brain, based on its own meaning, hence resulting in an action that is also representative of its meaning. In other words, the brain outputs action based on the meanings it receives.

The first effects are received at the date and time of birth, which determines the observable capabilities and skills. Based on these, the brain begins to convert the relevant meanings into action. That is, the actions a person outputs are determined by the meaning and strength of the cosmic signals he receives.

Hence what we call the 'personality' is formed.

Since the brain is essentially from the One, it encompasses all ninety-nine Names. It's all about the interplay of these Names; how much they are expressed and in what proportions, i.e. composition, that leads to all the infinite variations of expressions. This composition is determined at the time of birth.

Emotions are the channels through which we 'feel' this composition.

Actions that we see through the body form the temperament or the character of the person.

When the composition of these names reflects on to the body, the 'nature' or the natural disposition of the body is formed.

That is, 'nature', 'temperament', 'emotion' are the meanings of the compositions in respect to the body, character and the emotions respectively.

This divine composition is your Rabb. The One who rules over the body, drives it, moves it, and controls it.

Every individual is absolutely dependent on their Rabb. There is not a single iota of existence that isn't dependent on its Rabb and who does not fulfill the commands of their Rabb.

The 56th verse of the 11th chapter of the Quran expresses this truth as the following:

> **There is no animate being that He does not hold** (program with the Name *Fatir*) **by its forehead** (brain) (i.e. subjugate to His command)..." [31]

That is, the expression of the divine names at the level of *Rububiyyah* means the fulfillment of the command of Rabb at that level.

Potentially all of the meanings of all of the Names are within you! It is your unique composition that either allows or disallows their expression at the level of acts.

What is the secret behind the words "*Man arafah*" in the phrase that is generally accredited as a hadith narrated by Hadhrat Ali (ra), "*Man arafah nafsahu faqad arafah Rabbahu*"?

---

[31] Quran 11:56

It is a direct indication of what I explained above! The word "*man*" means **he who**, "*arafa nafsahu*" means **knows his 'self'** i.e. his essential reality (note that it says **HE WHO** knows himself, because there is still an identity-personality, i.e. a composition at this level!) Therefore, he who knows the reality of his identity-personality, his compositional make-up, will realize that his 'self' is nothing other than a unique composition of the divine names! Hence when the person becomes aware of this reality he becomes aware of his Rabb! For his Rabb is the composition of the names that comprise his existence, which we see and identify as the person. In reality however, it is nothing other than the One.

46

WHAT IS RELIGIOUS OBLIGATION AND WHY IS IT NECESSARY?

What is obligation?

What are the different types of obligations?

Who is obliged?

Let's talk a little about these...

What is an obligation? It is something by which a person is bound, or a situation in which a person is required to do certain things. In other words, a proposal is made and you are *compelled* to do it. This state is an obligatory state; you are obliged.

But if our existence is comprised of a composition of divine Names and we can observe this as our Rabb, how can our Rabb be obliged? How can Rabb be bound by something or compelled to fulfill something?

When you realize that your essential being is the One, you become exempt from the state of obligation. Can the One be obliged? If you can consciously say "no" to this, you become exempt.

But is this really so?

This is the pivotal point!

If understanding and realizing meant full exemption, then religion should only be valid until this point and inoperative after this point. But that's not the case!

It is still valid. Why? Let's see...

In respect to your Name composition you have a set of qualities and characteristics as a human being.

As long as you exist as the manifestation of this Name you are actively engaged in the dhikr of your Rabb regardless, you are fulfilling the purpose of your existence. But there is a fine point.

Externally, as long as you exist as this particular composition, the external actions put forth by this composition do not allow the spirit to form a specific energy. You can eat, drink, see and know but you can't produce this energy to strengthen your spirit. Due to this you can't escape hell after death and you can't pass the *Bridge of Sirat* to go to paradise. This is the external reason...

As for the internal reason, because you are the servant of your Rabb, even though essentially you are no other than the One, if you can't escape the limitations of your Rabb and reach the unlimited One denoted by the name Allah you are deprived of experiencing the reality of Allah.

The name Allah is the sum total of all of the 99 Names and in fact all of the infinite Names and qualities. But as long as you are confined to the limits of your particular composition, even though these names may manifest through you, they will be filtered by your compositional make up and hence become subject to the same limitations. In other words, they will only act to strengthen you, "your identity", and they will dominate over this identity. You will be under their dominion!

In the same way, after you leave your biological body with death, they will continue to impose their limits and thus form your hell. This is the suffering of hell.

Besides this, the biggest suffering is being deprived from knowing and experiencing Allah!

Why? Because you are bound to live within the limits of certain conditions and measures. Hence you are deprived from the limitless nature of your essential self. You can't escape the limits of your Rabb!

The inability to escape the limits of your Rabb means not knowing Allah!

To reach Allah there are three conditions:

The first is based on the dictum **"He who knows himself knows his Rabb"**. First you must know yourself so that you may know your Rabb.

The way to know your Rabb goes directly through knowing your "self". This is the first step.

The second is the mystery of expanding and overcoming the boundaries of your Name composition.

Knowing Allah is only possible by strengthening the weaker Names in your composition so that they are equal with the rest. The Names should not be operative over you in default mode, whereby you are automatically subject to their effects. On the contrary, you should discern their meanings, and gain the autonomy to manifest their meanings whenever, wherever and in whichever way you like.

To overcome the boundaries of your Rabb and reach divine vastness you must express the Divine Names equally.

To express meanings outside your composition is achievable through action and application. Remember Name equals action. An act is a name and a name is an act! So, when you don't perform an action you won't be expressing the meaning of that Name. Performing the act is to manifest the meaning of the Name.

To observe the meaning of the Name is to see it at the level of acts. They are the same thing. If you engage in actions outside the scope of your composition the meanings of these actions will transform from potential to observable action.

The people of bliss in the hereafter are of two groups:

1. The people of paradise
2. The people of Allah

In principal anyone who doesn't belong to the people of hell belongs to either one of these groups. The people of paradise are those who practice the religion of Islam; they observe the laws called "sharia" and are hence saved from hell. But how?

Everyone has a unique compositional make -up right? The laws of sharia that are practiced at the physical level impose a challenge to their composition. Salat, fasting, ablution, alms and charity, pilgrimage etc. These are all challenging practices, but out of the "fear of Allah" they do it anyway.

So, by observing these practices they inadvertently begin to cause certain minor changes in their compositions which enables the expression of new meanings. In other words, by forcing themselves to engage in these practices they begin to manifest qualities that are outside their compositional make-up! Hence, they free themselves from hell. This is how the general masses will go to paradise.

Then there are the people of Allah...

The person actively puts into application the meanings of the Names that are dormant in his composition, and hence activates these Names and their meanings to know Allah with His names. When you know your Rabb by "knowing yourself" (*man arafah*) when you recognize and observe this reality, you reach the level of *ilm al-yakeen* (the knowledge of certainty).

When you can make the transition from the limitation of your Rabb to the vastness of Allah, this expansion allows you to reach the level of *ayn al-yakeen* (the eye of certainty).

As for the third condition: As a result of this expansion, the boundaries of your composition are lifted from your consciousness, and you become free to take any meaning, express and manifest any name you like. This is the state referred to as "dying before death".

To die before death is to remove your identity and become free to take any form, any name, any meaning you like...

This brings us to our next topic...

47

AS FOR "RUBUBIYYAH" ...

What is the station of *Rububiyyah*? Where does the Rabb execute His laws?

When we talk about the domain of witnessing (*shahadah*) we don't refer only to the physical realm as some do.

The domain of the angels is also included in the realm of the acts. Everything outside the domain of the Names comprises the realm of the acts.

The domain of witnessing encounters the realm of the spirits, the realm of the angels, and the realm of the jinn. They are all a part of the realm of acts.

The Rabb of all of the beings within the realm of the acts is Allah.

In other words, the Rabb of the worlds is the One denoted by the name Allah. Allah is the Rabb of all the infinite worlds! Allah is the Rabb, the *Rububiyyah*, that forms, reigns, and administers the worlds and all the beings within them.

What is this "Rabb" concept and what is meant by it? The domain of the Names comprises the "Rabb" phenomenon. That is, the station of *Rububiyyah* is formed by the domain of the Names. i.e. What we know as the Divine Names, that which is denoted by the beautiful names is the station of *Rububiyyah*!

All of the worlds are nothing other than the outward manifestation of the meanings of the Divine Names. Nothing exists in the world other than the meanings of the Divine Names.

However, this outward manifestation comes about via the compositional structures.

The outward manifestation of the domain of meanings at the level of acts, is subject to the law of compositions. This must be understood well...

At the level of names all of the names are whole. They are 'one'! There is no differentiation between the names. At the level of names, for descriptive purposes, we say existence is "One". One single existence which encompasses all of the meanings. All of the meanings exist as a single meaning in this singular existence.

When these meanings are outwardly expressed, compositions are formed according to their manifestation. This is what brings about multitude. Multitude is formed, but the essence of multitude is singularity (oneness)! Even though different names form the multitude, because they pertain to the same existence, it is essentially one.

For example, say there's someone with various attributes. Generosity, intelligence, fear, aggressiveness, etc. Do not these qualities all belong to the same person? Because there are multiple qualities does it mean there are multiple people? On the contrary, they are different attributes of the same person; the different meanings and aspects of the same person.

Similarly, even though there are many names, there is only one meaning and one existence.

At the level of the Names the meanings of the names exist as a single meaning. The level of acts, which includes the angels, the jinn, humans and all other beings, is formed with different proportions of these meanings coming together as various compositions.

We can see the meanings of the 99 names on humans at different levels at different times. When we look at an animal maybe we can see the meanings of 70 names, and maybe 30 on a mineral.

What makes humans different from each other is the difference in their compositional make-up. These names and their meanings are what comprises their "Rabb" and since these names pertain to Allah, the person's Rabb is Allah.

A person's Rabb is the composition of the names that form his charecteristics. Since the meanings of the divine names belong to Allah the person's Rabb is Allah.

That is Rabb and Allah are not two different things! They are one and the same!

The meanings of Allah's names are observed at the staion of *Rububiyyah* and Rabb is the One who enables the manifestation of these names at the level of acts.

I'd like to take this opportunity to re-define or present a different perspective on the concepts *Haqq* (the Ultimate Reality), *halq* (the common), Rabb and *abd* (servant).

What is the common (*halq*)? The domain that comprises the whole of the divine names.

What is *Haqq* (the Ultimate Reality)? It is the domain that encompasses all of the divine names. Since all of the names are as a whole Allah can also be called the Ultimate reality (*haqq*). Most of our discussions in regard to religious matters are either from the level of acts and hence *Rabbani* (pertaining to Rabb), or from the level of the names and hence it is *Haqqani* (pertaining to *Haqq*). It is very rare that we say anything outside of these two domains.

What do we mean by talking from the level of the names? Talking about the meanings of the divine names are *haqqani* since they pertain to the *haqq*. When we talk about the names we are in effect talking about the Reality.

Halq has been created, it has come into existence from a state of non-existence. So, when the divine names are expressed as compositions they are defined as *halq*.

Abd "servant" means one who fulfill the purpose of his creation; one who fulfills the wishes and commands of the one to whom he is in servitude. Hence if there is a Rabb then by definition there must be a servant and if there is a servant then there must be a Rabb.

As for what is that which is referenced by the name Allah?

In respect to his Absolute essence (*dhat*) He is free from all thought, conception, imagination. In respect to his Self, there is nothing other than Him, to Him belongs all the names that He has let us know of, and He is the One who has created the worlds from nothing and continues their existence with His own.

The chapter *al-ikhlas* answers this question in the best way.[32]

We have provided explanations in respect to the Absolute essence, Attribute, Names and Acts. If either one of these are not included, then it is an inadequate explanation.

One must observe from all four of these stations. If either one of them is denied, then since He is the essence of that station one will be inadvertently denying Him.

If only one of these are taken into consideration, then this will be limiting Him to this station alone. Either way, He will either be pushed to some conception of 'far and beyond' or limited to a particular locality.

Yet if in your programming and composition there is the tendency to consecrate or limit then you will inevitably conceive It as such. However, the absolute truth is that He is free from all forms of limitation!

---

[32] You may find detailed information on this in *Muhammad's Allah*.

48

WHAT IS A HUMAN?

A human; is the existence that has the capacity to express and manifest all of the divine names.

The entire existence, including animals, are compositions, yet the potential to be the vicegerent of Allah is specific to humans.

A human is what we call man in respect to his compositional make-up.

"I too am a human like you!" (Hadith)

This means: "My existence, like yours, is nothing other than a composition of divine names.

49

ON 'RABB' AND THE REQUIREMENTS OF *RUBUBIYYAH...*

My Rabb is the One who trains and guides me toward a certain level of maturity and perfection. Whatever comes forth from my Rabb is perfect! The absolute perfection that reflects from my Rabb is the perfection of my Rabb.

The perfection of *my* Rabb is different to the perfection of *your* Rabb. Sometimes they even seem to contradict one another. But both my Rabb's perfection and your Rabb's perfection are none-other the perfection of Allah.

"My Rabb" refers to any of the compositions of the meanings of the divine names that comprise my being.

When one says "I" he is referring to his unique composition of divine names and their meanings. Since these pertain and belong to Allah your existence belongs to Allah.

These meanings may come together as one composition in one person and another composition in another person.

Hence person A is from Allah while the Rabb of person B is Allah! Both can say with certainty that their Rabb is upon an absolute state of perfection. Though their actions may be in contradiction with one another. This contradiction or seeming opposition is only due to the differences in their compositional make-up.

So then will everyone go to hell if they are all manifesting the will of their Rabb? Why would fulfilling the commands of ones Rabb lead him to hell? Will every being go to hell, and why? Most importantly, why will man go to hell in the first place?

Not every being will go to hell for fulfilling the commands of their Rabb, only 'man' will go to hell. Not every being will go to hell because they have no other choice but to execute the program of their Rabb. They do not have the capacity to **know Allah**!

Their compositional make-up does not carry the potential to know Allah. Due to this, they will fulfill the requirements of their Rabb and hence manifest their perfection. Done and dusted.

But man will go pass through hell!

What will cause him to pass through hell, either permanently or temporarily?

Like all beings, man has also been created to fulfill the requirements of his Rabb, but with one difference. Man's compositional make-up allows him to get to know Allah, based on his compositional make-up!

"Everyone will see the truth when he dies" means, "everyone will observe the divine within"!

And after one sees the divine within himself, the fact that he lived a life deprived of this knowledge, the fact that he was not able to move beyond the limits of his Rabb and reach that divine within, will form his spiritual hell.

Hell is a prison! It is a state of constant suffering... Spiritual hell, is being stuck within the limits of one's compositional make-up and not being able to activate the quality that allows one to know the essential reality of his composition. This quality is what causes him to suffer. When one is unable to overcome the character, temperament and conditioning etc. formed by his composition through 'moralizing' himself with the morals of Allah, this leads to hell.

If one can overcome and escape the boundaries of his composition spiritual hell will cease to exist. He will be of those who go to heaven while still on earth. One must first overcome the limits of his composition! His composition is his Rabb! As long as one exists with the 'personality' formed by his composition he is bound to the commands of his Rabb. Statements such as "This is my character", "This is who I am" etc. is another way of saying, "This is what my Rabb demands of me."

Sufism explains this as the following...

The reality of the self (ego) is *Rububiyyah*! The ego-self is made of the substance of *Rububiyyah*.

This means, what you call your 'self' is the same as the composition of the meanings of the divine names.

So, when you say "I do as I like", or "I can't help myself, I can't stop myself from doing a certain action" what you're actually saying is, "I'm fulfilling the requisites of my composition" and the natural consequence of this is hell.

When you're bound to your compositional structure, you will encounter difficult situations, you will be prone to suffering and problems. And there is no external existence out there that can have mercy on your soul and forgive you! For you are not doing wrong to something out there. You are doing wrong to yourself! You're wronging yourself because **you're not transforming the perfection of *Rububiyyah* comprising your essence to the perfection of *Uluhiyyah*!**

To point to this truth the Rasul of Allah (saw) says, "Moralize yourself with the morals of Allah."

This means to openly express the meanings of the divine names within **yourself**, which is comprised of the mystery and perfection of *Rububiyyah*. To manifest the different divine qualities within your essence is to moralize with morals of Allah.

One cannot reach Allah as long as he deifies himself. One cannot unite with Allah as long as he serves his Rabb. They say "So and so is *Rabbani*…" everybody is *Rabbani*! Every iota of existence is *Rabbani*!

When you stop being *Rabbani* and become *Divine*, that is when you will have reached Allah! Hence those who unite with Allah are called the "*ahlullah*" i.e. the people of Allah.

In general, everyone is *Rabbani*, the people of the Rabb! As everyone is automatically fulfilling the requisites of their composition. When you can actually say my Rabb is Allah, that is when you can unite with Allah. Otherwise your Rabb is the composition of the divine names comprising your composition.

To say "My Rabb is Allah" you must overcome the boundaries and limitations of your composition and moralize with the morals of Allah. The meanings that are expressed through you after that will show whether your Rabb is Allah or not. Otherwise to simply claim my Rabb is Allah does not in any way mean you have actually united with Allah. As long as you don't moralize with the morals of Allah, no matter how much you may think you have reached unity and oneness, you will only be deluding yourself!

In reality you will have only united with the deity in your imagination; and this God will not be Allah, it will be a production of your Rabb!

This is the difference between Rabbani and Divinity…

However, when we say divinity let us not think there are no names here! The names are present and manifest at the level of the divine too. But this manifestation is not bound to limits of the compositional structures. Here the Grand Intellect can assume any expression of the divine names it likes. These are two very different states of expression.

The *Rabbani* expression is an automatic expression derived from the compositional structure of the divine names involved. It is bound by the limits and requisites of the composition.

The Divine on the other hand, expresses the names which comprise its essential reality as It likes, assuming the form of whichever meaning It wills.

A life devoid of this boundless flexibility is driven by the *Rabbani* force.

Within the *Rabbani* life, if the person complies with the general rules; fulfills the recommendations and abstains from what is forbidden, the result will be paradise; he will be of the people of paradise. However, only if he can escape and overcome his composition and moralize with the morals of Allah, then he will find the meanings of all the divine names within himself and he can take on whichever meaning of whichever name he likes. He will not be bound by them, but will administer over them. This is when he will unite with Allah, and consequently he will become divine. He will appear to be a servant but he will be the **servant of Allah**! While others are the servant of *Rahman*, the servant of *Kareem*, the servant of *Wahhab*, the servant of *Samad* and so on…. The divine one is the servant of ALLAH! (*Abdullah*)

Now let us move on to another fine point.

Let us say you became divine. You moralized yourself with the morals of Allah.

Can you say, "I have overcome the boundaries of my Rabb and expanded myself to the vastness of Allah. I have discovered and observed all the names and now I can do as I will whenever and however I will…."

Is this a valid approach?

Once you find the divine names within yourself you will no longer have certain desires. The reason why wants and desires were strong in the past was because their meanings were present as compositions and so as a result of the most dominant names in the composition certain actions were automatically produced. When the meanings of the Names are present evenly and equably this balance automatically nullifies what we call humanly wants and desires, they disappear!

For at the core of humanly wants and desires lie the qualities of your composition. These divine names exist at different strengths and proportions in your composition. But when you come out from this specific form of existence and overcome its boundary the names start to manifest equally and thus humanly desires dissolve and are no longer formed.

You begin to produce actions aligned with the divine laws at the level of actions! That is, you start to act in ways that aid others to reach eternal bliss.

What does this mean?

It means you start to engage in actions that help others to overcome their own compositional boundaries and unite with Allah, for their sake!

The Quran depicts this as **"Those who advise each other of the Truth."**[33]

Advising of the Truth means to advise others to manifest the names comprising their essence evenly and equably. That is, the practices you recommend to them will naturally bring them to this state.

The Quran also uses the expression "As the Truth" (*bilHaq*) meaning to advise from the level of the Names. That is, to help them to become aware of their Rabb and advise them to act accordingly.

This is one of the mysteries of *Nubuwwah*! To advise as the Truth! **"You have no responsibility other than to advise the Truth"** and **"Religion is an advice, a recommendation"** allude to this!

---

[33] Quran 103:3

Hence, becoming divine is not the same as becoming *Rabbani*!

So, if you've become moralized with all of the divine names, and you found all of the names within yourself, and you saw that all of the observable actions in the world are your actions, can you do as you will? Absolutely not! All of the actions in the world are the actions of Allah for the names that drive them pertain to Allah! **But these actions do not belong to Allah! Those actions belong to the Rabb of their doer!**

This is a fine but imperative point and must be understood well!

Allah is both the owner of an action and not the owner!

He is the owner because the names that create and drive the action belong to Allah. But the doer of the action is not Allah! That action comes about in that particular way because the names that drive it are bound by a composition. If it weren't for that particular composition that action would not have come about in that particular way!

Thus, my friend, that action was from your ego-self!

50

FROM ALLAH OR FROM YOUR 'SELF'?..

"Whatever good comes to you it is from Allah, but whatever evil comes to you it is from your self"[34]

Since the meanings of the names that drive an action pertain to Allah, it is good and belongs to Allah. Yet since it is bound by the limits of a composition and is processed by a composition, it is evil and belongs to the ego-self of its doer.

The self (ego-identity) is altogether the manifestation of the Rabb!

I explained in previous chapters that what we call the self is the name composition comprising your being, governed by *Rububiyyah*.

That is, your essential reality is a composition of divine names which is your Rabb. So, when we refer to your compositional make-up, we say Rabb. In this light, he who obeys his self (*nafs*) obeys his Rabb!

This is a natural state of dhikr. Therefore, when we see an action, if this action is driven and produced by the composition, which is most often the case, then it is driven by the self (*nafs*).

If an action is not produced by the compositional effect, then it is from Allah, which was the case with all the Nabis and Rasuls, as *wilayah* necessitates "dying before death". To die before death means you overcome your compositional boundaries and hence all actions that come forth from you afterwards is driven directly by Allah and not the 'self'.

---

[34] Quran 4:79

Nevertheless, a Nabi takes ownership of his actions out of ethical code and morality, for no composition is lifted forever!

Overcoming your composition means you begin to live at the level of the Names and at the level of Attributes, with the observation of Allah, and consequently you become a **servant to Allah**.

Despite this, an action still comes out from the composition. For if there is an action then there must necessarily be a composition that produces that action. There is no way for it not to exist. Hence the effects of a composition cannot be lifted indefinitely!

A common mistake of those who misunderstand "oneness" is based on their misinterpretation of statements such as "I came from Allah, to Allah is my return" which leads them to deny heaven and hell. It is nothing other than a total misunderstanding.

Regardless, if the divine laws and regulations are observed the person may still go to heaven, but due to his misunderstanding he will not have reached a state of perfection. If he complies with the divine laws and fulfills the necessary practices yet dies with this misunderstanding, with death he will realize this and see the truth. This will not perfect his state however, he will simply observe the truth of the matters he misunderstood.

Yet again, all of this is with the condition that the person complies with the divine laws, for only then a person may be subject to divine grace.

51

ON ONENESS AND UNITY

Now let us discuss the topic of "ONENESS" ...

On one side we're talking about the existence of heaven and hell, the visible physical bodies in this world that we're experiencing, and the dimension of acts!

On the other hand, we're trying to explain the concept of oneness, the unity of existence and we're talking about the different levels and stages of unity and the different degrees of oneness.

Now if existence is one, how are these actions formed, where are they coming from? If existence isn't one, if it's multiple, how are we talking about a SINGLE existence within this multiplicity?

What do unity and oneness mean and what do they *not* mean? Let us talk a little about these...

Oneness (*tawhid*) is to observe and witness the ONENESS of Allah.

Unity (*wahdah*) is the act of Allah witnessing His own Oneness.

If you don't accept that the source of existence is one and this source is Allah, then you will inadvertently accept a "god" outside and beyond this realm.

The moment you adopt the idea of a god out there, since no such being exists, you will inevitably assume and hence create a god with the attributes fitting your own comprehension of it.

Hence you will create in your head a god based on your own understanding and conception and you will believe and accept it.

Consequently, you will become a servant to an imaginary god that you created with your own hands in your own head!

The vast majority of the human population deify and pray to a god that they conceived and created in their imagination based on their conditionings and expectations. They attribute to it the very qualities that are aligned with their own personal make-up and then they name it 'Allah' and claim, "Allah is like such and such…" describing a god shaped by their own thoughts and imagination.

In light of all the things we discussed regarding the make-up of existence, the universe and man, it is evident that the seeming multiplicity of existence, all of the innumerous beings are sourced from the same essence, a single origin.

Does this mean that many different beings were formed from that one single source? No.

Let me explain with an example: Think of a seed that you sow, how it grows and blossoms and eventually becomes a tree that bears fruit! That seed is present in every fruit of that tree. That tree is nothing other than what is contained in that seed.

Of course, this is simply an example of multiplicity it can't be completely reflective of the truth. Nevertheless, it may help to get a better idea of it.

52

"THE PART MIRRORS THE WHOLE"

The abode we call existence has not lost or parted from its original qualities. Evert iota of this existence still carries all of the qualities and attributes of its original form.

Yet the one who looks cannot see this and so the illusion of many separate forms of existence comes about!

Even though all of the qualities within the essence of existence is present in every form, one cannot see this due to the limitations of his compositional make-up, for example the five senses. Due to his own incapacity, that is, because he isn't able to activate and express the potential qualities that are also inherent within his being, he can't see it on other forms either. Hence, he cannot observe the oneness of existence.

When one is dependent on the limited sensory perception tools like the five senses one cannot see the oneness of existence and delusively assumes there are many separate forms of existence. Yet he claims, "There is ONE existence beyond the MANY forms!" and thereby he invents a "god"!

In order to prevent this misconception of a god beyond all the many multiple forms of existence the concept of UNITY was elucidated.

The ONE or ONENESS exists in every point of existence, and therefore the invitation is to "*know* existence" rather than to deify or externalize it as a "deity". It is a call to become conscious of your existence and to be aware of the consequences of your actions!

The religion of Islam is based on the principles of unity and oneness.

So, observe existence in this light, with the awareness that every situation you encounter is nothing other than the manifestation of the divine names and their meanings, never forgetting however, that it is bound to the compositional structure from which it is expressed!

Then you will never question, "Why is this so?" yet you may recommend and advise on how it should be so...

To come to this point of observation you need the light of Islam and religion. Once you really understand the truth of religion you will never apotheosize, idolize or deify again!

You will simply fulfill your servitude.

53

IF ONE FAILS TO REALIZE HIS RABB AND RECOGNIZE ALLAH…

When one knows his Rabb through 'knowledge' Sufism refers to this as the state of *"kufr"* (denial-covering of the truth)! Complying with the commands of his Rabb in this state will not save him from going to hell!

For he knows his Rabb but does not accept the divine commands, and thus prepares his future with his own hands, i.e. a necessary stop by hell.

But beyond knowing his Rabb, if he also accepts Allah, and as a result of confirming Allah if he allows the divine laws to take precedence over his natal programming, and thus acts with the divine laws, he will overcome his *Rabbani* conditions and limitations. Then and only then can he attain paradise. Otherwise, he will most definitely go to hell, even if temporarily, because there is no other way of resolving the situation.

There are two very important and necessary points to be aware of. We must take these two points into consideration and be conscious of them at all times.

The **first** is, existence is whole, complete, and functions as a mechanism. It executes its command based on the condition and state of each instance.

There is no secondary 'other' being outside that can interfere with this.

The **second** point is no matter what form or name something takes in this world, it is nothing other than the densification of the meanings of the divine names, the process of them going from a potential to an actualized state, from force to action, from ethereal to material. Hence whatever object or form you look at you must remember that it is a densified materialized state of the forces of the divine names, and thus, see the face of Allah!

The face of Allah means the meanings of the names of Allah. That is, to see the face of Allah is to observe the meanings of Allah.

All the Names, whether known or unknown to us, once they become manifest, they are considered as "the face of Allah".

The face of Allah is the divine meanings; the domain of the names, which may only be observed through the eye of consciousness.

Comprehension is not an action; it is a meaning. You can't see "comprehension", nor can you touch it. You can't sense it with your five senses. It is a meaning, and hence it sees meanings; the meanings of the divine names.

Therefore, everything you comprehend is a composition of the divine names, regardless of whatever its name or label is.

In this light, to see Allah, to see the One, is nothing other than a comprehension or discernment, it is knowledge!

The essence of discernment is knowledge. It is to know the meanings of the names, to feel and experience them and to find them within yourself. It isn't an object that can be seen and held.

What you claim to see with your eyes is nothing other than an illusion!

Real seeing is knowledge, it is comprehension!

How real are the objects and the people you see on television? You see them on the screen but are they really there? What you claim to see with your eyes is simply the decoding of the bioelectrical impulses that reach the brain via the cranial nerves. In order for the brain to decode this electrical message it has to have prior knowledge about it, otherwise it cannot understand its meaning. It will project an image, but it won't know the meaning of the image.

So, what forms in the brain and what gets uploaded to the spirit is meaning, not an image! It is not a 'thing'!

Matter only exists as matter according to the five senses, a very rigid range of information. If you look from a wider perspective with a broader sense mechanism, there is no such thing as matter!

You see the houses, buildings, mountains etc. because of the segmental capacity of your eyes. If your eyes were a lot more sensitive, you would have seen the atoms and the space inside them just like you see the stars in space. Your feelings would have been affected and shaped by what you see and hence your judgment and evaluation would have been different.

This being the case, everything that exists in all the worlds are essentially only meanings! The meanings of the various divine names. The rigid ranges of the limited tools of perception that make us perceive the illusion of 'matter' is only there to enable 'man' to understand his essential reality and observe the qualities of his true being. They are merely samples to serve a greater purpose. They invite you to evaluate what we see and contemplate on what more there can be in comparison to what is so you can know yourself!

Not your identity-self of course, your real self! First know your Rabb, understand the essence of what you think you are, comprehend what you really are, how you were formed and what your essential reality is! And then try to find your 'self' at a greater universal level!

Of course, this isn't as simple as said! One must really commit himself to do this! This has to be one's most significant issue in life! His existence must be for this! Why? Because existence is a single mechanism and every gear is subject to its own laws!

There is no room for assumption and illusion in this mechanism!

The mechanism is comprised of endless gears! There isn't a single imaginary illusory gear in it! They are all inter-connected with one another, forming the beginning and the end of each other.

Whatever manifests through you, its consequence is eventually going to come back to you!

54

EVERYTHING IS WORSHIP!

The purpose of the creation of man and jinn is as the verse states:

"I have created the jinn and men only so that they may serve Me (by means of manifesting the qualities of My Names)."**[35]**

As can be seen from the verse, it is to worship only Allah!

This act of worshipping is fulfilled by humans and jinn at all times; they are constantly engaged in the act of worshipping Allah. The verse doesn't say "they may worship me if they like…" It is an absolute statement. The fact that they are created for this purpose means they are all fulfilling this whether they like it or not, without exception.

So, then the first meaning to take from this is humans and jinn are constantly in a state of worship to Allah, which is by *natural composition*. Here are two verses that further clarify this:

> **The seven heavens** (all creation pertaining to the seven states of consciousness), **the earth** (the body) **and everything within them exalts Him** (*tasbih*; fulfill their functions by constantly manifesting in different ways to express His Names)! **There is nothing that does not exalt** (*tasbih*) **Him with** *hamd* (evaluation of the corporeal worlds created with His Names, as He wills)! **[36]**

---

[35] Quran 51:56
[36] Quran 17:44

Say, "Everyone acts according to his own creation program (natural disposition; *fitrah*)"[37]

Acting according to one's creational program, i.e. manifesting the meanings of the names that comprise their existence, **is their very worship!**

This is how they fulfill the purpose of their creation.

The second meaning to take from this is that a group of humans and jinn will *know* Allah. One of the learned followers of the Rasul (saw) construes the word "serve" as "know" i.e. to know Allah!

Surely this points to a small minority amongst humans. And if we take this as the only meaning then the prior meaning, that man and jinn is created to worship Allah, is rendered invalid.

But the verse, **"Everyone acts according to his own creation program** (natural disposition; *fitrah*)"** makes it evident that everyone acts according to the meanings of the names that comprise their existence. Hence, your actions reflect the meanings that compose you! So whatever name you are given, that name, say Ahmed, is a name that is given to the particular *form of expression* of the names manifesting from that composition. There is no separate existence from the meanings, i.e. the names aren't separate from the meanings they reference.

Since there is no other existence, whether we call these meanings Ahmed or Cemile, every act that is expressed under these names, are simply the expressions of the meanings that comprise their being.

This being the case, the temperament of that person, their natural disposition, or what we call their emotions, are just the manifestations of the names that make them up. In other words, it is the natural output of the meanings of the names that compose their existence.

Hence, anyone who lives with this natural output is necessarily fulfilling their natural worship!

But alas, the result of this natural worship in the future, is the experiencing of hell.

---

[37] Quran 17:84

55

TRANSFORMING YOUR COMPOSITION

The Quran constantly warns, reminds and urges us to "think" …

"We give you many examples, will you still not think? Will you still not contemplate? Will you still not take heed?"

The very fact that the divine names that comprise us are in compositional forms and thus manifest at different specific amounts and ratios tells us that they can in fact be expressed at much greater strengths! If this much is expressed via the composition then imagine what more can be!

Allah is present with His Absolute Essence (*dhat*) and Attribute in every form that openly manifests the meanings of His names. If He so wills, He may also enable other meanings to manifest from that point.

If your intellect and consciousness meet the One to whom these meanings and names are based, and you become aware of this, can you then have the power to manifest the names that aren't currently expressed?

Of course, you can!

Then, going beyond the acts that are the outcome of your natural disposition, if you comply with the rules and regulations of Allah you may possibly reach closeness to Allah!

Everything that transpires through you, your nature, emotions, conditioning and habits are the results of your natural programming, where some of the names are activated into action.

But if on the contrary you turn towards things that go against your natural inclination, then you may begin to activate other names. There is no other way of achieving this!

Let's say for example you're sitting somewhere relaxing and suddenly you hear the call to prayer. Your natural inclination is to continue sitting comfortably. Getting out of that comfort zone and going to the mosque, taking ablution and standing to prayer requires a lot of effort and goes against your nature! But if you can succeed in doing this you will be activating a willpower to do something against your natural inclination!

The greatest factor that contributes to suffering is the failure to use one's willpower! This is due to an inactive or weak expression of the name *Mureed* in one's brain. Chanting the name *Mureed* in dhikr will strengthen the attribute of willpower. The use of willpower is tied to one's knowledge.

Knowledge stimulates will, as is evident in the many people who know many things but fail to put their knowledge into action. This is because they lack the willpower to do so!

"I felt like it" we say… To say "I felt like doing/not doing such and such" is to say "my composition imposed this on me". Everything you do because that's what you think you feel like doing will push you deeper into the bog of your illusory self!

What drives you to do something? A conditioning. Is it consciousness? No. Consciousness is unity with Allah, it is to experience Allah.

Are your actions driven by this force? No. In that case you are driven by the natural programming of your composition, which is only taking you deeper into hell.

This is because instead of choosing to moralize yourself with the morals of Allah you are following a 'temperament' that is expressed through your compositional make-up.

Just because you know that your existence is the existence of Allah and that your actions are His actions does not mean you can go to paradise!

As the verse says:

> **And man will only accrue the results** (consequences) **of his own deeds** (what manifests through him; his thoughts and actions)!
>
> **And the results of his efforts will soon be seen!**[38]

---

[38] Quran 53:39-40

Just as your hunger isn't satiated until you actually get up and fix yourself a meal, that is without action progress isn't made and results aren't met, in the same way, in the life after death you will experience the results of what you do or fail to do here!

If you can't unite with Allah here in this world, don't think of uniting with Allah in the hereafter! It's impossible! If you can't discover the divine realities here in this world, there's no way you can achieve this in the hereafter! For the spirit is forever stuck with whatever the brain uploads to it in this world. Once its connection to the brain is ceased there's no possible way for new information to be uploaded to it!

Here's the proof:

> **"And whoever is blind** (unable to perceive the Truth) **in this life** (outer life) **will also be blind in the eternal life to come** (inner life) **and further astray in way** (of thought)."[39]

One may be do good, abstain from evil and be honest all he likes! He will still go to hell and stay there for a long time… because all of this is the output of his natural programming! None of it is done with consciousness! The names that compose him drive him to act this way!

If he hasn't put the effort in to really know Allah, if he hasn't rid himself of his illusory self, then his knowledge means nothing and will give him no benefit!

Think of someone who is aware of Allah's existence, knows that his acts are the acts of Allah and that everything in existence is the One and that there is nothing other than Allah. On the other hand, he still goes about his daily life feeling like the person he is and reacts to situations like the person would react. As long as this is the case he is in a state of hidden duality.

As long as one feels like a person and is thus unable to observe from the perspective of the One that person is in a state of hidden duality and all his deeds are like the deeds of the ignorant ones who are unaware of this reality.

The Rasul of Allah (saw) explained hidden duality to Abu Bakr (ra) in the following hadith: Rasulullah (saw) said:

---

[39] Quran 17:72

"O Abu Bakr! Shirk (duality) is more hidden than the crawling of an ant." It is shirq to say, "Allah willed so I willed" and it is shirq to say, "If it weren't for this person, that person would have killed me…"

Should I teach you a supplication that if you recite it, you will be freed from minor and major shirk? Recite this three times a day:

"Allahumma inni audhu bika an ushrika bika shay'an wa ana a'lam wa astaghfiruka limala la a'lam."

"O Allah! I seek refuge in You from ascribing any partners to You knowingly, and I seek Your forgiveness from that which I am unaware of."[40]

This is an important hadith to help us understand hidden forms of duality.

Essentially the whole point of Sufism is to remove hidden duality and cleanse one from the conditioned belief "I exist".

Unity (*tawhid*) consciousness cleanses one from the concept of relative existence, derived from the five-sense perception, and enables one to witness the reality that nothing exists other than Allah.

---

[40] Al-Jami' al-Kabir - Al-Suyuti

56

THE GRAND SPIRIT WITHIN THE ESSENCE OF EXISTENCE

One of the most precious books written on the reality of Sufism is the "Universal Man" by Abd al-Kareem al-Jilani. Its Ottoman Turkish translation is done by Abdulaziz Mecdi Tolun and its Turkish translation is done by Abdulkadir Akçiçek. It contains paramount information regarding the Great Spirit (*Ruh al-Azam*) and the Grand Spirit (*Ruh al-Quds*).

Abdulkareem al-Jili is a descendant of Abdulqadir Jilani and the Rasul of Allah (saw). In his "*Universal Man*" he talks about the *Ruh al-Quds*, one of the dimensions of existence that permeates through the entire universe. He says:

"*Let it be known that the Grand Spirit is the Spirit of Spirits*" that is, the essential Spirit forms all other individual spirits, i.e. that of humans.

"And, It is free from being subject to the command "Be!" You cannot call it a creation. For it is one of the pure faces of Allah. Existence subsists with that face. It is a Spirit but nothing like other spirits! For it is the Spirit of Allah and it was this spirit that was blown into Adam. As the verse says, "I have breathed into him of my spirit" (Quran 38:72)

As can be seen from this meaning, the spirit of Adam was created but the spirit of Allah was not! For it is the Grand Spirit, it is free from all creational deficiencies."

Creational deficiencies, i.e. the limitations pertaining to the compositional make-up. The Grand Spirit is free from such constraints.

"This Spirit is that which is referenced as the face of Allah of creation, and the verse refers to it as:

SO WHEREVER YOU TURN, THERE IS THE FACE OF ALLAH
(Quran 2:115)

Another way of saying this is, the Grand Spirit is that with which Allah has given life to existence and keeps it alive."

Existence depends on this Spirit as it comprises the essence of all life.

"Hence wherever you turn with your external senses in this world of emotions and wherever you turn your thoughts and intellect there is the Grand Spirit with all its perfection and grandeur.

For it is the divine face! And existence subsists with the divine face. The divine face encompasses everything. For it is the spirit of Allah. The spirit of a thing is one and the same of that thing, it is its being. Hence in this case existence subsists with the being of Allah, i.e. with Allah. The being of Allah is the Absolute Essence.

Know that everything has a spirit and its form depends on it. The spirit of a form is like the meaning of a word, its existence depends on it. This spirit is the Grand Spirit. When one looks at the Grand Spirit and sees it through the eyes of a human he will see it as a creation. For it is not possible for two superiors to come together.

Now let's take the human being as an example; it has a body, that is its form... It has a spirit, its meaning... It also has a face that is the Grand Spirit, the divine mystery.

When the requirements of the human form, the body, takes precedence the spirit begins to adopt natural (animalistic) qualities. Since the spirit is the essence and source of the form, its world begins to get mixed up due to the bodily qualities placed in its form. Its spiritual freedom is lost and becomes dependent on the form. It thus enters the prison of nature. Its life in this World resembles the sijjin (underworld dungeon) in the hereafter. Perhaps it is the same as the sijjin of the hereafter. However, the dungeon of the hereafter is within a perceivable flame! In other words, 'sijjin' is hell. Hell is experienced as its meaning (i.e. suffering) in this world, but in the hereafter all meanings have an actual, physical, observable form. Understand this well!

Now on the other hand...

If spiritual practices take precedence over someone, whereby they eat less, talk less, sleep less, and contemplate more... and abandon the things pertaining to the body!

Then the form (body) also becomes light. It may become so light that one may walk on water, levitate and fly. Walls will not hide its form, distant places will become near. His spirit will reach a state where it will overcome the obstacles pertaining to the body.

Thus, he will reach the highest of stations, the realm of the spirits; freedom. He will become free from all dependency to form. Some may even go further than this. The state of observing the names and attributes of Allah. Such a person is a noble elevated being, both in respect to his form and spirit.

The requirements of the human form are the things that are necessary to keep the body alive. As for the nature and spirit, one may desire honorable things like rank and status. For the spirit of man is noble and thus seeks nobility. But if one leaves all of this aside and observes the secret (mystery) of his essence instead, then the divine secret may begin to reveal itself. Then the form and spirit of the person will come out of the bog of the body and elevate to the pinnacle of nobility, where the One will become his ear, eyes, hands, and tongue..."

What the sage is trying to say in short is: You have a specific temperament and a world of emotions shaped by your compositional make-up. This is your human nature! That is, your humanoid or homo sapien aspect!

As long as one is bound by these natural and emotional tendencies he will continue to live within the boundaries of his composition. He may contemplate, imagine, and observe all he likes, he will not be able to overcome the limits of his composition!

He may even know his essential reality. He may know that his being is comprised of the names of Allah. He may be aware of the reality **"He who knows his Rabb will know himself"** and that his "Rabb" is the Divine names … He may be fully aware of the fact that these Names are driving and administrating his being. He will even observe the reality that his existence is nothing other than the divine names!

Yet despite all of this, **his nature and emotions** will dominate over him! He will be driven by events rather than driving the events himself! Because the composition will be in charge and thus will rule over him.

One who is ruled and driven by events in this world will be prone to the suffering of hell in the hereafter. One who is able to take charge and drive the events himself today, will be in paradise tomorrow. He will be able to escape hell because he will be able to come out of the blind-follower state and overcome his natural tendency and thus go to paradise as "Allah manifests Himself anew at every instant."

Otherwise, **just because one knows the reality of his being does not mean he knows himself.**

To know the reality of your being is to know your Rabb.

To know Allah, your real self, your quintessential reality, is only possible by overcoming your composition, reaching a state of being able to shape, modify, drive and transform events, and abandoning the desires of your nature and emotions.

To comply with these is to allow the composition to execute itself. In this case, you will be subject to the laws of your Rabb, the essence of your composition, and this will form your hell.

What does it mean to be driven by events?

You have a specific composition!

This natural composition activates particular circuitry in the brain and thus certain habits and tendencies are formed. When you encounter a particular situation, you give an automatic habitual reaction determined by your composition. This is what it means to be driven by events; you have no control over it.

So how to take control and drive the events instead of being driven by them? How must one act?

Your actions should not be the result of your automated-habitual tendencies and conditionings. Rather, you must observe the divine order and mechanism at play and do the most appropriate action you are capable of. The action you output should aid with your bliss and happiness! It should not be done out of habit and conditioned data, lest you become driven by events and hence prone to suffering.

Isn't the whole purpose and point of religion to teach us the divine laws that will enable our infinite bliss?

What do we mean by bliss?

To know your true self beyond the compositional conditioning and limitation. To attain this state, you must forego your natural inclinations driven by your compositional temperament and align yourself with the unlimited unrestricted meanings of the divine names. If you can do this you will overcome your compositional constriction and base your actions on the expansive nature of the divine names.

These actions will then give direction to events rather than making you succumb to them.

Let's say you encounter a situation that propels you to act in a way that is either 'profitable' in the material or worldly sense, or it is an action based on societal conditioning.

For example, every time you see a friend you say "Hi". This is an automatic output of your conditioning. Now change that "Hi" to *Assalamu alaikum*" (Salam be upon you)!

"*Salam*" means a state of emancipation from the restrictions of the bodily life and the experience of 'certainty' (*yakeen*).

To be emancipated from the 'self' and the composition.

Salam is to swim in the ocean of meanings, to observe and experience them! This is only possible by knowing Allah. That is, when you say "Salam be upon you" you must be conscious of its meaning; you must consciously wish freedom and emancipation to your friend from the limits of his compositional identity.

When you do this not out of habit or conditioning but **consciously** then you are genuinely connecting with your friend and outputting a mindful, conscious behavior. Thus, you are no longer driven by events! Now you are in a position to give direction to events. **Consciously**! For everything that is done unconsciously is just an autopilot habitual output of your compositional programming....

57

THE FACE OF ALLAH

"And to Allah belongs the east (the place of birth and origin) **and the west** (setting – disappearance – death). **So, wherever you turn, there is the Face of Allah** (you are face to face with the manifestation of Allah's Names). **Indeed, Allah is all-Encompassing and Knowing."**[41]

Notice the verse doesn't say "faces." It says, **"The Face of Allah** is everywhere". Clearly, this word isn't used for the purpose of defining an individual. We've already established the fact that what you perceive as separate individual beings is due to the inadequacy of your sight.

If with an elevated consciousness you remove this inadequacy you will develop 'insight' with which you can see that there is no multiplicity in creation. What eyes perceive as many, 'insight' perceives as one - the face of Allah.

The meanings denoted by all of the names are not separate meanings, they are all one. A single meaning is being referenced via many seemingly different names!

Since all of these names belong to the ONE, there is only ONE meaning in ONE existence. Different meanings need different names. So, whichever meaning you take essentially you are dealing with the same singular existence, the single source! Hence the concept of multiplicity and unity adjoin here, and one becomes many.

---

[41] Quran 2:115

That is, it is the names that bring about multiplicity. Since there is only one meaning, but because that one meaning is expressed in many different ways it seems as if there are many meanings, it is a relative concept. It is *relatively* many but principally *one*. This one meaning pertains to the single Spirit, as there is only one spirit!

This single spirit expresses its meanings, qualities and attributes in many different ways leading to the perception of multiplicity. In essence there is only one existence but it is observed in many different ways!

Let us give an example. Let's say there is a man called Ahmed. Ahmed has many attributes; he is generous, he is courageous, he is humble… All of these qualities pertain to the same Ahmed. These attributes or 'meanings' of Ahmed do not bring about different Ahmeds. They are merely different aspects of the same person.

If we see him run and hide when faced with a difficulty, we call him a 'coward'. Hence the names and attributes are generated by his actions. Ahmed's actions are interpreted as meanings and those meanings are given a name.

If you remove the names, existence will be seen as singular and the unity of existence may be observed! On the other hand, if in reference to actions different names are given, it will seem as if there are many meanings and many names!

Names are dependent on actions! If there are no actions, the meaning of a name won't exist.

Another way of looking at this is, Allah's names have come about after the manifestation of existence.

Before existence came about at the level of acts, there were no domain of names and hence no meanings.

In Sufism they say "meanings were intrinsic" to express this truth… It was embedded, within the essence of the One, unexpressed. How can we know this? Based on observable actions… If there is no activity, there is no meaning. Meanings come about later…

Hence there is only one face, if you can observe the realm of acts with insight you will only see one face. One existence!

The oneness observed with insight and the multiplicity observed at the level of acts should be observed holistically and at the same degree. If one overweighs the other, you will fall into a state of denial.

Denying the many is denying the One. Denying unity is denying the One.

In any case, whether you accept the many and deny the One, or you accept oneness and deny multiplicity, eventually you'll be denying the One.

Existence is wholly and utterly His Existence!

58

SHARIA - HAQIQAH

Shariah is the name of *haqiqah* (reality) at the level of acts.

Hence, he who denies *sharia* is indisputably denying the reality.

Sharia encapsulates actions that are founded and built upon the principles of the reality.

This being the case, he who denies sharia is obviously ignorant of the reality. For *sharia* is based solely on the reality. When the label '*sharia*' is removed what remains is the reality. If the actions of the reality are the actions required by *sharia*, then it is considered as *sharia*.

In short, whoever denies any part of *sharia* is denying that reality.

All of the activity we see at the level of acts are based on the reality.

Reality is the outward manifestation of the One and Its meanings. However, since they manifest in the form of compositions, we say it's man-made.

If any man-made product or activity is the result of a composition it is an expression of habits based on nature, conditioning, and emotions.

Since the expression of habits, conditioning, nature, and emotions are the automatic output of a compositional program it is contrary to the divine laws. Reason being, it is a limited expression confined within the boundaries of humanly conditions.

This, inevitably, is the very process that creates one's hell.

59

THE PURPOSE OF SHARIAH

The laws of sharia are the orders and the prohibitions of Allah. These orders and prohibitions are the means by which one can overcome his compositional imposition.

At the very least, complying with these orders and prohibitions will create a state of paradise... At best, it will eliminate one's bond to his composition and remove his identity! When the composition is removed the person unites with Allah. When one unites with Allah the meanings of the divine names are expressed through him as Allah likes.

In short, one's eternal bliss depends on his ability to overcome his compositional imposition and to know Allah, to moralize with the morals of Allah, so that all of the divine names can be expressed from him.

On the contrary, if one knows the reality but despite this knowing he continues to comply with his compositional and habitual inclinations then there is indeed suffering awaiting him in the end. This is the suffering known as the 'stop-over at hell' for believers.

This very long 'stop-over' is a forceful compelling way to enable the abandoning of habits and conditioning that one failed to in this world. Hence, we can say the pain and suffering of letting go of worldly ties is predestined for such a person.

So, when we comply with the laws of sharia we partly overcome the composition and become moralized with the morals of Allah.

On the contrary, actions that are driven by compositional motives naturally create one's hell. When the person continues to act in congruence with his compositional inclinations he consequently creates a state of suffering. This is the result of not obeying the laws of sharia.

Sharia consists of the Quran and the recommendations of Rasulullah (saw). The Quran comprises the absolute divine laws. All else is humanly interpretation derived from the compositional make-up, which don't have any effect over the divine laws and thus there is no obligation to apply them.

This is a very fine point and it must be understood well.

Laws that are not revealed through *Uluhiyyah* are formulated by humans and are thus outputs of humanly compositions.

If a person is a Nabi his teachings may be followed and applied but if he isn't a Nabi then he is not notifying you of the laws of Allah. He is simply sharing the laws construed by his composition. It is not mandatory for you to follow him.

If you, however, find meaning in these laws that propel you towards divine bliss then you are free to follow and apply them, but if you don't, then you do not have to follow and you are not responsible for it either.

This is why when one dies, he will not be asked of his specific religious school or *tariqah,* as these notions will not be valid. One will only be called to account and faced with the consequences of whether he complied with the **divine laws** or not.

60

THE ACTION OR THE DOER?

There is an often overlooked detail in the sharia instruction. The Rasul of Allah (saw) states:

"To condemn for the sake of Allah is to condemn the action not the doer."

Let's say Ahmed did a bad deed. We have to condemn his deed not Ahmed.

For the being we're referring to with the name Ahmed is the existence of Allah, in the form of a composition, at a particular location.

So, when we condemn Ahmed we are condemning the meanings of the names, and hence Allah. This will veil us from the One.

This is why sharia tells us to condemn the action not the doer!

But why condemn the action? Because that action forms the composition, which forms the conditioned thought patterns, which create one's hell. One should detest such actions and abstain from doing them.

As long as the doer continues to engage in these actions we may continue to condemn. As soon as he stops, we must feel love and immediately approach the doer with love. For it is the action that creates hell but the doer is the manifestation of the One.

So to hate and condemn for the sake of Allah is addressed to the action and not the doer - the doer is no other than the One.

If we confuse the two and direct our contempt to the doer, we will be directing animosity to the One which will cause us to become veiled, deprived and distant from Him. Resultantly this will form our hell.

So long as we are condemning the doer of such actions, we are in effect creating our own hellfire.

The due and correct response is to condemn the action alone!

Love is similar. Our love should be for the One. To love a person because of their humanly qualities is to create suffering for ourselves. To love someone because of the divine qualities we observe on them is doing justice to love.

Our hatred must be directed to the action, our love must be directed to the One! We must see the One who is present in the essence of the person. If we fail to see the One and claim to love a person as someone separate from the One we will be doing grave injustice and betrayal to love and to the One. This will take us to duality.

By saying "I love my wife, I love my daughter, my money, property, assets, etc." you are effectively engaging in duality... for the One resides within all of the above!

To love these things besides the One, as though they are independent of Him is nothing other than a state of duality.

Then, you must observe and experience the One, and when you encounter an action that spawns composition, habit, and conditioning, condemn that action. And when you encounter someone who is engaging in actions to overcome his composition and habitual programming then love those actions.

These are the measures we must take when feeling love or hatred for the sake of Allah.

61

OBSERVING ALLAH THROUGHOUT EXISTENCE

Regarding the observation of Allah...

Based on the instruct, "Do not contemplate on the Absolute Essence (*dhat*) of Allah" I will not make any claims regarding His Absolute Essence.

Yet we know that the qualities of life, knowledge, will, power, speech (expression), hearing and sight pertain to Allah.

These seven qualities bring us to the eighth-quality referred to as "*Taqween*".

'*Taqween*' means to create or form existence...

That is, the *Hayy* and *Aleem*, uses His attribute of will (*Mureed*) to manifest existence, thus displaying the attribute of '*Taqween*'...

Some translate the word '*Taqween*' simply as 'to create' but it is 'to create existence', to manifest the worlds, not randomly or through any external source, but from within Itself!

Since there is nothing besides Its existence, clearly the manifestation and creation of the worlds (*taqween*) must take place from Itself!

It outputs an act, which carries a meaning. Now take care to understand this well:

This Being with certain qualities outputs a particular act based on His Knowledge. This act carries a meaning. Based on this meaning we give it a name. Hence even though we are giving this name to the act, essentially we are naming the meaning it carries. So, this meaning pertains to the doer of the act, but it does not in any way restrict its doer or creator!

How does this work?

He creates and forms the meaning, but He is not bound or restricted by it!

That meaning belongs to Him. He outputs the meaning just as He expresses many other meanings. He does as He wills!

This means that it's all about the divine will. That is, He wants and wills and then displays the power to manifest His will, which expresses the quality *Taqween*.

> **"Indeed, Allah will admit those who believe and fulfill the requirements of their faith to Paradises underneath which rivers flow... Indeed, Allah does as He wills** (He forms what He wills to manifest from His knowledge with Power; Knowledge – Will – Power).**"**[42]

> **"Indeed, Allah does what He wills."**[43]

These verses notify us of the presence of the qualities of will and power.

Through narrating these verses to us, the Rasul of Allah (saw) is telling us that Allah has the power to do as He wills...

Such a being, who has the power to do as He wills, cannot be bound or constrained by anything! It's impossible!

If He is, then He can't have the power to do as He wills. If he has the power to do as He wills, then he can't be restricted in any way!

Whether we say the world, the universe, or the multiverses... all of it is created!

How were they created?

They were created by the One who does as He wills, from "nothing", they were brought into existence from 'non-existence'.

What does this mean?

Remember the verse:

---

[42] Quran 22:14
[43] Quran 22:18

"Has there not been a time, when man was not a thing even mentioned? (Man was not yet manifest; he was the unmanifest within the dimension of the Names)!"[44]

That is, the meaning referenced by 'man' was not yet existence at that time.

At which time? Is this talking about time as we know it, or a different dimension?

The verse is talking about a dimension, not time! It is talking about the dimension of attributes, the dimension of *wahidiyyah* (unity) which is he unmanifest state of the divine qualities, there are no names or meaning at this level and hence no manifest 'beings'!

The dimension of attributes is not where creation takes place, this is where the divine qualities are known by the Divine but not yet expressed.

Knowledge at the level of the attributes is Allah's knowledge of Himself! His knowledge regarding his existence, attributes and qualities...

Knowledge at the level of the names on the other hand, is about the observation of the meanings of His names. There is a difference of dimension between the two!

What does 'difference of dimension' mean?

It is the difference between the divine knowledge observing;

1. Itself
2. Its meanings
3. The actions formed by these meanings.

These are the differences of dimension.

Time is a relative concept that applies to the dimension of acts. The differences between these stations is not about time, it's about dimension.

The process of condescension of Allah from the Absolute Essence to the Dimension of the Attributes, to the Dimension of Names and so on, is about the dimensional differences, and all of this is a matter on an instant!

Instant should be understood as time!

---

[44] Quran 76:01

Essentially, the time zone referred by the word 'instant' belongs to the being called "*Dahr*"!

As I explained before, based on the hadith al-qudsi '*Dahr*' is Allah. So 'instant' is the time unit in the sight of Allah. Only those who can reach the stations of the Absolute Essence and Attribute may know this. It is not possible to understand this through the five senses and the concept of time shaped by mass conditioning.

The masses conceive time as a linear concept at the level of acts, the determinant of the position of one event in comparison to another.

There are no acts or activity at the level of Allah. It can only be explained as the absolute knowledge observing itself, perhaps this is the closest way to express it. This self- observation can be divided into three stages: observing itself, observing its existence, and observing it meanings.

Observing Itself is to observe the absolute essence, to observe the attributes is to become aware of these attributes, observing its meanings pertains to the level of acts which is the natural and mandatory by-product of the level of names.

All meanings spawn actions that are based on its own meaning.

This process of outputting action as the natural product of inherent meanings marks the beginning of the process of "creation".

This is the point at which the worlds are created.

This is the point at which multiplicity is formed.

This is the point at which the meanings of existence and non-existence, creator and creation, Rabb and servant begin to manifest at the level of acts.

The meanings of the actions bring about the activity at the level of acts. Depending on which meaning the One wants to manifest and which He chooses not to...

Life that is present at the core of the dimension of names belongs to the Grand Spirit! It is the Grand Spirit not the "big" spirit as such concepts, i.e. big, little, full, part, etc. do not apply to spirit. The Spirit is one and single, it permeates the entire existence and hence it has been referred to as the Permeating Spirit, Single Spirit and the Grand Spirit.

Since the Grand Spirit encapsulates all of the meanings of the names and pervades and penetrates through the entirety of existence, all of the meanings within the Grand Spirit are present in all the forms and manifestations throughout existence.

In this light, all of the animate and inanimate beings and creatures in the universe are simply the meanings of the Grand Spirit observing each other from different angles.

Since existence is fully comprised of these meanings, then in this light, the realm of acts is rendered invalid! For, the existence of the realm of acts is relevant and is based on an observer. The realm of the bees is different to the realm and world of humans or to the realms of the subatomic particles.

There are species that are born, that grow, multiply and die all in a millionth of a second. There are species that are born and reach their maturity in ten million years then begin to debilitate and die in another ten million years. All of these exist in their own dimension, their existence is relative. In respect of the latter, the prior may seem inexistent!

So, what am I really saying?

Allah, the Rabb of the worlds, is present with His Absolute Essence (*dhat*) in all the dimensions of life!

In every iota, there is nothing other than His existence, and it is Him observing Himself!

The act of creation is the process of meanings becoming manifest at the level of acts. Thus, any activity that becomes observable at this level is 'created'.

Creation takes on various names. Human, mineral, animal, etc. Despite the fact that they are 'created' they derive their life entirely from the One. They exist and subsist with the name *Qayyum* within their essence. And they each know exactly what to do as the name *Aleem* is also present within them.

Of course, their strength of manifestation depends on the individual make-up.

Every action is expressed based on the meaning it is manifesting. And all of this nothing other than the will of Allah.

Your Rabb is Allah. You are the servant of your Rabb! If you fulfill your servitude to your Rabb you will be fulfilling the commands of Allah. But in any case, you are accountable of fulfilling all of the commands of Allah, besides those of your Rabb. If you fail to do this you will be doing wrong to yourself and hence be subject to suffering.

The essence of yourself is the essence of Allah…

Self is the being of something, and the being of existence is Allah.

By doing wrong to yourself you are not giving the due of Allah as you are unable to observe your essential reality.

If you know the different aspects of your being, your servitude, your Rabb, and how Allah comprises your essence, and give its the due, then you will reach divine bliss and unite with Allah and be of those who enter paradise while still on Earth!

62

OBSERVING THE UNIVERSE THROUGH THE EYES OF CONSCIOUSNESS

Until now we've been examining reality from a religious perspective...

Now let us look at it from another angle, from the perspective of existence itself, getting to know itself.

We know scientifically that the world wasn't always like this. Our planet the Earth, the Sun and our solar system were not always in this state, they gradually evolved to this form. Just as a child is born, grows, ages and dies... The primary principle of the universe is that things are born, they grow, multiply, and die, or 'transform.'

This applies to everything! Since everything is subject to the same law it is evident that all beings come into existence from a non-existent state, they grow, multiply and eventually return to the non-existent- state from whence they came.

This also applies at the universal level. The universe came into existence, or was 'created' from a non-existent state so that the essential meaning of this universe, which is existence (life) may observe itself.

Observing the meanings is synonymous to the 'creation of the universe'. The observation of the meanings of the names in the greater sense, is what started the creation of the universe.

The entire universe is nothing other than the meanings of the divine names... and they are being observed inside its being, not from outside itself!

Due to this, the universe is the existence of the One in and through which His divine names become manifest.

However, the divine names do not have an end, neither does the universe... The universe has a relative end but in respect of its activity it is eternal as it depends on the divine names and the names are eternal!

Every action that transpires in this universe is a transformation of meaning into action. Everything that exists within this universe is a projection, a manifestation of the meanings of the divine names. And hence a sacred locus for the projection of the existence of Allah and His attributes.

To manifest His meanings Allah created the universe, and to observe it, He created Adam!

This observation can't take place at the level of the Absolute Essence or the Attributes and hence the creation of the worlds becomes necessary. So, what is the observation about?

To understand the observation of Allah take yourself as an example. When you look at something you see an object, a person, a thing. Can this be the case for Allah?

When you look at the world do you see separate entities?

The eyes send certain signals to the brain and this bioelectrical message is converted by the brain to produce an image. The brain perceives the meanings and converts it into an image to aid its understanding of it.

But is there really an image in the brain?

The brain only perceives and cognizes. Imagery is only a supporting factor.

Do you not see? To see is to perceive and understand! To have the insight to comprehend that thing, what it is, how it is and why it is the way it is...

The observation of Allah is to perceive with His knowledge the meanings that are inherent within Him. It is Allah enveloping his meanings with His knowledge.

So, do the worlds actually and physically exist or are they merely assumed to exist?

We said every single form and being that exists in this world derives its existence from a divine meaning. These are meanings that Allah observes within Himself, <u>not 'assumes'</u> but observes!

However, for these meanings to manifest as actions they go through the process of 'creation' which brings together a composition of meanings and projects them as activity. This projection is the illusion that we 'assume' into existence. Despite this, even the illusion of existence belongs to the meaning of that composition. Hence, illusion pertains to the 'servant'.

At the divine level, it is Allah observing his Absolute Essence and Attributes, which is the result of the qualities we mentioned above.

We can't talk about illusion regarding Allah. Even though it was used in the past to reference Allah's observation of His meanings, it was only used for the purpose of simplification, to make its comprehension easier. In the real sense, it is unacceptable to relate illusion to Allah.

Allah did not 'accept' or 'assume' the world exists, He 'created' the world and brought it into existence.

The meanings with which the universe was created were already implicitly inherent within It and became manifest at the observable level.

Creation is thus the transformation of meanings from the ethereal level to the material level.

But were the names created, do they really exist?

In respect of their 'name' they were created! But in respect of the 'named' it belongs to itself and were not created. Meanings were implicitly and inherently existent. But their names were created, as names were formed *later*.

To summarize, the universe and everything within it is created, as they appear at the dimension of acts, everything before the dimension of acts isn't created.

The angelic dimensions are included in the level of acts, as they are also the manifestations of the divine forces.

The dimension of names comprises the original meanings of the activity, beings and forms at the levels of acts. That is, the meanings observed and perceived by the Absolute One with His knowledge. None of these meanings are created because the One isn't created.

The fact that you were created will never change. For you can never leave the level of acts. Just as you exist at the level of acts now a million years or a billion later you will still be at the level of acts.

The level of acts may be the material domain today or the radial level tomorrow, but it will always be the dimension of acts.

Only in respect to the meanings within your essence that pertains to Allah you are not created. You are created in respect to the dimension of acts alone.

So, if you can be aware of both and give both their due right, then you can attain eternal bliss.

Otherwise if one aspect veils the other aspect of yourself, you will eventually and most definitely be led astray from the reality.

63

YOUR DIMENSIONAL REALITY

Now let's talk about you... Your existence is a composition of the meanings of the divine names... That is, different compositions of the divine names at different times manifest to comprise your existence.

There is also a 'you' that is observing these meanings that are manifesting as you.

When you dive into your own depths and ask yourself, "Who am I?" you can't really find a definitive answer... You can say "I have this quality, or that quality" but you can't say "I am this" ...

You can't say 'I am this' regarding your absolute essence. This is not possible. But you can define your qualities and attributes and you can claim, based on your qualities, that you will not become non-existent with death, that you will live forever...

Based on your attribute of **knowledge** you have the ability to cognize and comprehend all of this...

Based on this comprehension certain desires and wants bring out the attribute of **will** in you.

Then to turn these wants into action you exercise **power**... Using power, you fulfill your wants. Even if you can transform one of your wants out of a thousand into action, you have the attribute of power...

You can talk about your qualities; you can articulate them. Hence you have the attribute of **speech**.

You can **perceive** your environment and observe the meanings around you. Based on all of these you continually turn meanings into action throughout your life…

Therefore, all of the qualities and attributes we've been discussing at the universal level are all present within you! If, to the best of your capacity, you don't give the due right of all of these faculties, you will be doing wrong to yourself.

If and when you can give each of these faculties their due right, then you will have done justice to yourself.

Every level, aspect and dimension of yourself that you deny, means you are doing injustice and wrong to yourself.

When you can do right by your absolute essence, your Names, attributes and acts, you will be doing right by your existence.

Only by knowing Allah and divine nearness can you truly attain this.

The extent to which you reach divine nearness you will know yourself, and the extent to which you know yourself you will know Allah!

Let us remember the words of Rasulullah (saw):

"Where is Allah? On earth, or in the heavens?"

"Allah is within the hearts of the believers."

(Imam Ghazali – *Ihya-u Ulumuddeen*)

You may unite with Allah, but can you comprehend Him? No!

There is nothing that resembles Him![45]

Vision (sense perception) **perceives Him not but He perceives** (evaluates) **all that is visible.**[46]

And they found a servant from among Our servants to whom We had given (gifted) **grace** (enabling him to experience his reality) **and had disclosed through him Our Knowledge** (the

---

[45] Quran 42:11
[46] Quran 6:103

manifestation of divine attributes as the pleasing self [nafs-i mardiyya]) **from Our ladun.**[47]

Let us know this truth with certainty... If you have accessed this knowledge, this is due to the grace of Allah, who has disclosed this knowledge to us. One can't acquire this knowledge with effort. It is only with divine grace that it is disclosed to us, for it is His Knowledge!

If He so wills, he will disclose it to you, with His grace, not because of your comprehension! For nobody has the capacity to comprehend the entirety of Allah's meanings. Allah is infinite and thus knowledge is infinite and endless.

Essentially, knowledge is the observation of Allah.

One may only observe Allah with and through knowledge!

Any other observation is illusory!

For all other observations of a 'god' entails the concept of a deity that is created. The Divine cannot be created!

And the non-created One cannot be physically observed!

Man is created, we've already discussed this.

The created cannot encompass and see the Creator!

Only Allah can see Himself! Any time you claim to have 'seen' or 'heard' Allah; you have been deluded! It is the Rabb in your imagination that you have seen!

Thus, to unite with Allah means nothing other than the manifestation of Allah's knowledge through the composition called 'you'!

---

[47] Quran 18:65

64

ON HEAVEN AND HELL

Now let us move on to another point…

If existence is comprised entirely of the meanings of the divine names, how do heaven and hell exist?

To understand this, we must understand existence. If we don't correctly understand the existence of the world it is not possible for us to comprehend the existence of heaven and hell.

How did this world form? Isn't Earth the densification of the meanings of the divine names?

If man is the densified manifestation of the divine names, then so is Earth and so is the universe!

Just as the word 'earth' or 'world' references the materialized form of certain divine names and meanings, so do the words 'afterlife', 'heaven' and 'hell'…

Thus, anyone who denies heaven and hell will be denying Allah. All forms of life, whether worldly or otherworldly, are manifestations of the divine names and their meanings as various compositions.

So whenever one denies heaven, hell, the intermediary realm, the angels, the devils, the jinn, or the Satan, etc. he is inadvertently denying the names of Allah and hence denying Allah.

In short, denial is nothing other than being ignorant of Allah. It is a state of being veiled. He who is in a state of denial, will be prone to the suffering caused by the very thing he denies.

Previously I had said, "Religion is the name given to the manifestation of the reality" and discussed how the divine laws are the mandatory regulations, necessitated by the reality.

I had said, "He who denies any of the divine laws or the laws brought by the Rasul of Allah (saw) will be denying the Reality!"

Then, just as the reality is not separate from the divine laws, it is one and the same as the manifest world and the world of acts. Therefore, the reality is completely present at the level of the names and acts. But due to the veils of the perceivers it may not always be observed at the level of acts.

One veils himself from observing the reality first with his words, then with his conditioning, and then with his illusory identity.

It is your delusive assumption creating this veil!

Don't look for the reality in your assumption, look for it in the direction of the divine laws!

Only then may you be of the observers of the reality.

As the Quran says;

> **But they have no knowledge (proof) thereof... They follow only unverifiable assumptions, and indeed, never can assumption reflect the Truth!**[48]

Let us know with certainty, the first station of knowledge is to know what is referenced by the word 'Allah'... Only then can you realize the reality of your 'self'!

---

[48] Quran 53:28

65

THE REALITY OF THE 'SELF'

Here's an excerpt from the *Perfect Man* by Abdulkareem al-Jili:

"Allah also created the self (nafs) of Rasulullah (saw) from His Self.

'Nafs' is the self of something. He formed the Muhammadan realities from His own reality... After creating the self of the Rasul (saw), He created the self of Adam as a form, from the self of Rasulullah (saw). As a result of this fine mystery, despite Adam was forbidden from eating the fruit in paradise, he ate it! For he was made from the substance of Rububiyyah and Rububiyyah cannot be restricted. This principle remains applicable on earth and the afterlife.

Based on this fine mystery, whatever the self was forbidden from doing, it was drawn to, whether the forbidden thing was for his bliss or suffering.

When the self does something, it does not consider whether it will give him happiness or harm. It simply does it as the necessary functioning of its existence due to the principle derived from Rububiyyah...

Do you not see how he ate the fruit in paradise? He did it without any heed. Even though he knew through divine warning that it was going to cause suffering for him. As Allah warned:

"...do not approach this tree lest you suffer...[49]"

That fruit was nothing other than the misery of the bodily life! Allah had created the fruit of the tree as an example of the bodily life. Hence, He made it forbidden. For He knew that it will cause him to be rebellious and

---

[49] Quran 2:35

deserving of being reduced to the miserable level of the bodily life and thus to a mode of complaint and suffering!

*That tree is described in the Quran as "**the accursed tree** (bodily life)."[50]*

When he went to that tree he left the vicinity of the spiritual and the divine and became distant. This is what 'descension' means. Being forbidden from eating the fruit went against the unrestrained nature of the self; this was confusing. The self was stuck between actualizing the 'Bliss of Rububiyyah' that it had acquired and taking heed of the 'divine warning' that eating the fruit will cause his demise.

This being the case, it relied on its own knowledge and because he was drawn to eating the fruit he didn't heed the divine warning at all.

This confusing situation applies to all who has knowledge. Those who fall into complaint and suffering do so because of this confusion.

They abandon the clear warnings confirmed by the Nabi's and Rasul's.

Man is always in a situation of either having faith in the divine warnings and abandoning his own desires or succumbing to his bodily nature and rebelling against the divine warnings."

As can be seen the behavior of a person is either shaped and driven by the divine names in his composition and we call these the things we *wanted* to do, *chose* to do, *willed* to do, because we *felt like* doing it! Or, they are things we do, despite not wanting to, just because they are divine warnings.

We had previously discussed what divine laws mean; actions that enable one to overcome their composition and observe his absolute service to Allah…

Hence the things we "feel" like doing because we enjoy them, are the very things that veil us from Allah.

"I'm so used to doing this!" "But I like it!" "But this is how I've been created!" This is my make-up!" "I enjoy it, I love it…" etc… all such statements are driven by one's composition.

And since the composition is made of the divine names and in essence comprises one's Rabb, when one becomes aware of this, he easily falls into a form of carelessness. Knowing that the essential reality of his self is the

---

[50] Quran 17:60

One makes him complacent and careless, he begins to think he can do whatever he likes, however he likes.

He accepts no restriction, which further pulls him into the prison of the bodily life, thus he inadvertently creates his prison with his own hands.

If he continues to comply with the divine laws even after this realization, then he will eventually overcome his composition and unite with Allah reaching eternal bliss. The name as-Salam will manifest in his life.

Complying with these laws despite the contrary desires of one's composition can be achieved via the expression of the name *as-Sabur*. He must show patience, undeterred by the *Rububiyyah* principle in his make-up. And he must do this with a strength he gains from his 'self', otherwise it is not possible.

And when this is not possible, he will live in compliance with his 'nature' and hence create his hell!

Actions are based either on cognition, or fear and illusion. Cognition brings submission, fear also brings some form of submission…

In the end, both will submit, but what is in their foundation? Did he submit because he cognized why it is such and this knowledge made him submit, or was it out of fear?

Similarly, people submit to Allah in two ways… a Nabi or a Saint submit to the divine laws out of their cognition.

What matters is that you submit not out of fear and illusion, but with cognition and discernment. The purpose is to reach this cognition, even if one temporarily falls into fear, he must eventually overcome it.

For some, their make-up is suitable and they can directly cognize, but in general the majority begin at more primitive 'states and work their way up.

The point is to submit to Allah through cognition and discernment. Remember the words of the Rasul of Allah (saw):

"O Allah, I seek refuge in YOU from YOU…"

What does this mean?

To seek refuge in Allah from His administration over you…

Say (recognize, realize, comprehend, experience)**: "I seek refuge in the Rabb** (the reality of the Names comprising the essence) **of the *Nas*** (mankind).**"**

"The Sovereign of man," (The *Malik*, the One whose sovereignty and administration is absolute over *Nas*, mankind.)

"The God of man," (The reality of *Uluhiyya* that resides within the essence of every human, with which he subsists his existence, and mistakenly thinks this state pertains to a god outside of himself!)[51]

Three states are being highlighted here:

The Rabb of the people: Seeking refuge in the Rabb of the people at the level of acts in which the operation of *Rububiyyah* is in force.

The Sovereign of man: This points to the Domain of Names and their meanings.

The God of man: This is the recognition and observation of the station of *Uluhiyyah*, formed after the previously mentioned observations.

The second station, the recognition of the Domain of Names is described as grasping the mechanics of creation (*mubdi marifah*). This is the understanding of how the various qualities of Allah take form to create compositional meanings.

And last but not least, the third station is the ascension towards Allah through 'Death before dying' (*mutu kable en temutu*).

It is not possible to experience 'death before dying' prior to grasping the mechanics of creation!

First you must unite with your Rabb, then the observation of the meanings of the divine laws will take place, and you will reach the station of the Names, resultantly, you will observe what "Sovereignty" is...

After this, as a result of observing sovereignty, you will become free from the conditions of the names, and will become one with them through death before dying.

This is another way of expressing the state of uniting with Allah...

---

[51] Quran 114:1-3

Similarly, looking at the different states of certainty, we can say the first corresponds to the knowledge of certainty (*ilm al-yakeen*). He who knows himself will know his Rabb... "*Mubdi marifah*" corresponds to the eye of certainty (*ayn al-yakeen*) and 'death before dying' corresponds to the reality of certainty (*haqq al-yakeen*), showing how the reality of certainty can be reached.

Considering that saints who have reached the state of '*haqq al-yakeen*' are very very few it is very unlikely and unrealistic for someone to claim, "I have overcome the conditions of the names and am now one and whole with them."

This state of becoming one with the names can only be attained by those who have reached the state of '*haqq al-yakeen*'. Grasping the mechanics of creation is described in the Perfect Man as those who give the due right of the names and actualize them. To state of certainty accrued through the process of dying before death entails servitude to Allah! To serve Allah in respect of existence, not the names.

In his *Perfect Man*, the section on the 'Form of Muhammad', Abdulkareem al-Jili explains the necessity of overcoming one's compositional make-up in order to escape hell:

"The bodily nature in the world is similar to this: One becomes ecstatic and captivated by Allah and goes into a state of self-restraint and abstinence to purify and cleanse himself of his bodily conditions. In the end, if you say 'his bodily nature has been annihilated" it is true. If you say, "His bodily nature has become inactive by the purification of divine light" this is also true."

Why?

Because abstinence and self-restraint require the performing of certain actions, which in turn activate specific names enabling you to manifest their meanings.

The only way to activate and express the dormant inactive names in one's composition is through self-restraint and abstinence. Otherwise they remain dormant, passively forming your "nature" which generates your hell. In this case you may say it is inactive beneath the divine light but you may not say the bodily nature is totally annihilated.

Did you manifest certain names? Yes, you did. When those names became manifest did the other names, those forming the nature of your composition, disappear? No. They are still present.

They are still present and active but because the new expressions are stronger their effectiveness has subsided, they no longer play an active role in driving the persons actions. In fact, due to manifestation of the new names expressed via new actions we may say the other names are now 'covered'. To put it simply, at the level of acts, the person has broken his habits by taming his bodily nature.

One is a description at the level of acts, the other is at the level of the names.

In the end, the names that form one's nature never become totally annihilated. They continue to exist.

They only lose their strength and effect over the person, as new names are expressed at stronger degrees, they lose their executive power, and this leads to a change in one's composition.

This is also known as "the clear manifestation of divine light".

As for the laborious and burdensome practices such as self-restraint and abstinence…

The only reason something feels laborious and burdensome is because it goes against your nature… When you are 'comfortable' you are aligned with your nature. That which causes discomfort and disturbs you challenges your bodily nature.

Such laborious actions take the place of the suffering the people of hell will encounter in hell. Since there are many degrees and variations of suffering in the afterlife, all spiritual practices such as dhikr, prayer, alms, abstinence and self-restraint are necessary.

Unless one totally suppresses his bodily nature the purification of the body-nature cannot take place. One must be determined and put in a lot of effort!

One must be conscious at all times.

One must constantly consider the consequences of his bodily inclinations and consciously do the opposite. One must never succumb to his addictions or habits. One must never act out of automation or the natural inclination of his bodily nature. This requires serious effort and strenuous exercise!

Those who don't have strong desires don't have to observe extreme measures of abstinence of course. The deeper and stronger desires are rooted in one, the more effort one needs to put in order to be cleansed of it. A little inclination may be eradicated with a little effort. Such is the position of those who will go to hell for a temporary time before going to heaven.

Some will suffer more in hell and some only little.

Depending on how rooted your habits are and how strong your natural programming is, the degree of your suffering will change.

People can't even give up their habit of smoking! The very thought of it gives them torment! Obviously, the suffering on the other side is going to be a lot harder for such people... Same goes for excessive eating, sex, and other bodily habits... the more addicted and inclined one is to such things the harder it will be to let go, and thus the more the suffering.

Dhikr, constant self-restraint and abstinence, are the pleasures of the people of Allah.

Only the servants of **Allah**, as opposed to the servants of their **Rabb** take immense pleasure from such practices.

They perceive every practice that help them overcome their identity as a means of getting closer to Allah and take immense pleasure!

They take pleasure from self-restraint, abstinence, dhikr and everything that goes against their identity (*nafs*)!

This pleasure is the pleasure of getting closer to Allah and observing Allah! If one can't take pleasure from such practices then he is still the servant of his Rabb!

As the verse points out:

> **And there is none among you who He will not pass through** (experience) **Hell! This is, by your Rabb, a definite decree.**[52]

Everyone until a certain age, in terms of their birth, formation, composition etc. is subject to the bodily life. This is the entrance to the life

---

[52] Quran 19:71

of hell! If one can overcome this in the world, he will be exempt from hell in the hereafter!

If on the contrary one can't overcome his bodily nature with spiritual practices like dhikr, abstinence and self-restraint, then with death he will enter the hell of the grave, and after a certain period of suffering, he may eventually be purified and enter paradise! Otherwise it is not possible to go to paradise...

But if one can overcome this in the world he will not be prone to the suffering of hell in the hereafter.

The suffering one endures in this world corresponds to some form of suffering of the hereafter.

As Rasulullah (saw) says:

"Ague is a delight of hell for the believer".

If ague, malarial fever, is likened to the fire of hell, then you imagine what abstinence and self-restraint feels like! Yet this self-combat is more powerful and more intense than anything. It is more painful than the most painful experience one has. As, it is an extremely toilsome process to outroot habits and tendencies that have been established over many years... It requires tremendous effort and willpower. And it is a continuous process, as thirty, forty, fifty years of conditioned, programmed, constructed identity needs to be cleansed and dissolved! Hence it is extremely intense until the self finds its essential purity... then the difficulty will begin to subside...

This is why Rasulullah (saw) referred to self-combat as the "greatest of combats"!

And comparatively, he referred to physical war as a 'small combat'.

Indeed, it is much easier to draw your sword and fight with an enemy than it is to war with oneself!

66

WHAT IS RELIGION?

Religion is the totality of divine laws. They are necessarily divine laws and can't be human laws, as human laws are generated by the human composition and a composition always reinforces its own make-up and thus takes you back to the composition.

Divine laws on the other hand, are free of compositional restrictions. Rather, they enable one to overcome their composition and become moralized with the morals of Allah.

Hence when asked "What is religion?" the answer given by the Rasul (saw) was "Religion is a state of perfect morals" i.e. "the morals of Allah".

Thus, it is the totality of divine laws which can be categorized into four:

The first are the laws that address human nature.

The second address the compositional make-up.

The third are related to knowing one's essential reality.

And the fourth are the laws that enable one to know his Self...

Only the followers of Muhammad (saw) have been blessed with the last set of laws.

The previous three are from the perfection and nobility of other Nabis and Rasuls, while the last category is specifically for the followers of Muhammad (saw).

Now let's say someone engages in certain practices to overcome their natural disposition. With some effort and determination this will lead them to other practices which will eventually enable them to reach some form of enlightenment. Yet they will never find the divine reality and hence end up in a state of suffering, or hell, regardless.

Religion is not just about overcoming your nature!

The religious practices that enable one to overcome their nature *strengthen one's spirituality* while simultaneously saving them from the hellish state of being stuck in their nature.

If spirituality strengthening practices are insufficient the person will still be subject to a period of suffering…

Just because one can rule over their bodily nature does not guarantee them a place in paradise!

It may give one supernatural abilities in the world but as long as one lacks the sufficient spiritual strength they cannot attain paradise.

Only the actions prescribed by the divine laws can enable this…

The second set of laws regarding the composition are practices that allow one to adopt the morals of Allah.

Your morals are formed by your composition which are comprised of the divine names. But these names, when merged together to form your being, comprise your Rabb and you can't overstep the laws of your Rabb.

The names that comprise your existence define your perspective and constantly preserve it. But as you begin to moralize with Allah's morals your thoughts and perspectives begin to shift and change - which can only take place and be known with divine laws.

The laws related to one knowing his essential reality does not mean identifying with the absolute essence of existence!

In other words, claiming things like "Since the essence of existence is comprised of the divine forces that also comprise and compose my being, I am one and the same as the universe" are generated by philosophical analysis and do not reflect the reality. One who makes such claims has not found his reality. For this kind of self-discovery transpires at the level of acts. The self identifies with the universe, with the universal "consciousness" but all of it is taking place at the level of acts, rather than the level of Attributes, where the discovery should really be taking place.

Again, this can only be known, found and experienced with the religion of Islam.

Finally, the fourth set of laws are about discovering one's absolute Self! This is based on the teachings of Muhammad (saw) aligned with the divine laws.

In short, if we say, "religion is the path to bliss" this will be an insufficient and inadequate claim. It is more correct to say, "Religion is the path that takes one to divine bliss" or "What allows one to reach true bliss is the totality of the divine laws". As only through complying with these laws can one reach true happiness.

Alternatively, he may reach 'natural' happiness based on bodily pleasures, but the counterpart of this in the hereafter will be nothing less than the suffering of hell.

First, we talked about the physical make up of humans. Then we spoke about the presence of the One under the guise of a 'human'... This leads us to explore what Islam and religion is... why it came, why it is necessary etc.

We established that a person has a specific composition, composed of divine names. A name-composition that forms a personality is what we call a "human." Hence the word human refers to a specific composition of names. However, the laws that stem from the composition cannot constantly direct the future of the composition to bliss! For it is not possible for the name composition to change!

Only the laws coming from the divine level of attributes which is the essence of the name composition, the laws of the Absolute Self can alter, destroy and completely change the composition.

To put it simply, you can't come out of a depression with the same mind-set with which you went into depression; you need a higher intellect, that's why you ask for advice or seek therapy. How can you come out of a depression with the same mind that caused you to go into depression in the first place? You need the guidance of another intellect.

In the same way one can't change his composition with his composition, as it is the composition itself that caused him to become the way he is. He needs the divine guidance and administration coming from the level of Attributes, i.e. from Allah, to override his current programming or to get to know his composition at a greater scale.

That's why we said the *totality of divine laws*, not the totality of human laws.

Hence any and all religions stemming from 'human' laws cannot be a means to true salvation. The religion of Confucius can't save humanity!

For despite containing some truths, which it obviously does since Confucius is also a composition of Allah, they are constrained and limited truths derived from a composition.

Truths that are born of one's composition are not sufficient to enable one to overcome his compositional make-up and unite with Allah.

This is why humans can only reach salvation with the divine religion. Religious ways devoid of divine administration can never give salvation.

This is why "the religion in the sight of Allah is Islam" says the Quran, describing what religion is.

It is making it evident that religion is Islam and only Islam.

What does this mean though?

The result of a composition is its natural output and it is limited to the space it occupies, it can't go further than that.

The religion of Islam however, encourages you to express the meanings of different names by advising you to engage in activities that will enable this.

It recommends certain practices to help you to activate and express the dormant qualities within you so that you may expand and enhance your composition, and fortify your spirit or spiritual energy.

So, what does the religion of Islam ask of us?

Firstly, it asks that we give our word of testimony…

To say "*La ilaha illallah*", to actually witness this truth, and to accept the Rasul who has taught us this…

So, let us now explore the meaning of the word of testimony.

67

ONE MEANING OF THE WORD OF UNITY

What does "*La ilaha illallah?*" mean?

"*La ilaha*" means *there is no god.* "*Illa Allah*" means, *there is only Allah!*

Let's examine it in sections:

La ilaha; there is no god, i.e. there are no other beings other than Allah.

Now there are two significant denotations here:

The first meaning is there is no god, the second, more implicit meaning is, yes there are other seemingly separate forms of existence but they all exist and subsist with Allah.

The first meaning is warning you against conceiving separate forms of existence… It's saying there are no separate beings, there is only Allah, the *Wahid* and *Ahad*.

There is only an inseparable, indivisible, unified existence: Allah!

In this light, neither you nor anyone else exists.

The second meaning is saying there are separate beings but what you conceive as separate is nothing other than Allah, in respect of the dimension of names and acts. For what we call the dimension of acts is dependent on the human or compositional laws.

There are seemingly separate forms, but they are nothing other than Allah! For there is no existence besides Allah.

That is, they only exist as points of manifestation of the divine names.

The second implicit meaning is hidden in the word "*illa*". *La ilaha* **illa**: there is no god **but, only, besides**… this is what the word "*illa*" implies.

Therefore, the meaning of "*La ilaha illallah*" not in respect of the Absolute Essence (*dhat*) but in respect of the dimension of names is, "there is no god there is only Allah"! There is no existence besides Allah, the *Wahid'ul Ahad*. This is the first meaning.

The second meaning, at the level of acts, is that there are loci of manifestation of the divine names, thus there are seeming separate forms or 'compositions' of existence. But all of these compositions are compositions of the names of Allah and hence they are nothing other than Allah. They are from Allah, they belong to Allah, they are extensions and manifestations of Allah.

For the common people the Word of unity "*la ilaha illallah*" simply means there is no other deity, there is only one creator to be worshipped and that is Allah.

The truth is, **there is no existence besides Allah**, and hence nothing to worship and deify!

Have I been able to make my point?

There is no deity, only Allah! You can find more details on this in Muhammad's Allah.

To accept something first you need to know what it is, first you need to understand it and comprehend it then you can choose to either accept or reject it.

If you can understand the meaning of *La ilaha illallah* as I've just explained then you are given an invitation to accept it.

Do you accept it?

If so, then you can claim "*La ilaha illallah*, but only if, beyond a mere acceptance, it is an observed reality for you…

On the other hand, you may not be in observation of it but it may make sense to you and it may be aligned with your compositional make-up and you can still accept it, simply because it makes sense to you and your composition.

But if you can observe the meaning of *La ilaha illallah*, at least at the level of acts, then you are asked to witness it. Hence the Word of Witness is an expression of an actual 'act of witnessing' that has taken place. The Word of Witness is for those who can **observe** and **witness** this reality.

If you can observe it then you can lawfully say "I witness that…"

How can you be a witness?

You can only be a witness to something that you've actually seen right?

Hence to witness this reality is to see and witness that there is no other being besides Allah.

Then you can claim *"Ash hadu an la ilaha illallah"*.

"I witness that nothing exists besides Allah. It is only Allah that exists!"

Who is able to bear witness in this way?

According to the Quran:

"Allah knows with certainty that none exists other than He. He is *HU*, there is no other, only *HU*…"[53]

This verse is a clear indication that nothing exists other than Allah; and everything that "seemingly" exists is nothing other than Allah.

Then, *La ilaha illallah* can only be proclaimed once in a lifetime, in the real sense, with the prefix "I witness" …

Many can object to this. Especially when so many spend their entire lives chanting the Word of Unity over and over again. Yet repeating something is one thing, observing its meaning is another thing altogether. Observing that there aren't "many" creations but a singular existence, and that this singular existence is only Allah, is a one-time experience. This observation takes place once. It doesn't happen again and again because existence isn't destroyed and re-created for you to see this again for the first time.

Once you've seen it you've seen it. The first time you look at something and see it, you've seen it. The next time you look at it you're merely continuing an observation you've previously made. You can look at it again and again, but all of these will be extensions of the initial look, a more detailed seeing of what you've already seen.

---

[53] Quran 3:18

So, if you can say "*La ilaha illallah*" once, in the real sense, then every time you say it thereafter will just be a repetition and a validation of your initial observation.

Hence why Muhammad (saw) says;

"When you see the Kaaba for the very first time, make a prayer, as that prayer will most definitely be accepted."

He doesn't say this for "every time" you see the Kaaba or if you continually stare at the Kaaba. The first experience is a one-time experience.

Observations after the initial observation are not disregarded, but the first is the real deal. For once you've seen something you've seen it; you can no longer unsee it! All other following observations are but the continuation of the first.

68

THE SERVITUDE AND RISALAH OF MUHAMMAD (SAW)

Once we can proclaim, "*Ash hadu an la ilaha illallah*" we are charged with another duty.

That is, to be able to declare, "*Wa ash hadu anna muhammadan abduhu wa rasuluhu*".

"*Wa ash hadu*" I witness... "*anna*" with certainty (without doubt) "*muhammadan abduhu wa rasuluhu*" that Muhammad is the servant and the Rasul of HU.

The name "Muhammad" is a reference. Hence the being that is referenced with the name "Muhammad" is first the servant then the Rasul of *HU*.

Servitude is a higher station than *risalah* and is thus mentioned first.

Can you imagine... a higher station than being a "Rasul"!

"I was put ahead of all the Rasuls that have come in the past" he says...

Risalah is the highest station one can reach, and he was put ahead of all the other Rasuls! Additionally, his servitude was put to the forefront with "*AbduHU*" advancing him to an even higher station!

What is meant by "servitude" of the one who is referenced by the name "Muhammad"?

Muhammad is "*AbduHU*" ... Here, the word "*Abd*" (servant) is tied to the word "*HU*" ...

Hu points to *Huwiyyah* – The Absolute Divine Essence...

Hence his servitude is his divine essence, meaning he is a servant to the divine essence of Allah.

This means, he encompasses the station of the Absolute Essence (*dhat*) which is the core of the dimension of acts, the dimension of names and the dimension of attributes.

Therefore, everyone who claims to bear witness, consciously or unconsciously, is accepting and confessing that Muhammad comprises all of these dimensions.

To be a servant of the divine essence is a state that is only observed on Muhammad among all other Rasuls.

The essence of something is the very thing itself, hence the fact that he is the servant of the divine essence is because he has observed the divine One through himself!

Muhammad (saw) is the first human to have observed the Divine Essence within his own essence.

Hence his rank is an unmatched unique rank beyond description.

The name of no other Rasul can be mentioned near his!

The heirs of Muhammad are the heirs of this meaning and hence they are mentioned among the other Nabis and Rasuls in the "realm of meanings".

Who are his heirs?

Only the "Perfect Man" can be his heir!

The perfect man isn't a man with perfect qualities!

The "perfect man" is a station that refers to those consummate enlightened masters who have attained "*gawsiyyah*" – they are the "essences of their era"!

Existence revolves around them and with their verdict!

Hence even though the word "servant of *HU*" is generally and grammatically conceived as the servant of Allah, the observation of the reality reveals that *HU* designates *HUWIYYAH* - the divine essence!

Servitude to the Divine Essence requires the attainment of the dimensions of the Names, Attributes and the Absolute Essence!

Only after this, the station of *Risalah* comes... What does *risalah* mean?

The meaning of *Risalah* is actualizing the laws of *Uluhiyyah* – specifically those that are related to man's eternal bliss – at the levels of acts. It is realized and actualized at the level of acts.

After one proclaims the *Shahadah*, that is, witnesses the servitude and *risalah* of Muhammad (saw), he becomes *Islam* and is thus called a *Muslim*.

One who makes this proclamation can only do so because the following verse becomes manifest through him:

> **And whoever submits his face** (consciousness) **to Allah as a doer of good, has surely grasped a strong handle... All affairs return to Allah!**[54]

The name "*Muhsin*" (blessed) is one of the names of Allah not included among the 99 names. To submit one's face to Allah is to confess that there is no other than Allah in his observation and perception!

Remember the verse, **"So wherever you turn, there is the Face of Allah"**[55] i.e. whatever or whomever you look at you will see His face, just as when someone else looks at you, they too will only see the face of Allah...

Hence, he who proclaims the Word of Witness has returned the trust to its owner by submitting his face back to Allah, its lawful owner, and has thus become freed of being labelled a 'traitor-betrayer'.

Now that we've explained the meaning of *Risalah* let us move on to *Nubuwwah* and *Wilayah*...

---

[54] Quran 31:22
[55] Quran 2:115

69

WHAT IS A NABI AND A RASUL?

What do the words Nabi and Rasul denote? What do they mean?

A Nabi and a Rasul are born with the capacity of being a Nabi and Rasul!

One who lacks this capacity cannot develop it later. It must be inherently present at birth.

With this capacity and the presence of the One within his essence, he overcomes the conditions of his composition by engaging in certain practices and observes Allah in his essence!

After observing Allah within his own being he submits to Him. He delivers the commands of Allah, the laws of *Uluhiyyah*, to the people, as the laws that will construct their eternal bliss.

This is precisely what a Nabi does; he delivers laws.

A Rasul on the other hand does not bring new laws but reminds the people of the laws that were previously delivered.

What differentiates a Nabi and a Rasul from a *wali*?

A *wali* observes that existence is the One. As he rises in spiritual rank he begins to observe Allah. Eventually the *wali* becomes a conduit to Allah's administration over the realm of existence.

The *wali* does not administer, Allah does!

However, a Nabi and a Rasul, beyond the administration of the worlds, relays the divine laws to the people, explaining the divine meanings and hence aiding and supporting others to unite with Allah.

A Nabi invites people to Allah, as someone who has reached the essence and the reality of existence.

The fact that Muhammad (saw) is the final Nabi is due to the fact that he has explained and clarified all of the human and divine realities; there is nothing left to be explained.

When he claimed, *"I am the final Nabi"* he was actually saying "I have explained everything that needs to be explained, I have left no need for another Nabi".

The greatest person to come after him can only be one who provides the details of his teachings…

He can perhaps shed some extra light on to the matters that Muhammad (saw) left mystifying but he can never reveal a totally new reality.

70

REGARDING THE QURAN

The Quran is the totality of the divine laws and mysteries we discussed thus far.

There are two types of verses in the Quran:

Muhqam – Absolute

Mutashabiha - Allegorical

The absolute verses notify us of the actions and practices one must engage in to be cleansed of and overcome his natural predisposition.

It tells us which actions will lead to suffering and create our hell in the future by keeping us imprisoned within the limits of our natural make-up. It also tells us how we can know Allah and the necessary practices and prohibitions we must observe to achieve this.

Allegorical verses, on the other hand, are symbolic or metaphoric verses that convey deep divine mysteries and secrets for those who have the capacity to bear it.

No matter how much one thinks he understands these divine realities, if he hasn't actually and totally grasped them, he will most definitely find a contradiction between his assumption and the laws let known by the Quran and the Rasul of Allah (saw).

If he completely discerns these realities, that is if he reaches the station of "Heir of Rasulullah", then he will most certainly find the counterpart of every sharia law inside the "reality" and every "reality" within the sharia laws. He will observe them in their perfect place. If at any point he is convicted otherwise or develops an alternative opinion, this is a sign that he hasn't completely and totally discerned the matter.

71

REGARDING THE ANGELS

Why is it so important to have faith in the angels? Why is it included among the six pillars of faith?

Faith in Allah, His Rasul (saw), and the Quran are completely understandable; they are the means by which we are notified of the divine laws.

But angels? Do we ever see an angel in our life? No!

Is it possible to see an angel? Can it talk to us? No!

So, what's the deal with having faith in angels, what does it matter if we know and accept them or we don't? Why is it one of the pillars of faith? It is even included in the "*Amantu*"! Why is it so necessary to have faith in them?

The word "*malaiqah*" is plural, its origin comes from the word "*malq*" which means "force"!

Angels are the divine forces of Allah, they are like transmitters of divine power, every force carries a meaning!

Just as you accept the existence of Allah, it is evident that existence is a manifestation of certain "forces".

When you produce something, a potential force is transformed into action. When it is in the state of a force, it may not be observable, but it is present in your essence.

Observing it is possible via manifestation…

Divine forces are also observed at the level of acts. In other words, observation of the dimension of names and acts is possible through the "divine forces" i.e. the angels…

For example, what we call "radiation" is a meaning present in a star which reaches Earth as cosmic radial rays... In the past they used to describe this as "laws being carried down from the 3rd or the 7th sky."

Thus, recognizing these divine forces is a step towards knowing one's self...

Due to this, one must accept and confirm the presence of these divine forces, so that he may recognize and know them in order to be able use and administer them with the power of Allah.

How can you accept something you don't know?

You must know and accept it first so that you can begin to administer it!

And when you do, it will be the administration of Allah, not the servant.

Hence the necessity of having faith in the angels is on account of the angels comprising the divine forces!

It is through these angelic forces that the meanings of the divine names transform from the state of pure potential into activity. Hence to deny the angels is to deny the meanings of Allah!

On the other hand, it is said that angels are the mediators between the servant and Allah.

Isn't a servant a manifest composition at the level of acts?

And isn't Allah the absolute essence? So then the relation of the stages between these two points are implemented with these forces.

Your ascension from the level of acts to the level of the names is possible via angelic forces!

As a matter of fact, during "Ascension" the Rasul of Allah (saw) was accompanied by an angel.

But only up to a particular point! After that the angelic forces can go no further. For they have emerged at the level of the names. So, at the level of names the angelic forces must be abandoned before moving on to the level of attributes.

Angelic forces take various names as the divine names become manifest.

In other words, every angel, or all of the angelic forces derive their power from a divine name.

72

WHAT IS FATE? HOW TO HAVE FAITH IN FATE?

This is perhaps one of the most commonly misunderstood, or the hardest to "grasp" topic of all ages!

So many have presented opinions on this topic throughout history but not many have actually done solid research on what the Quran and the Rasul (saw) have said about fate.

It's actually quite interesting, there are so many books on the topic of fate, but close to none of what the Rasul of Allah (saw) has taught regarding this topic can actually be found in them.

In order to validate the concept of "free-will" verses regarding fate have been pushed under the rug!

My understanding of good virtue is that if one falls impotent in explaining a particular verse or a hadith he should admit his impotence and inadequacy rather than pushing it under the rug.

Those who adopt the view, "One determines his own path in life with his free-will, and faces the consequences of his own choices" are called the "*Qadariyah*" about whom the Rasul (saw) has said, ***"The Qadariyah are the Zoroastrians amongst my followers."***

The *Qadariyah* believe that a person determines his own fate, and Allah, from afar, watches and observes it all!

In point of fact the Quran invalidates this concept with countless verses.

There are also other views such the "*ahli sunnah*" and "*jabriyyah*" however I don't wish to discuss these here as I am not trying to assert a particular view, everyone's view is for themselves.

I only felt the need to touch on the topic of fate after examining the make-up of man, the effects he lives under, the mechanics of his being and existence…

All of this naturally brought us to the topic of fate, for **we must also accept this truth**!

What is the value of man's will, power and possessions next to the glory of Allah, his Sublimity and Greatness?

In short, how much power does man have in the sight of the One denoted by the name Allah?

What is the value of man in the sight of the One who created the hundreds of billions of galaxies full of stars so much greater than our Sun?

Here is a hadith al-qudsi:

The Rasul of Allah (saw) said:

Allah says:

"O my servants! All of you are misguided other than those among you that I rightly guide. Ask of me so that I shall grand guidance to you.

All of you are poor, other than those among you that I make wealthy; ask of me so that I shall grant provision to you.

All of you are sinners, other than those among you that I have forgiven; he who knows my mercy and forgiveness and asks to be forgiven, I shall forgive him regardless (of the greatness of his sins).

If all of you, from the most precedent to the most proximate, the living and the dead, the wet and the dry, were to have the heart of my most pious servant it will not add the worth of a mosquito wing to my dominion!

If all of you, from the most precedent to the most proximate, the living and the dead, the wet and the dry, were to have the heart of my most impious servant it will not lessen the worth of a mosquito wing from my dominion!

And if all of you, from the most precedent to the most proximate, the living and the dead, the wet and the dry, were to come together and each of you asked for as much as his heart desired, I will give to each and every one of you all of your wants and this would still not lessen anything from my dominion; it will be no different than if one you dipped the tip of a needle into an ocean to take some water out!

I DO AS I WILL!

Both my forgiveness and my punishment are my promise.

If I will for something to be, I say "Be" and it will be!"

So, what do you think?

Is this hadith enough to put us into our place?

In the sight of the One who likens stars that are millions of times greater than our Sun to the tip of a needle, what do you think is the place of our much arrogant and boastful human race?

Do we have the power to do anything "despite" Allah!?

So now we come to the topic of FATE…

In the section on astrology, I had explained how the life of the brain is programmed with cosmic effects and that this program was not subject to change under normal conditions. In other words, the fate of the person is written during the formation of the brain with the "cosmic pen" whose ink has *dried* and is hence *unalterable*.

The fate of man…

Does he have any control over his fate?

Is everything predetermined?

Is everything done and dusted?

Let us see what the Quran and the Rasul of Allah (saw) have to say about this…

73

THE TOPIC OF FATE-DESTINY IN THE QURAN AND HADITH

"You cannot will, unless Allah wills."[56]

"...While it is Allah who created you and all your doings."[57] (Quran 37:96)

"No calamity befalls you on earth (on your physical body and outer world) **or among yourselves** (your inner world) **that has not already been recorded in a book** (formed in the dimension of knowledge) **before We bring it into being! Indeed for Allah, this is easy.**

"We inform you of this in order that you don't despair over your losses or exult (in pride) **over what We have given you, for Allah does not like the boastful and the arrogant!"**[58]

"There is no living creature which He does not hold by its forehead (brain; the programming of the brain by the name *Al-Fatir*)**."**[59]

"Say: Everyone acts according to his creation program (*fitrah*). **This is why your Rabb** (who is the *Fatir*) **knows best who is on**

---

[56] Quran 76:30
[57] Quran 37:96
[58] Quran 57:22-23
[59] Quran 11:56

the right path!"[60]

Say: 'Allah' and let them amuse themselves in their empty discourse (their illusory world) in which they are absorbed."[61]

"The doer of what He wills!"[62]

"He is not questioned (called to account) for what He does! But they will be questioned (they will live the consequences of their actions)!"[63]

"Indeed, We have created everything with its program (*qadar* – fate)."[64]

There are many more verses in the Quran regarding fate, so I will suffice with this much for now and share some hadith regarding fate from both the Sahih Muslim and Tirmidhi collections...

Abu al-Aswad reported that Imran ibn Husain asked him:

"What is your view on what the people do today in the world and strive for, is it something decreed and preordained for them or will their fate in the Hereafter be determined by the fact that their Rasul and Nabi brought them teachings which they did not act upon?"

I said: "Of course, it is something which is predetermined for them and preordained for them."

He then said: "Then, would it not be an **injustice** (to punish them)?"

I felt greatly disturbed and said: "**He is not questioned for what He does! But they will be questioned**" (Quran 21:23); thereupon he said to me: "May Allah have mercy upon you, I did not mean to ask you but for testing your intelligence."

Two men of the tribe of Muzaina came to Allah's Rasul (saw) and said:

---

[60] Quran 17:84
[61] Quran 6:91
[62] Quran 85:16
[63] Quran 21:23
[64] Quran 54:49

"O Allah's Rasul, what is your opinion on what the people do in the world and strive for, is it something decreed for them; something preordained for them and will their fate in the Hereafter be determined by the fact that their Rasul brought them teachings which they did not act upon and thus they became deserving of punishment?"

Thereupon, he said:

"Of course, it happens as it is decreed by fate and preordained for them, and this view is confirmed by this verse of the Book of Allah:

By the self (the individual consciousness; identity) **and the One who proportioned it** (formed the brain)**; then inspired it as to what will lead it astray from the Truth and the system, and how to protect itself...** (Quran 91:7-8)"

***

Jabir reported that Suriqa b. Malik b. Ju'shuin came and said:

"Allah's Rasul, explain our religion to us (in a way) as if we have been created just now. Whatever deeds we do today, is it because of the fact they have been predetermined and written, or is it our doing that determines them?"

Thereupon he said:

"Everything has been predetermined and written. The pens have dried and destinies have begun to operate."

(Suraqa b. Malik) said: "If it is so, then what is the use of doing good deeds?"

Rasulullah said:

"Act, for everyone is facilitated for what he intends to do. He who does good will be facilitated towards the good." (Muslim, Tirmidhi)

***

Abdullah Ibn Masud (r.a.) narrates:

Rasulullah (saw) to whom the truth is revealed and who always speaks the truth, told me:

"Substance from your parents are gathered in the mother's womb for forty days, then in another forty-day period it becomes a clot of blood, then in another forty-day period it becomes a small flesh. (After the

120th day) Allah sends an angel and asks it to record four things: Its livelihood, its sustenance, its death, and whether he will be of the fortunate or the unfortunate ones."

Ibn Masud continues;

"I swear to Allah in whose hands of power the life of Abdullah lies, after the angel records these, the spirit is blown into it (the fetus comes to life).

One may do so many good deeds such that between him and Paradise will remain only an arm length yet at this point the record (written by the angel in the mother's womb) will come into effect and obstruct the person. After this, he will begin to do the deeds of the people of hell (and be cast to hell).

One may do such bad deeds that between him and hell will remain only one step distance, yet at this point the record (written by the angel) will come into effect and obstruct the person. Then he will begin to do the deeds of the people of heaven (and go to Paradise)." (Bukhari, Tajrid 1324)

***

Anas Ibn Maliq (r.a.) narrates:

Rasulullah (saw) said:

"Allah appoints an angel to every womb, and the angel says, 'O Rabb! A drop of discharge (i.e. of semen), O Rabb! A clot, O Rabb! A piece of flesh.' And then, if Allah wishes to complete the child's creation, the angel will say. 'O Rabb! A male or a female? O Rabb! Wretched or blessed (in religion)? What will his livelihood be? What will his age be?' The angel writes all this while the child is in the womb of its mother." (Bukhari, Muslim)

***

Ali (r.a.) reported that one day Rasulullah (saw) was sitting with a twig in his hand and he was scratching the ground. Suddenly he raised his head and said:

"There is not one amongst you who has not been allotted his seat in Paradise or Hell."

They said: "O Rasul of Allah, then why struggle, why not let everything go and submit?" Thereupon he said:

"No, do perform good deeds, for everyone is facilitated in that for which he has been created. The fortunate will be facilitated in doing the deeds of the fortunate ones and unfortunate will be facilitated in doing the deeds of the unfortunate ones!"

Then he recited this verse:

"As for he who gives to the needy and seeks refuge in Allah and confirms the Word of Unity, We will facilitate him toward Paradise. But as for he who withholds and considers himself free of need and denies the Word of Unity, We will facilitate him toward Hell (Quran 92:5-10)." (Bukhari, Muslim, Abu Dawud, Tirmidhi)

***

Imran bin Husain (r.a.) narrates:

"Once I asked Rasulullah (saw): "O Rasulullah, have the people of paradise been distinguished from the people of hell (with Allah's preordainment)?"

Upon which Rasulullah (saw) said;

"Yes, they have been distinguished."

"If the people of heaven and hell have already been predetermined then why should those who do good deeds and engage in prayers continue to do so?"

"Everyone will do what he has been created for, whatever has been predestined for him, he will carry that out" he answered. (Bukhari, Tajrid 2062)

***

Abu Huraira reported Allah's Rasul (saw) as saying:

"Verily, a person performs deeds for a long time like the deeds of the people of Paradise. Then his deeds are terminated like the deeds of the people of Hell and, verily, a person performs deeds like the people of Fire for a long time, and then this deed of his is ultimately followed by the deeds of the people of Paradise."

Sahl b. Sa'd reported it from Allah's Rasul (saw) that a person apparently performs the deeds of the people of Paradise in public, while he is destined to be among the dwellers of Hell, and a person acts apparently like the people of Hell, while in fact he is destined to be among the dwellers of Paradise.

***

Muslim narrated that Tawus al-Yamani said: I found some of the companions of Rasulullah (saw), saying:

"Everything is by decree."

Tawus added: I heard Abdullah ibn Umar say that Rasulullah said:

"Everything is by decree – even incapacity and ability."

***

Abu Huraira reported Allah's Rasul (saw) as saying:

"Verily Allah has fixed the very portion of adultery which a man will indulge in, from which he cannot escape. The adultery of the eye is the lustful look, and the adultery of the tongue is the licentious speech, the heart desires and yearns, which the parts may or may not put into effect."

***

Ubayy b. Ka'b reported that Allah's Rasul (saw) said:

"The young man whom Khadir killed was a non-believer by his very nature and had he survived he would have involved his parents in defiance and unbelief."

***

Aisha, the mother of the believers, reported that a child died and I said: "There is happiness for this child who is a bird from amongst the birds of Paradise."

Thereupon Allah's Rasul (saw) said:

"Don't you know that Allah created Paradise and He created Hell and He created the dwellers of Paradise and the dwellers of Hell?"

Aisha, the mother of the believers, said that Allah's Rasul (saw) was called to lead the funeral prayer of a child of the Ansar. I said: "Allah's Rasul, there is happiness for this child who is a bird from the birds of Paradise for it committed no sin nor has he reached the age when one can commit sin."

He said:

"Aisha, per adventure, it may be otherwise, because Allah created for Paradise those who are fit for it while they were yet in their father's loins and created for Hell those who are to go to Hell while they were yet in their father's loins."

***

Narrated by Abu Huraira (r.a.):

Rasulullah (saw) said:

"Adam and Moses argued with each other. Moses said to Adam, 'Are you Adam, whom Allah created with His own hands and blew into from His Spirit, and made His angels prostrate before you, and made you live in Paradise in comfort and ease, yet with your mistake you expelled us all from Paradise!?'

Adam said to him, 'Are you Moses, whom Allah selected as a Rasul and to whom He spoke directly and conferred upon you the tablets in which everything was clearly explained and granted you the audience in order to have a confidential talk with you. What is your opinion, how long ago was the Torah written before I was created?

Moses said: Forty years before.

Adam said: Did you not see these words: Adam committed an error and he was enticed to (do so).

He (Moses) said: Yes.

Whereupon, he (Adam) said: Do you then blame me for an act which Allah had ordained for me forty years before He created me?"

Allah's Rasul (saw) said:

"This is how Adam evidently prevailed over Moses."

***

Abdullah b. 'Amr b. al-'As reported: I heard Allah's Rasul (saw) as saying:

"Allah ordained the measures (of quality) of the creation fifty thousand years before He created the heavens and the earth, as His Throne was upon water."

Abu Huraira (ra) reported Allah's Rasul (saw) as saying:

"A strong believer is better and is more lovable to Allah than a weak believer, and there is good in everyone, but cherish that which gives you benefit (in the Hereafter) and seek help from Allah and do not lose heart, and if anything in the form of trouble comes to you, don't say : If I had not done that, it would not have happened so and so, but say: Allah did that what He had ordained to do, for your "if" opens the gate for the Satan."

***

Tirmidhi narrates:

Omar (r.a.) asked: "O Rasulullah, what do you say, are our activities created as we engage in them, or have they already been predestined?"

Rasulullah (saw) answered:

"O Hattab's son, everyone is facilitated to carry out that which has been predestined for him. He who is from the good will strive for the good, and he who is from the bad will strive for the bad!"

***

Narrated by Salman (ra):

"Nothing increases one's lifespan except good deeds, and nothing repels Divine Decree except prayer (supplication)."

***

Abu Khizamah narrates:

The Rasul of Allah (saw) was asked: "Do you think the medicines with which we treat ourselves, the readings by which we seek healing, and the means of protection that we seek, change the decree of Allah at all?"

He said:

"They are also a part of the decree of Allah. The son of Adam was created with ninety-nine deaths before him, if he can overcome these dangers, he will eventually come to old age and die."

***

Hadhrat Ali (ra) narrates:

The Rasul of Allah (saw) said:

"Until the servant has faith in the following four things he is not a believer: That there is no God but Allah, that I am the Rasul of Allah, that death and life after death exists, and that destiny is a reality."

***

Jabir bin Abdullah (ra) narrates:

The Rasul of Allah (saw) said:

"Until a servant believes that good and bad is from fate, that whatever has reached him could never have missed him, and what has missed him could never have reached him, he cannot be a believer."

***

Narrated by Abdullah bin Amr...

The Rasulullah (saw) came upon us as though holding two books in his hands and asked us,

"Do you know what these books are?"

"No O Rasul of Allah, we may only know if you tell us."

Upon this he showed the book in his right hand and said,

"This is a book from the Rabb of the worlds. In it are the names of those who will go to paradise, their father's names and the names of their tribes. It contains every name in detail, there will be no addition to it nor will there be any subtraction from it anymore."

Then he showed the book in his left hand and said,

"This too is a book from the Rabb of the worlds and contains the names of those who will go to hell, their fathers' names and the names of their tribes. Every name has been recorded in detail, there will be absolutely no addition to it nor any subtraction from it anymore."

We asked, "O Rasul of Allah (saw) if it has been predetermined then what is the purpose of our deeds and practices here?"

He said;

"Be righteous and moderate, for he who will go to paradise regardless of whatever deed he may have done in the past his final deed will be the deed of the people of paradise. And he who will go to hell, regardless of whatever deed he may have done in the past his final deed will be the deed of the people of hell. Our Rabb has determined the fate of His servants.

One section is in hell."

***

It was narrated on the authority of Abu Hurairah (ra) that the Rasul (saw) said:

"There is no Adwa *(no disease is conveyed from the sick to the healthy without the Permission of Allah),* ***nor Haamah*** *(i.e. owl),* ***nor Safar."***

A Bedouin stood up and said, "Then what about my camels? They are like deer on the sand, but when a mangy camel comes and mixes with them, they all get infected with mangy."

The Rasul (saw) said:

"Then who infected the first one? There is no adwa and safar, Allah has created every soul and preordained its life, sustenance, and every incident he will encounter!"

***

Abu Hurairah (ra) narrates:

Rasulullah (saw) said,

"Nobody's good deed will take him to paradise."

"How about you O Rasul of Allah (saw)?"

The Rasul (saw) answered:

"Yes, including me. I will go to Paradise only out of the bounty and grace of Allah. Therefore, my companions, refrain from going to extremes in your work and your worship. Follow the right (moderate) way to get closer to Allah. And let none of you wish for death. For if it is a person of good virtue, he may increase his good virtue and if he is a sinner then he may repent before death."

Bukhari, Tajrid Hadith number 1918.

***

Abdullah ibn Amr reported:

The Rasul of Allah, (saw) said,

"Verily, Allah Almighty created His creation in darkness and He cast over them His light. Whoever is touched by that light is guided, and

whoever misses it is led astray. Thus, I say the pens have been dried upon the knowledge of Allah."

***

Zaid ibn Thabith (ra) narrates:

Rasulullah (saw) said,

"If Allah were to punish the inhabitants of His heavens and of His earth, He would do so and He would not be unjust towards them. And if He were to have mercy on them, His mercy would be better for them than their own deeds. If you had the equivalent of Mount Uhud in gold, or the equivalent of Mount Uhud which you spent in the cause of Allah, that would not be accepted from you until you believed in the Divine Decree and you know that whatever has befallen you, could not have passed you by; and whatever has passed you by, could not have befallen you; and that if you were to die believing in anything other than this, you would enter Hell."

***

Suraqa ibn Malik asked: "Allah's Rasul, are 'deeds' tied to the fact that the pens have dried after recording them and destinies have begun to operate or are they based on the future (unaffected by the past)?"

Thereupon he said:

"Deeds are tied to destiny which is written, and the pens have dried. Everyone is facilitated towards that for which he has been created."

74

QUESTIONING THE AUTHENTICITY OF HADITH

If any alleged "learned" dares to question the authenticity of the hadiths I shared, here is another hadith from the Rasul of Allah (saw) as a warning:

Narrated by Abu Hurairah (ra):

The Rasul of Allah (saw) said:

"Let none of you, upon hearing my hadiths, say, 'Leave the hadith aside and tell us something from the Quran instead so we know it is authentic. For this is my word!"

To present other perspectives about what the Rasul says is to inadvertently claim that those people are of equal value, which is a grave insult and a proof of ignorance.

This is why Abu Hurairah (ra) said to Ibn Abbas (ra):

– My dear nephew, when I narrate a hadith from the Rasul (saw) do not give me examples and opinions from others!

We must accept the words of the Rasulullah (saw) without questioning them. Then, if we want to understand them, we can do our research. If through research we understand their meaning, great, but if we can't, then we must accept it without questioning it and leave it to time to get a better understanding of it.

If we deny or refuse it we will eternally deprive ourselves from that knowledge.

We know for sure through the words of Allah, **"He does not speak from his opinion"** that the Rasul of Allah (saw) has informed us of all the truths and realities of existence.

But this information necessarily had to be given in a symbolic and metaphoric language due to the limitations in his time. So we must decode and decipher them and we can only do this to the extent we deepen our knowledge.

Without doubt narrowminded people who can't think outside the box will criticize those who have been created to research and get to the bottom of things, they will put them down and even accuse them of being 'unbelievers'.

Unfortunately, it is because of such narrowminded imitators that religion can't find the reputable place it deserves in our modern world.

In 1967 I wrote in my book *The Great Awakening* the following sentence:

"IF YOU CAN'T COMPREHEND IT, AT LEAST DON'T DENY IT."

Let us not forget that the Satan became IBLIS because he denied what he could not comprehend!

75

HOW TO APPROACH THE TOPIC OF FATE

For he who has insight there is no difference between the mystery of unity and the mystery of fate!

For he who wants to see the reality, there is no mystery!

For those to whom this knowledge has been eased, it is very simple:

Allah willed and desired to manifest His infinite meanings.

With His attribute of **Power,** He manifested the meanings that He chose with His attribute of **Knowledge**.

Essentially everything took place at the level of knowledge.

Later, that which transpired at the level of knowledge, was transformed from *force (energy)* into *action*. The essence of existence is the meanings of the divine names and attributes.

The infinite compositions of these infinite names have brought about infinite manifestations, all of which exist and subsist with His existence.

Let us understand this well:

Just as you can choose to make a hat or a shoe with the same piece of leather, and just as your foot does not say, "Why couldn't I be an eye?" nothing has the right to question its existence.

And if they do? If a virus inside a cell in your body was in complete rebellion or complete submission to you, what would that mean to you?

Fate, in essence, tell us that all things are within the knowledge, will and power of the ONE.

The Unity of Existence that Sufism teaches also tells us that there is no "multiplicity" in existence but rather the multiple forms of manifestation of the SINGLE existence.

Both convey the same message!

76

FAQ ON FATE

Question 1

– If my fate is predetermined, and what will be will be, and what won't be can't ever be, then why should I strive for anything, I'll just sit and do nothing!?

Answer 1

– If you've been created to sit and do nothing then you may go ahead and do so. Otherwise, whatever you've been created for, that will be facilitated for you and you'll naturally be drawn to it.

Question 2

– If Allah had preordained Hell for me and has facilitated the deeds of Hell for me, how is this my fault?

Answer 2

– The Sovereign One may rule and administer His sovereignty however He desires. Just as you have full right over your property and none has the right to intervene in your discretion, Allah is the Absolute owner of the universe and has absolute right to do whatever He likes, without being constricted or limited by any condition.

Question 3

– Is Allah "making" me do this by force?

Answer 3a

– Allah is *al-Jabbar*, He does as He likes and none has the right to question that!

Answer 3b

– Essentially Allah doesn't make you do anything. Because you don't even exist. You are merely a name. You are a virtual reality formed by the five senses. You are a relative illusory being. If we were to examine you at the cellular level you are a mass of a countless number of cells. At the level of light, you're beams of colors… In respect of your brain structure and programming you're a cosmic robot programmed to fulfill particular functions. And yet together with all of this, in respect of your essence, you carry within you all of the infinite qualities of the universe!

Question 4

– *If I don't have a separate existence and if there is nothing other than the One, why should Hell exist and why should I be subject to suffering?*

Answer 4

– You don't have a separate being right now either yet you are constantly going from one state of suffering to another. Just as there are physical and psychological sufferings now, it will be the same in the hereafter.

Question 5

– *If my fate is predetermined then I'm not going to pray or engage in any spiritual practice. If I am destined to go to heaven I'll go to heaven, and if I'm destined to go to hell I'll go to hell anyway!*

Answer 5

– Allah facilitates for the people of paradise, the deeds of paradise, and for the people of hell, the deeds of hell. Whichever you've been created for, its deeds will seem easier and more attractive to you. You will be naturally drawn to engaging in the deeds of whichever one you've been created for.

Question 6

– *Prayer can prevent misfortune. Isn't this changing fate?*

Answer 6

– The prayer to prevent misfortune is also predetermined and is a part of your fate!

Question 7

– Do I not have any will power then?

Answer 7a

– Neither the Quran nor the hadiths, as far as we know, mentions willpower!

Answer 7b

– Since your being is entirely from His being, it is His will that is in effect at every level, and He is the possessor of Absolute Will. If he wills to remove the veil that covers your insight you will see that everything you think you own belongs to Him! Willpower is the Absolute Divine Will manifesting through the person. They are one and the same! Existence is One!

Question 8

– So then all of my shortcoming, mistakes, and faults belong to Him!?

Answer 8

– These are relative qualities based on the illusory being you have identified with. In reality there is neither a "you" nor any inadequacy, shortcoming, or anything faulty!

Question 9

– How about the contemptible things? Are they also Him?

Answer 9

– For the eye that perceives contempt, the contemptible things are not Him. For those with insight, nothing is perceived as contemptible anyway. Their brains don't depend on their sight. Their sight depends on their brains!

From the inferior level of having their "thoughts defined by their sight", they have elevated to having their "sight defined by their thoughts" and hence have realized that there is nothing in existence other than the One!

Question 10

– I don't' understand most of what you're saying but I don't feel like refusing them either, what shall I do?

Answer 10

– Learn! There is no limit to learning! Research and find the truth from whoever and whatever source possible. Until doomsday knowledge is attainable. Always research from the source. Follow the recommendations of the Rasul of Allah (saw) and examine their deeper meaning with knowledge. If Allah has willed good for a person he will give him an understanding in religion. Always seek wisdom and truth and don't waste your time with gossip.

Question 11

– I don't get what you're saying.

Answer 11

– Then just follow the recommendations of Rasulullah (saw) and don't stand in anyone's way!

Question 12

– If I'm destined to study and acquire knowledge I'll do it. But if that knowledge is destined to come to me it'll come to me even if I don't study for it!?

Answer 12

– Creation is linked to causality. If you are destined for a particular outcome you will also be channeled to its cause. If you're not destined for it, then you will feel repelled from engaging with its cause and hence won't reach that outcome.

Question 13

– Some verses and hadith state that if a person does good deeds he will reap its rewards, and if he doesn't then he'll be deprived of them. Doesn't this show the person has a choice?

Answer 13

– Everyone will see the results of his actions. Good or bad. But this doesn't invalidate the fact that his actions are preordained!

Question 14

– *So, will I see the results of everything and anything I do?*

Answer 14

   – You will inevitably feel attracted to and engage in the actions aligned with what has been preordained for you and eventually you will see its results and experience its consequence.

77

IS MAN A COSMIC ROBOT!?

In the previous chapter I referred to man as a cosmic robot.

The brain, with its innumerous infinite qualities, is programmed by the cosmic rays that permeate from the infinite number of stars in space, and the person conducts his life based on this programming.

In more religious terms, with Allah's words, the angels write and record the fate of a person, the lifespan, sustenance, deeds, and whether he will be of the fortunate or the unfortunate ones.

Ok but is this all? Is it this simple?

No!

This is only one side of the story. There is another side to man: his essence and origin.

Although the human brain is programmed with cosmic rays (Nur - angels), in respect to the vicegerency quality inherent in man, he possesses the capacity to evaluate the entire creation with all of their qualities!

In other words, man exists to mirror the divine names and qualities of the One denoted by the name Allah.

If the brain reaches the capacity to function at its highest level with the realization that all of the qualities he manifests are the qualities of Allah, and that he does not have a separate existence, that he is literally a divine composition, that's when the other aspect of man becomes apparent!

That is when Allah becomes the sole operator of this cosmic robot whereby, He becomes the one who sees, hears, talks, holds and walks in the guise of what seems to be a cosmic robot. In fact, the robot dissolves, disappears, and the Eternal One sees nothing in existence other than Itself!

In short, the being that came from non-existence goes back to non-existence and only Allah the *Baqi* remains, in spite of the "apparent forms."

Pre-eternity, post-eternity, the past, the future, all of it in the sight of Allah is one and the same thing!

In short, if you are destined to, you will realize and experience your nothingness and that it is Only the One that exists…

78

WHY THE TOPIC OF UNITY?

Unity is based on two perspectives: The first is creation from the perspective of Allah, and the second is Allah from the perspective of man!

The verses from the Quran and the hadith I shared previously cover much about creation from the perspective of Allah. As for Allah from the perspective of man, I have covered this in various chapters both in this book and in detail in "*Know Thyself*".

The reason I went into the topic of "Unity" immediately after the topic of fate is because I wanted to underline the "most honorable" **vicegerency** quality of man, in addition to his robotic aspect. For both are equally valid and true. Taking a one-sided approach will most definitely be misleading and result in deprivation!

One will either be deprived of the external aspect or the internal!

Whereas Allah is both the apparent (*Zahir*) and the obscure (*Batin*)!

This being the case, being deprived of either one means being deprived of Allah!

So, it a duty upon us to examine existence both from its external and its internal aspects, that is, both from its aspect of consciousness and from its energetic-material aspect.

If, with the unawareness of our inherent vicegerency quality, we think of ourselves only as cosmic robots, we will in effect be turning down such grave blessings that its inescapable remorse will lead to suffering no less than that of physical hell!

In fact, I covered more on fate in this book than any other book you can find on shelves today, for the reality of fate and destiny is still largely unknown in our present day, which leads to digression from the path of Unity.

In Bukhari Rabia bin Abi Abdurrahman (ra) is recorded to have said:

– One who has knowledge but keeps it to himself (does not share his knowledge) is undeserving of it!

At this point she points to the neck of Abu Zarr Ghifari, one of the prominent followers of Rasulullah (saw) and says:

– If you put a sword to my head, in fear that I may not have enough time to share what I have heard from the Rasul (saw) before you execute me, I will explain it right away!

Having faith in fate is one of the six pillars of faith, but one must first know *what* it is to have faith in it.

If the Rasul of Allah (saw) had said, "Have faith in Tangu" surely you would say, "Ok, but who or what is Tangu!? Teach us about it so that we may know and place our faith in it. How can we have faith in something we don't know?"

This is why I tried to share as much as I can on this topic so that you may understand it.

It is entirely up to you whether you want to accept the teachings of the Rasul of Allah (saw) or not.

But I felt it mandatory to narrate the hadith regarding fate so that people know what they're placing their faith in.

These hadiths can be construed and interpreted but they can never be doubted!

Abu Huraira narrates:

One day, as we were engaged in an argument about fate and destiny, Rasulullah (saw) came over. He got so angry that his cheeks went red as though pomegranate juice had spilled on them.

He said:

"Is this what you have been ordered with? Is this what I have been sent to you for? When the people who came before you argued over the matters of fate they were destroyed. This, I swear to you, that you may not argue with each other, I swear to you!" (Tirmidhi)

Unfortunately, some books translate the last sentence of this hadith as "I swear to you that I will never talk about this topic, I swear to you" even though he is warning his followers no to "argue" about fate.

Thus, we must get our act together and accept the message of the Rasul of Allah (saw) without arguing and doubting.

Whoever argues about the validity of hadiths has most definitely chosen the way of destruction!

Sadly many "sheikhs" today belittle the intellect and denounce knowledge, they even claim things like "knowledge has been removed from the world" confessing their ignorance.

On the other hand, Imam Ghazali has reported in his revered collection "*Ihya-u Ulumuddeen*" the following from Tirmidhi:

The Rasul of Allah (saw) said:

"Allah has not created anything more valuable than the intellect!"

The Rasul of Allah (saw) said to Ali (ra):

"If people attain closeness to Allah with their good deeds you attain closeness with your intellect!"

Rasulullah (saw) said to Abu'd-Dardaa (ra):

"Increase your intellect so that you may get closer to Allah!"

"May my mother and father be sacrificed for you O Rasul of Allah, how can I increase my intellect?"

"Refrain from what Allah has forbidden and follow his commands, this will make you intellectual."

Narrated by Said bin el- Musayyab:

Hadhrat Omar (ra), Abu Hurairah and Ubayy Ibn Kaab (ra), asked the Rasul of Allah (saw):

"O Rasul of Allah! Who is the most learned among the people?"

"The intellectual ones!"

"Who are the highest in worship?"

"The most intellectual ones!"

"Who are the highest in virtue?"

"The most intellectual ones!"

"O Rasul of Allah, is not an intellectual a reputable person who is generous and well-informed?"

"All of this pertains to the worldly life. The hereafter is for those who protect themselves."

In another hadith the Rasul of Allah (saw) says:

"The intellectual one is he who believes in Allah and his Rasul and follows his orders."

The qualities the followers ask about in the above hadith are worldly qualities. The intellect, on the other hand, allows one to think comprehensively, to evaluate extensively, to comprehend the life after death and then to duly prepare for it.

This is why man can reach the honor of faith with his intellect.

The intellect will take you to Allah. He who denies intellect and knowledge displays his ignorance, may Allah save him from the pit of ignorance and honor him with knowledge and intellect is all I can say...

To sum up...

We must utilize the most valuable thing Allah has created, our intellect, an even if we can't discern the wisdom behind some of Rasulullah's teachings we must accept them as they are without questioning, doubting or debating over them.

A hadith al-qudsi narrated by Bayhaqi and Ibn Najjar Anas (ra) is as follows:

"Whoever is not satisfied with my fate and preordainment let him find himself another Rabb!"

Abu Hind ad-Daaari (ra) narrates from the Rasul of Allah (saw) as Allah saying:

"Whoever is not pleased with my preordainment and does not show patience to my trials let him find himself another Rabb! (Tabarani)

My intent for writing this book was to touch on and clear up many topics so I don't want to go into a lot of detail here. Allah willing, I will cover in greater detail in my future books the things I didn't elaborate on here.

79

GOOD AND EVIL ARE FROM ALLAH!

One of the six pillars of faith is: *"That all good and evil are from Allah."*

Whatever good comes to you it is from Allah, but whatever evil comes to you it is from your self (from complying with your conditioned beliefs including your alleged 'moral codes'). **We have revealed you as a Rasul for the people. Sufficient is Allah, as your essence with His Names, as a Witness for you.**[65]

The verse preceding this is:

Death will find you wherever you are. Even if you were within tall and sturdy towers... But if good comes to them, they say, "This is from Allah"; and if evil befalls them, they say, "This is from you." Say, "All of it is from Allah!" What is the matter with people that they do not try to understand the reality![66]

"If good comes to them... if evil befalls them..."

Let us first examine and understand what the word "evil" denotes in this verse...

What is evil? To whom do we do evil and how? To whom do we do good and how?

What do the words good and evil mean?

When I do something that is aligned with your natural programming I will have done good to you, *according to your understanding and*

---

[65] Quran 4:79
[66] Quran 4:78

perception!

And when I do something that goes against your nature I will have done "evil", again, *according to your understanding and perception.*

But in reality, it's actually the other way around! It's when I do something *against* your nature that I do good to you, and when I do something *aligned* with your nature that I do evil by you! **This is according to the REALITY!**

> **Fighting has been ordained for you, even though you despise it. Perhaps you dislike a thing that is good for you and like a thing that is bad for you. Allah knows, but you know not.**[67]

Basically, what we call evil is something that goes against your nature, temperament, compositional make-up. This is from the perspective of your "composition."

Say: What you perceive as evil is from Allah i.e. not from Muhammad!

The concepts of good and evil are only valid from the perspective of your composition.

Anything that suits your composition you call good and anything that doesn't suit your composition you call it evil.

But in reality, only Allah knows what good and evil are.

Therefore, we must accept that both good and evil are from Allah.

Since the essence of the self is a composition of divine names, when we say it is from you, your 'self' (*nafs*) we are in effect saying it is from Allah, i.e. from the composition comprising your being.

In this light, is not the source of what we call evil, Allah?

Not Allah, Rabb!

Because there are no opposites with Allah. Opposites and limits are only applicable to the composition.

Even though the essence and source of the composition is Allah, because it is in the form of a composition, it is described as the 'self'! Hence any evil act is prescribed to the self not to Allah! The fact that it is *evil* is according to the self anyway. Nothing is evil in the sight of Allah!

---

[67] Quran 2:216

You only call it evil because it discomforts your compositional make-up. If you elevate to higher levels of consciousness and overcome the limits of your composition you are no longer going to perceive it as evil, you're simply going to say it is from Allah and go about your day… Neither good nor evil is going to remain in your sight!

To reiterate, evil is anything that goes against the composition, and it is according to the composition, or any action that constricts and confines your composition.

In the divine sense and as a divine warning, the word evil refers to things that protect and preserve your composition.

Evil used in this sense seems attractive to you because it befits your composition and allows you to remain in your comfort zone. On the other hand, this is considered evil in the divine sense, because it keeps you confined to your illusory identity, so even though it seems good to you it is evil in reality.

But in the end, they are all from the effects of the divine names, hence the verse says:

> **Say, "All of it is from Allah!" What is the matter with people that they do not try to understand the reality![68]**

> **And indeed, Allah has determined a measure** (fate) **for all things.[69]**

"Things" in the verse above refers to everything, form, meaning etc. All of it has been created upon a particular fate and lives according to this. In the general sense things refers to humans and hence it is said, "Allah has determined his fate" indeed "the fate of man is the hands of Allah!"

What does it mean for man's fate to be predetermined by Allah?

As we have already discussed, the being referred to as a human is nothing other than the manifestation of the different compositions of the divine names.

The manifestation of these meanings in this way is again generated by the Being that encompasses all of these meanings. Once it is determined that this unit of existence will be formed with this particular proportion of

---

[68] Quran 4:78
[69] Quran 65:3

these particular names, its fate is set!

Fate should be examined in two aspects:

The first is the formation of capability, the second is the formation of skill...

Both capability and skill are from fate. However, because the being to which this capability and skill has been given, is essentially comprised of the divine names and forces, he has the ability to act and assert power within this configuration.

Hence the determination of capability and skill by the divine power is "fate" but the assertion and actualization of this within the limits of the individual configuration is the person's "will", i.e. personal will power is the usage of the names that are inherent within one's specific composition.

When you manifest these names you are in effect using your willpower!

To what extent can you use your willpower?

To the extent of the power of the names in your configuration.

But if you can reach your essential reality and recognize and experience the absolute essence and attributes of Allah within your own being, then you may be able to extend and increase their usage, and your 'personal willpower' will transform into 'divine willpower.'

In reality there are no separate personal and divine willpowers of course, there is only a single will, and that is the will of Allah. It is only when this will is configured to operate from a 'person' is when we call it a personal will.

So long as you live within the limits of your composition you will have a so-called 'willpower'!

But if you can overcome your composition and expand its limits, divine willpower will begin to manifest through you, whereby when you will for something to happen the divine forces will operate to make it happen. That is, the "divine will" will execute itself through you.

Your composition defines your fate and the means by which your composition is formed is the "*Lawh-i Mahfuz*" the Preserved Tablet.

The preserved tablet is the recorded and preserved cosmic information that defines your make-up, in other words it is the effects that you received from the zodiacal signs and planets which has formed your immutable archetypal reality (*al-A'yan al-Thabitah*).

The miniature expression of your preserved tablet is your brain, while at the cosmic level, it is the star signs and planets!

Your immutable archetypal reality is the cosmic programming your brain received on the 120th day after conception. It is the life program you are destined to live!

The preserved tablet can change but the *al-A'yan al-Thabitah* is totally unalterable. Why?

Because the effects it creates in the brain are fixed. It has been hardwired; it can no longer change!

Your preserved tablet, on the other hand, can change in two ways:

It can change with the effects of the planetary transits. And, when the brain undergoes certain experiences, new circuits are wired and activated, which can also cause changes to your preserved tablet.

The first is achieved by saints (*walis*) on duty and those with the power of administration. They have the ability to strengthen or weaken certain effects.

The second can take place via the practices one person does to overcome his composition; as he abandons his habits and natural tendencies he allows his composition to change by firing and wiring new neural networks in his brain, eventually changing his preserved tablet.

The verse says:

> **No calamity befalls you on earth** (on your physical body and outer world) **or among yourselves** (your inner world) **that has not already been recorded in a book** (formed in the dimension of the knowledge) **before We bring it into being! Indeed, for Allah, this is easy.**[70]

The word "you" in the verse refers to the illusory existence of 'man' in the form of a composition!

Everything "man" is destined to encounter and experience, the "good" things and the "bad" things, is recorded in the divine book called the Preserved Tablet, which in modern terms, is his *astrological chart*.

---

[70] Quran 75:22

Man is under the administration of this chart, it is his fate! But in respect of his quintessential reality, he is also the creator of his fate.

In respect of the names comprising his composition man is *subject* to fate, in terms of the divine attributes and absolute essence within his essential reality, he is the *creator* of his fate!

> **And whoever is blinded** (with external things) **from the remembrance of *Rahman*** (remembering that his essential reality is composed of the names of Allah and thus from living the requirements of this)**, We appoint for him a Satan** (a delusion; the idea that he is only the physical body and that life should be lived in pursuit of bodily pleasures) **and this** (belief) **will become his** (new) **identity!**[71]

This verse makes it evident that one who is blinded from his essential reality, of the Divine Attributes and that comprise his being, and who thinks he is a 'person' turns away from the Rahman and delusively follows the Satan.

If you think of yourself as the name, the label, the body that you've been given and constructed throughout your worldly life, this is turning away from the remembrance of the Rahman (the infinite quantum potential) which is how "following the Satan" manifests at the physical level. Rahman is the awareness of one's infinite quantum potential, the attributes comprising his being.

The divine names are not observed singularly at the level of names, as separate meanings, they are observed at the level of acts, within a composition, as collective meanings. It is incorrect to think of the divine meanings as separate forms of existence. The One encompasses all meanings and is not in any way divisible.

There is no fragmentation, division, or separation in existence. He is *AHAD*, the One and Only, Single existence. And He is *WAHID*, meaning all of the seemingly separate meanings are in UNISON, they are not 'parts' of the One, *there are no parts!*

The ONE observes through you, His various different meanings as a whole, they are not separate from one another. These meanings that are derived from the level of Names are observed at the level of acts.

---

[71] Quran 43:36

There is no level of names beyond the level of acts that contains different singular meanings or groups of meanings!

80

AKHIRAH: LIFE AFTER DEATH

What is life after death, how many forms does it take?

The word akhirah comes from the root word "*akhir*" which means "after" and is generally used to refer to the domain of life after death. Its other meaning is "the end" of something, which refers to both the notion that there is life at the end of death and that there is an end to all things.

The end of all things...

The end of the human body is deterioration...

The end of the spirit is the hereafter, the domain of life after death!

Is this domain of life after death a place to which we all go after everyone dies and the doomsday takes place?

No!

The life after death begins immediately after one tastes or experiences the physical-biological process of death, when the bodily senses cease to function and the person begins to exist as the spirit rather than the biological body!

In other words, it is the domain of life without a biological body.

There are two stages of life after death:

The first stage is the Intermediary Realm or the Realm of the Grave. The second is the phase after the Doomsday takes place.

The Intermediary Realm or the Realm of the Grave is a transition phase and is purely spirit based.

In the second phase after Doomsday however, the spirit begins to densify and a new body begins to form. That is, in the second phase of life after death, after Doomsday, the spirit will develop a new body.

"To have faith in life after death" means to believe with certainty that after one experiences death and abandons his earthly body, he will continue to live with his spirit, a holographic radial body.

81

DID YOU KNOW YOU WILL BE BURIED ALIVE?

Let's say you're in bed and you realize you're not feeling too well... you snooze in and out of sleep, go in and out of dreams, get flashes of past memories or wonder around in future hopes... Then you want to move your arm and you realize you can't! How can it be? You literally can't move your arm! "Am I paralyzed?" you begin to think in horror... You want to scream out for help, but you can't!?

Then suddenly your daughter throws herself on you and starts weeping in anguish, "Mum! Mum! Please don't leave us.... Please don't die!"

Die?

You try to yell out "I'm not dead!!!" but not a sound comes out! You can't even move your lips!

At this point others begin to crowd around you, they're all crying and mourning in grief...

Suddenly you feel a sense of freedom to move so you get up and start walking around the room, you walk up to your friends and family and tell them "Look I'm here, I'm not dead, stop crying!" but nobody can hear or see you...

You daughter is a mess... her weeping gives you pain, you want to comfort her, you want to tell her you're ok but there's no way of making contact! You can't touch, you can't talk, you can't move an object...

They sit around you and start praying, and sharing their past memories of you...

Then after all the hustle is over, they wash you and wrap you in a shroud and place you in a coffin!

Meanwhile you're aware of all of this, you're watching and observing it all...

They take you to the cemetery and you see the grave that has been dug for you...

Slowly they place you inside... and they start burying you while you're alive! You're fully awake and conscious just as you are right now, while they are burying you! They start throwing soil on you, you know you're going to be prisoned under, buried alive, but you can't do anything to stop it!

An indescribable horrific pain and suffering begins...

Remember the hadith:

"People are asleep, with death, they will awaken!"

Hadhrat Osman (ra) would sit by a grave and cry until his beard would be soaking wet. When they asked him, "You don't cry when you hear about heaven and hell but you cry here before a grave?"

He replied, I heard from the Rasul of Allah (saw):

"The grave is the first station of the life after death. If one can pass this station the rest will be easier. But if he can't, the rest will be even more difficult. The grave is far more horrid than any horrific scene I have ever seen!" (Tirmidhi)

The person's bodily functions stop functioning, his brain stops operating, and his lifeless body is buried. Then....

Ibn Omar (ra) narrates:

"When the deceased person's worldly ties are cut off he is shown his future place, depending on whether he is a person of hell or heaven. Then he is told, "This is your place until Allah raises you again on Doomsday for *Mahshar* (the place of gathering)."

So, what does this mean? Let's examine this place of sitting and waiting in the grave a little further...

Abu Hurairah (ra) narrates:

The Rasul of Allah (saw) said:

284

"When one of you is buried, two angels, black and blue, come to him. One of them is called Munkar, and the other Nakir. They ask: 'What did you used to say about this man?' So, he says what he was saying (before death) 'He is Allah's servant and Rasul. I witness that there is no god but Allah and that Muhammad is His servant and His Rasul.' So, they say: 'We knew that you would say this.' Then his grave is expanded by seventy cubits, and it is illuminated for him. Then it is said to him: 'Sleep.' He asks: 'Can I return to my family to inform them?' They say: 'Sleep as a newlywed, whom none awakens but the dearest of his family.' And he sleeps until Allah resurrects him from his resting place.

If he is a hypocrite he says: 'I heard people calling him a Rasul, so I said the same; I do not know for sure' And they say: 'We knew you would say that.' So, the earth is told: 'Constrict him.' And it constricts around him, squeezing his ribs together. He continues being punished like that until Allah resurrects him from his resting place." (Tirmidhi)

This is the inevitable end of those who assume that they are their body! Just like you dream of things that you busy yourself most with during the day and you can't escape it in your dream... just like you can't change or stop a nightmare... in the same way the natural outcome and consequence of living a life based on identifying with one's body will be suffering in the grave. Everyone will see the direct outcomes of his actions in the world when he's in the realm of the grave.

If one hasn't consciously prepared himself for the life of the grave where his ties to his body will be ceased, then this will be his inescapable end.

How about if the deceased isn't buried but cremated instead?

The result of this is worse. In the grave you will suffer maybe fifty years, maybe a hundred or two hundred years, at some point your body will eventually totally decompose, but with cremation you're watching your body burn while you're fully alive and conscious! Can you imagine the pain this will cause!? Imagine you saw this in your dream? What a nightmare! And it's a constant state of suffering, over and over again, perhaps until Doomsday.

What about if the deceased is thrown into water?

Imagine seeing yourself drowning in your dream!

Burying and allowing the body to decompose is the wisest option, thus it has become the religious custom.

Are all the deceased imprisoned in the grave?

No!

The deceased are in two groups:

The first are the martyrs who have given their lives up for the sake of Allah, and the saints (*walis*) who have experienced the mystery of "dying before death". After they enter the grave and are called to account by the angels they are released to roam about freely until Doomsday.

The second group is further divided into the believers, who will suffer for a period before they are shown their place in paradise and put to sleep until doomsday, and the unbelievers, who also suffer for a period and then shown their place in hell before being out to sleep to see nightmares until doomsday.

When one experiences death and is left alone in the grave with his holographic spirit body he will be subject to immense suffering. Why?

Think about it... Under normal conditions you live your daily life with your biological body but when you see a nightmare you are terrified. It is not your biological body that is terrified, it is your spirit, or magnetic-radial body.

Your conscious mind has no effect while your dreaming, you don't feel like you are physical body in your dreams you feel more like your magnetic body.

And hence your nightmare gives you a hellish experience. Even though your physical body is sleeping in a comfortable bed untouched by it all.

Usually our dreams are affected by our conditioning, the cosmic effects we receive, our thoughts and emotions... depending on these we either see nice dreams or nightmares.

"SLEEP IS THE BROTHER OF DEATH!"

A part of life after death is of this kind.

All of the active qualities in your brain that you are aware or unaware of are uploaded to your astral body or spirit!

Your life after death will continue with your spirit body at the level of your consciousness at that very last instant just before you die.

You will begin to see all the things that you were veiled from seeing while alive due to the limitations of bodily senses. Your sight will become clear.

You will see clearly the conditions you are subject to, what you will live in the future, and the end of the world!

And you will realize that you have failed to develop and attain certain powers that you should have during your worldly life. And there is no way of having access to your brain, the loading machine which was your only tool to load those powers to your spirit.

A spirit can only be developed by its own brain; no other brain can upload any qualities to it.

So, when you die and your brain stops working you can no longer upload new forces and qualities to your spirit.

Your stuck with what you have. Forever.

This realization then will bring about such immense remorse that it is not possible to describe this pain.

You have an infinite life ahead of you and no way of attaining any other new skill, tool, power, or ability!

And thus, your new life begins.

But you are unable to shape or channel this life, just like when you are in a dream.

You are totally and automatically subject to the conditions of your new life without the ability to change anything because you haven't attained the necessary powers to do so!

Welcome to endless nightmares to which you haven't prepared yourself!

This is the suffering of the grave!

This is why the Rasul of Allah (saw) says,

"When the person is buried in his grave, he will scream with such agony that all of the beings, other than humans and the jinn, will hear it!"

To top it off, he will constantly be shown his place in hell and told "this is where you are going to go" and then he will be shown paradise and told, "this is what you missed out on" deepening his suffering.

This is the situation of the common people.

If he is a believer, on the other hand, if he has engaged in certain practices and prepared himself for the afterlife, he will be shown his place in paradise where he will go, and he will also be shown hell and told "this is what you have been saved from!"

He will be told, "this is where you could have gone but your preparative practices have exempt you from it!"

So far, I have been talking about the states of hell and heaven in the grave. Not the actual heaven and hell.

I will discuss them in detail later.

Now there is also another group in the intermediary realm. Those who have attained certain spiritual power... the Saints...

These noble beings are those who have reached and experienced their essential reality, have changed their compositions and have discovered their divine potentials to activate certain spiritual powers!

They will be able to interact with one another during this phase. They will come together and converse with one another. They will share their insights with one another and have discussions.

This realm also has an administrative system and these souls will be trained and recruited for certain activity. On earth, there is a hierarchy of administrators in the intermediary realm referred to as the 4's, the 7's, the 12's and the 40's, there is an active administration in the afterlife as well.

82

DOOMSDAY

Now we come to the second phase of the afterlife; the day of judgement or doomsday.

The second phase begins with the doomsday.

When is the doomsday?

None of the religious resources have provided specific information on this so it won't be correct to make any claims here.

We know from various hadith that when the doomsday takes place all of the spirits of all of the people who have lived on earth will be resurrected with a new body befitting those conditions, they will all be gathered together, the angels will pull and bring hell, which will totally engulf the earth, and then a bridge will over hell form from the earth to heaven, those who can pass it will make it to paradise and those who can't will be stuck in hell.

Of course, this bridge isn't like any other bridge!

So what kind of a bridge will be formed?

The Rasul of Allah (saw) explained:

"...Then the bridge will be laid across Hell."

The followers asked, "O Rasul of Allah! What is the bridge?" He said,

"It is a slippery bridge on which there are clamps and hooks like thorns. If one hasn't practiced salat then the hook for salat will come out and snatch him and throw him into hell and if he has incomplete fasting

the hook for fasting will come out and snatch him and throw him into hell, he will suffer there for some time then will be released."

This is a metaphoric expression!

Let me explain it like this:

After the second world war the Americans set up an air bridge, i.e. an air route to Berlin to supply food and clothing. Now when you say air bridge people immediately think of a literal bridge from America to Berlin. Obviously not! It is an air route connecting two places, making it possible for supplies to be transported.

In the same way, when the Earth begins to be engulfed by the Sun people will begin to escape from hell using the powers they were able to gain while alive.

The Rasul of Allah (saw) explains this event as:

"Some of the believers will pass like lightning, some will pass like the wind, some will pass like swift horses, some will pass like fast camels, some will walk, some will crawl, and some will be thrown into Hell."

How else can you explain it 1500 years ago?

Everyone has a different level of spiritual strength, based on this, some will easily flee from the gravitational pull of the earth and some will have an extremely difficult time.

It is a scientific fact that at some point the Sun will become 400 times bigger than its current size and it will engulf Mercury, Venus, Mars and Earth. The surface of the sun is 6000-6500 degrees. The earth will melt away and evaporate!

What will happen if the earth goes into the sun?

Will it liquify?

In one hadith the Rasul of Allah (saw) says:

"When the earth falls into hell it will melt and evaporate like a drop of water."

The size of the sun today is 1,303,000 times bigger than earth! On that day it will be 400 million times bigger!

Will the earth not be like a drop of water then?

Those who have attained enough power to escape the magnetic pull of the earth will try to help those with lesser power, but those who haven't done anything to gain any strength will forever remain in the Sun.

Can this really be true?

What we call the black holes in space today are extremely powerful stars. They are the size of the Moon yet the strength of their vacuum is such that they can even easily pull Jupiter or even bigger stars like the Sun within themselves, engulf them, digest them and make them disappear! Just like that!

Similarly, spirits who get stuck inside this horrific place called hell will forever be imprisoned inside!

If one fails to attain certain spiritual powers while on earth he will have no chance of escaping it. Ever.

If one *can* escape hell however…

By the way I'm not going into 'resurrection' here, that is another topic on its own…

If one can pass through and escape hell he will go to heaven…

The person with the lowest status in heaven will be given a planet 10 times bigger than this earth, according to hadith.

That is the smallest of stars in space… perhaps it is even bigger but the Rasul of Allah refrained from saying it lest it be taken as exaggeration.

The Rasul of Allah (saw) was not able to express the real extent of suffering of hell. The little that he did reveal was enough to make many extremely afraid and claim "it can't be true!"

Had he revealed the actual reality of it, nobody would have believed him.

It is a lot scarier than we assume!

There is no death in hell!

There is no death for anyone in the afterlife… There is no such thing as becoming non-existent!

Because your essential existence is your spirit. And your magnetic body can't become non-existent. It may densify, it may become injured, it may change but it can never become non-existent!

For the essence of the composition is the radial body! It is a holographic wave structure which can't be destroyed!

This is like when you die in your dream but then you live again, you can die and live many times in your dream because the energy body can't really die, death is inapplicable and invalid here.

Hence those in hell will experience dying again and again but they will keep on living!

This is why the verse says, **"For them awaits an infinite painful suffering."**

On the contrary, those who go to heaven, to the other stars within the dimensional depths of the universe, will find within themselves certain powers (based on the divine names) with which they will be able to manifest the meanings of the divine names, something that isn't really possible in this world!

In this world you have a dense physical body which makes it difficult to manifest your every thought and desire!

But in heaven you will have an ethereal body through which you can actualize all of your thought at once! And since those who go to heaven will also live forever, their joy and euphoria in paradise will also be infinite.

This is the afterlife in a nutshell!

83

HADITH ON THE AFTERLIFE

Let us now have a look at what the Rasul of Allah (saw) has to say about life after death and what awaits us there.

Narrated by Abu Hurairah (ra):

It was asked, "O Rasul of Allah (saw). Will we see our Rabb on the Day of Resurrection (doomsday)?"

He said, *"Do you have any difficulty seeing the moon on the 14th night of the month (full moon) when the sky is clear?"* They said, "No." According to a narration by Sa'id Al-Khudri the Rasul of Allah (saw) asked, *"Do you have any difficulty in seeing the sun and the moon when the sky is clear?"* We said, "No."

He said, *"So you will have no difficulty in seeing your Rabb on that Day as you have no difficulty in seeing the sun and the moon (in a clear sky)."*

"On that day the people will be resurrected and gathered together. I will be the Sayyid of the people, do you know why? Because on that day Allah will unite everyone on a flat surface and the announcers voice will be heard by every group."

Ibn Masud (ra) narrates:

"When the people are resurrected, they will look up to the sky for forty years nobody will say a word to them. During this time the Sun will be drawn near them and melt them, and everyone will be covered in sweat, they will remain like this until their sweat reaches their throat."

Tabarani narrates:

"On the day of resurrection (the place of gathering) some will be covered in sweat and it will begin to choke them. They will plead, "O Rabb throw us into hell so that we may be freed from this" ...

Muslim provides more detail:

On that day the people will be in sweat according to their deeds. Among them one will be covered up to his ankles, and among them will be one who is covered up to his knees, and among them will be one who is covered up to his waist, and among them will be one who is bridled with it.

According to the narration by Abu Sa'id al-Khudri (ra):

This period will be lightened and made easier for the believers such that it will last only as long as one of the *fardh* (mandatory) salats.

Or according to another narration:

That day will be shortened for the believer as though an hour of the day, and they will be given glad tidings.

Then the Rabb will announce, "Let everyone follow what they used to worship!"

According the Ibn Masud (ra) the Rasul of Allah (saw) said,

"Then an announcer from the heavens will say, 'While it was your Rabb who created you and gave you form and sustenance, you worshipped other things, is it not then divine justice for everyone to follow what they used to worship?'

"Yes, it is" they will answer.

Then it will be said, "Let every nation follow what they used to worship!"

Abu Hurairah (ra) adds:

Allah will ask one of his servants, "Did I not shower my blessings upon you and give my creation to your command?"

He will say, "Yes, my Rabb."

Then Allah will say, "Just as you forgot about me then, I will forget about you now!"

The he will ask another servant and he will say, "My Rabb, I had faith in you, your book, your Rasul, I performed salat and fasted…" upon which Allah will say, "Let us ask the witnesses" and then the servant will be tongue tied and the organs in his body will begin to talk against him, and reveal his hypocrisy!

And then it will be said, "Let everyone follow what they used to believe in and worship, thereupon some will go to the sun, some to the moon and some to various other idols. The companions of the cross will go with their cross, and the idolators will go with their idols, and the companions of every god will go with their god, till there remain those who used to worship Allah, both the obedient ones and the mischievous ones, and some of the people of the Scripture.

Then Hell will be presented to them as if it were a mirage. Then it will be said to the Jews, "What did you use to worship?" They will reply, "We used to worship Ezra, the son of Allah." It will be said to them, "You are liars, for Allah has neither a wife nor a son. What do you want now?" They will reply, "We want You to provide us with water." Then it will be said to them "Drink," and they will fall down in Hell instead. Then it will be said to the Christians, "What did you use to worship?" They will reply, "We used to worship Messiah, the son of Allah." It will be said, "You are liars, for Allah has neither a wife nor a son. What do you want now?" They will say, "We want You to provide us with water." It will be said to them, "Drink" and they will fall down in Hell instead. When there remain only those who used to worship Allah alone, both the obedient ones and the mischievous ones, it will be said to them, "What keeps you here when all the people have gone?" They will say, "We parted with them in the world when we were in greater need of them than we are today, we heard the call of one proclaiming, "Let every nation follow what they used to worship" and now we are waiting for our Lord." Then the Almighty will come to them in a shape other than the one which they saw the first time, and He will say, "I am your Lord," and they will say, "You are not our Lord." And none will speak to Him then but the Rasuls, and then it will be said to them, "Do you know any sign by which you can recognize Him?" They will say. "The Shin," and so Allah will then uncover His Shin whereupon every believer will prostrate before Him.

Abu Hurairah (ra) narrates:

"The first of man's deeds for which he will be called to account on the Day of Resurrection will be Salat. If it is found to be perfect, he will be safe and successful; but if it is incomplete, he will be unfortunate and a loser. If any shortcoming is found in the obligatory Salat, the Glorious and Exalted Rabb will command to see whether His slave has offered any voluntary Salat so that the obligatory Salat may be made up by it. Then the rest of his actions will be treated in the same manner" [Sunan al-Tirmidhi: 413].

Those who dispute about whether they should pray only the obligatory (*fardh*) salat or sunnah too should take this hadith into consideration.

Essentially the obligatory prayers are a total of 17 *rakahs*. Two at dawn (*fajr*), four at midday (*dhuhr*), four in the late afternoon (*asr*), three at sunset (*maghrib*), four at nighttime (*isha*), and three *rakahs* of *witr*, the final prayer of the day after *isha*.

The other salats known as "sunnah" are considered to be voluntary salats, whether the person intends it as a compensation for past missed salats or purely as sunnah.

After salat, the person will be called to account for all his other deeds.

84

SCENES FROM THE HEREAFTER

Let's continue with hadiths regarding the stages of life after death:

Narrated by Abu Hurairah (ra) and Abu Sa'id al-Khudri (ra):

"Then a bridge will be laid across Hell. I and my followers will be the first ones to go across it."

"An announcer will ask, "Where is Muhammad?" Upon this the Rasul of Allah (saw) will stand and all of his followers, the devout and the sinners, will follow him to the bridge.

Then the light of the believers will blind the sinners and they will begin to fall into hell until only the Rasul and the devout followers are left."

"All the other nations will move out of our way and we will pass through them with the mark of ablution shining on our body, our faces lit with Nur. The other nations will look at my followers and say, "They have come so close to becoming Nabis!" On that day none but the Rasuls will speak. And the invocation of the Rasuls will be "O Allah, keep us safe! O Allah keep us safe!"

"Then when they reach the Bridge 'as-Sirat' Allah will give Nur (light) to each of them. Once they pass over the inclined part of the bridge and reach the flat part the Nur will be taken from the hypocrites. The hypocrites will say to the believers, "Wait for us, let us borrow some of your light" and the believers will reply, "Our Rabb! Increase and complete our Nur…""

"They will be told, "Run to salvation according to your Nur!" While crossing the bridge some will pass in the blink of an eye, some will pass like lightning, some will pass like the wind, some will pass like swift horses, some will pass like camels, some will walk, some will crawl, and some will be thrown into Hell."

Ibn Masud (ra), explains the varying speeds as:

"The blink of an eye, the speed of lightening, as fast as a meteor, like the wind, like swift horses, like she-camels" and adds "some will have Nur only in their toes and crawl over the bridge dragging their arms and legs."

"There will be thorny hooks on the bridge like the hooks in hell called *as-Sadan*... Did you see as-Sadan? These hooks will be like the thorns of Sadan but none knows how big they are other than Allah. The hooks will snatch those with bad deeds."

Some will run, some will walk, and the last one will creep and crawl his way to heaven. Then he will ask, "My Rabb why did you leave me behind?"

And Allah will say, "It was your own deeds that left you behind."

The 8th verse of chapter *at-Tahrim* says:

> **"Their Nur** (light of knowledge) **will race before them and on their right. They will say, "Our Rabb... Perfect our Nur** (increase the scope of our observation) **and forgive us... Indeed, you are Qadir over all things."**

And the 13th verse of chapter *al-Hadid* says:

> **"On that Day the** (hypocrite) **men and two-faced women will say to those who believed, "Wait for us that we may acquire some of your light** (Nur; knowledge of the reality)**." It will be said, "Go back and seek light." And an** (unsurpassable) **wall will be placed between them with a door, its interior** (inner world) **containing grace, but its exterior is torment** (the condition of those who fail to experience the reality is suffering, whereas observing the qualities of the Names leads to a state of grace)**."**

"Both the hypocrites and the believers will be given Nur and as they begin to cross the bridge the hooks and clamps will snatch some away and the Nur of the hypocrites will be extinguished. In the end, only the believers will be saved."

"The first group to pass the bridge will be a group of seventy thousand believers. They will go directly to heaven without being called to account.

Those who come after them will be like the brightest stars in the sky. They too will pass with ease."

"There are hooks and clamps on each side of the Bridge and they catch on command. These hooks are the lustrous desires that surround hell. Those who are deluded by these desires will fall into hell and be destroyed. Some will eventually reach salvation after a period of suffering."

We asked, "O Rasul of Allah! What is the bridge?" He said, "It is a slippery (bridge). I have come to know that the bridge over Hell is thinner than a hair and sharper than a sword. Some will be safe without any harm; some will be safe after receiving some scratches, and some will fall down into Hell (Fire). The last person will cross by being dragged (over the bridge)."

Finally when Allah finishes His judgment, and intends to take out of the Fire whoever He wishes to take out from among those who used to testify that none had the right to be worshipped but Allah, He will order the angels to take them out and the angels will recognize them by the mark of prostration (on their foreheads) for Allah banned the fire to consume the traces of prostration on the body of Adam's son.

I swear by Allah in whose hand of power is my being, the invocation and prayers of those who are saved from hell for the salvation of their brothers who are still inside will be nothing like the beseeching and praying you have seen in this world. Those who are saved will say,

"Our Rabb, those who remain in hell are our sisters and brothers. They used to pray with us and fast with us and perform pilgrimage and do good deeds."

Then Allah will say, "Go then and save anyone with a *dinar* worth of faith in their heart."

Allah will forbid the fire from burning them. These intercessors will enter hell and take out their brethren.

Then Allah will say, "Go back and take out anyone with a half dinar weight of faith in their heart."

And they will go back inside and save them.

Then Allah will say:

"Go back inside and save anyone with an iotas weight of faith in his heart."

And hence they will go back inside and save more people.

Finally, all the Nabis, the Rasuls, angels, believers will have done their interceding to save the people. At last Allah will say "Now it is my turn" and He will send the remainder of my followers into hell. The people in hell will say to them, "You used to worship Allah in the world and never associated partners to Him, yet here you are in hell with us! You used to pray and fast, yet here you are in hell!"

Upon this, Allah will say, "I will free them from hell for the sake of my Honor and Glory" and then He will save them.

Then Allah will say, "The angels interceded, the Nabis and Rasuls interceded, the believers interceded. Only the Most Merciful One is left!"

Then some who have done no good deeds in the world and who have turned to coal in hell will be taken out. And they will be dipped into water, called *Ma'ul Hayat* (water of life), from which they will spring out like a seed springs out on the bank of a rainwater stream, with gold hoops around their necks so the people of paradise recognize them, and they will say:

"These are the exempt ones that Allah brought to paradise for the sake of their faith, even though they have done no good deed."

And Allah will say, "Go into Paradise, everything your eyes can see is yours!"

And they will say, "Our Rabb! You have blessed us with a blessing to which you have not given to anyone in the world!"

And then, one man, will remain in the middle of hell and heaven, with his face turned to hell, he will be the last person to enter paradise. He will say, "O Rabb! It's (Hell's) smoke has poisoned me and its flame has burnt me; please turn my face away from the Fire."

He will keep on invoking Allah till Allah says, "Perhaps, if I give you what you want, you will not ask for another thing?" The man will say, "No, by Your Power, I will not ask You for anything else."

Then Allah will turn his face away from the Fire. When he sees paradise the man will say, "O Rabb, bring me near the gate of Paradise." Allah will say to him, "Didn't you promise not to ask for anything else? Woe to you, O son of Adam! How treacherous you are!"

The man will keep on invoking Allah till Allah says, "But if I give you that, you may ask me for something else." The man will say, "No, by Your

Power. I will not ask for anything else." He will give Allah his covenant and promise not to ask for anything else after that. So, Allah will bring him near to the gate of Paradise, and when he sees what is in it, he will remain silent as long as Allah wills, and then he will say, "O Rabb! Let me enter Paradise." Allah will say, "Didn't you promise that you would not ask Me for anything other than that? Woe to you, O son of Adam! How treacherous you are!"

On that, the man will say, "O Rabb! Do not make me the most wretched of Your creation" and he will keep on invoking Allah till Allah smiles and allows him to enter Paradise.

But the man will cry: "O Rabb! Please don't make me the most miserable of Your creation!" and he will keep on invoking Allah until Allah, the exalted, will smile and allow the man to enter Paradise.

While narrating this part Ibn Mas'ood (ra) smiled and said:

"Why don't you ask me why I am smiling?"

They said: "Why are you smiling?"

He said: "This is how the Rasul of Allah (SAW) smiled and when they asked, "Why are you smiling, O Rasul of Allah?" He said: "Because when Rabb of the worlds smiles and tells him, "Make a wish!" the man will say, "Are You making fun of me when You are the Rabb of the Worlds?" and Allah will respond, "I am not making fun of you, but I am Able to do whatever I will!"

And the man will keep on wishing and wishing and asking for so many things until he can't find anything else to ask for. Then Allah will help him out and remind him saying, "How about this... and how about that?" And then, when the man is completely satisfied, Allah will say, "All your wishes will be granted... and doubled!"

Abu Hurairac (ra) added: "That man will be the last of the people to enter Paradise."

The Rasul (saw) explains,

I know the last man to come out of hell and enter paradise. He will come out crawling from hell and Allah will tell him, "Enter paradise" but when he goes there he will see it full and say, "O Allah, I found paradise to be full!" and Allah will tell him, "Go and enter paradise" again the man will find it full and again Allah will say, "Go and enter paradise, you will be given a place ten times bigger than the world"

And the Rasul of Allah (saw) smiled until all his teeth could be seen, and then he said, "This man will have the lowest rank and place in paradise."

It is reported on the authority of al-Mughira b. Shu'ba that the Rasul of Allah (saw) said:

Moses asked his Rabb, "Who amongst the inhabitants of Paradise has the lowest rank?"

Allah said, "The person who will be admitted into Paradise as the last of all among those deserving of Paradise. I will say to him, 'Enter Paradise.' He will say, 'O my Rabb! How should I enter while all the people have settled in their apartments and taken their portions?' He will be asked, 'Would you be pleased if you could have the kingdom of a king amongst the kings of the world?' He will say: 'I will be pleased my Rabb.' Then Allah will say, 'For you is that, and like that, and like that, and like that, and like that.' On the fifth repetition he will say, 'I am well pleased My Rabb'. Then Allah will say, 'It is for you and ten times like it, and for you is what your *nafs* (self) desires and your eye enjoys' He will say: 'I am well pleased, my Rabb.'

Then Moses asked: "Which is the highest of ranks amongst the inhabitants of Paradise?"

Allah said: "They are those whom I have chosen for Myself. I established their honor with My own hand and then set a seal over it and they will be blessed with Bounties which no eye has seen, no ear has heard and no human mind has perceived and this is substantiated by the Book of Allah, Exalted and Great 'No soul knows what delight of the eye is hidden for them; a reward for what they did.'"

85

WHY SHOULD WE FEAR OR FEEL AWE TOWARDS ALLAH?

Abu Dharr (ra) reported that the Rasul of Allah (saw) said:

"I see what you do not see. The sky has squeaked, and it has every right to do so, for it does not have a space of four fingers where there is no angel prostrating his forehead before Allah, the Almighty. By Allah! If you knew what I know, you would laugh little and weep much; you would not enjoy women in bed; and you would go out to the open plains loudly imploring Allah, the Almighty." (Tirmidhi)

> **"Among His servants, only those who have knowledge** (of what is denoted by the name Allah and who are aware of its Might) **are truly in awe of Allah** (realize their nothingness in respect of His magnificence)!"[72]

> **The Rasul of Allah (saw) says,** *"It is I who knows Allah best among you and it is I who fears Allah most!"*

Ok, but why should we fear Allah?

> **"O believers... Protect yourselves duly from Allah** (as He will definitely subject you to the consequences of your deeds) **and die only as ones who have experienced submission."**[73]

The word "*taqwa*" means to refrain from things that can harm and cause suffering. To have *taqwa* is to protect yourself by seeking refuge in a

---

[72] Quran 35:28
[73] Quran 3:102

powerful shelter.

There are two aspects of protecting oneself:

1. Protecting oneself against the potential dangers awaiting in the hereafter, as the Rasul of Allah (saw) has advised us, by complying with the compulsory protection measures.

2. Measures to protect one's self against being deprived of Allah, the One who comprises one's essential being.

Does the word 'fear' refer to an emotion or is it used in reference to the importance of taking the necessary precautions to be protected against potential dangers that are awaiting us?

The verse **"Only the learned ones will fear Allah"** shows us that he who has no knowledge cannot fear Allah!

Hence it is evident that only those who are learned and knowledgeable fear Allah consciously!

Just as the Rasul (saw) says *"It is I who knows Allah best among you and it is I who fears Allah most!"*

To think of the infinite existence denoted by the name Allah, as a "god" is duality (*shirq*)!

Since we can't think of Allah in this sense then we must turn our attention to His manifestations at the level of Acts.

The incidents that are to transpire at the level of acts in the future will operate like an automated mechanism.

The verse says:

"You will not find an alteration in Our Sunnah."[74]

Because it is an automated system!

The consequences are inescapable and irreversible. It is as though the Rasul of Allah (saw), the person who cares most for you, is warning you against the inevitable dangers awaiting you, telling you:

"You are being pulled towards a point at which you will encounter extremely dangerous situations. It is as though you are strapped on a band that is moving towards a saw! Please take the necessary precautions! Do

---

[74] Quran 17:77

not be fooled by the amusements of the world. Don't waste your time with gossip and empty discourse. Cease your ties to the band you're stripped on and escape the saw!"

Certainly, the life of the world is nothing but a fleeting pleasure, an illusory amusement. And no doubt, your belongings and your children are nothing other than distractions.

Do not waste your life by succumbing to these illusions. The inescapable end awaiting you is definite and absolute and relentlessly cruel. So, take your precaution while you still can in this world. That is all you can do. On that day, the child will run from his mother and the wife will run from her husband. Nobody will be of any avail to anyone.

If we believe that Muhammad (saw) is the bearer of the truth then we must take heed of his message. Even though, taking heed of his message goes against our current comfort zone, conditionings and compositional make up.

The divine laws advise that we cleanse ourselves from our natural programming, habitual make-up, conditioned temperaments, etc…

If we fail to do so, we will face a pitiless end.

If some shaking event took place now you would run for your life. Think of a scenario much worse than any you have ever seen or heard of.

The lightest of the pain awaiting us in the hereafter is the pain of separation from all our worldly ties, everyone and everything that we are attached to. And this pain lasts forever. Because the concept of time doesn't exist as it does here. And you do not encounter another situation to help you get over the previous one. You are stuck in that painful state!

In this world, you live a tragic event and then time passes and something else happens to help you get over that pain and misery, you can forget… But this isn't the case after death. Once the body decomposes and you become totally detached from your body, if you haven't been able to ascend to a higher level of life, a state of sleep overcomes you and you fall asleep.

Either to a dream or a nightmare which continues until the doomsday…

On that day the spherical structure of the earth will disappear and become like a flat surface. All of the people who lived on earth will be resurrected! Think of that crowd!

Think of a crowd of fifty thousand, one hundred or two hundred thousand people! Now think of a crowd of the millions and billions of people from the beginning of the world all gathered together, while the angels are pulling hell closer to the earth until it completely surrounds the earth!

Try to imagine that crowd and the flames of hell surrounding them. A single wave can melt the earth away!

And then it is announced, "Let everyone follow what they used to worship in the world"

And everyone inevitably and inescapably goes after what they used to follow and worship in the world.

And then a bridge that is thinner than hair sharper than a sword is laid upon which millions of people are going to start crossing over...

How can millions of people cross over a bridge thinner than hair sharper than a sword?

This is a metaphoric expression to describe the difficulty of this phase...

Ones ability and power to cross over depends on the energy they were able to accumulate through their practices in the world.

Remember the man who asks, "Why have you left be behind my Rabb?" and he is told, "It was your deeds that left you behind!"

Your inadequate deeds in the world, your incomplete prayers and practices will prevent you from gaining the necessary spiritual strength!

Consequently, you won't be able to escape the pull of the Sun! Nobodies light will benefit anyone!

Don't think the Rasul or a Saint or some master will run and help you! Each will be to his own!

The extent to which your spiritual energy is inadequate is the extent to which you will stay in hell.

The more you are attached to your habits, belongings, people, emotions, the longer you will suffer in hell.

This is nothing like our concept of time. The body will become like coal. Only the parts that took part in ablution and salat will be exempt from the fire. And this will go on for years and years!

Now if you say, "Eventually we'll go to paradise because we are believers, so let us live as we like now!"

You are free to live however you like but for five minutes of pleasure in this world, you are creating infinite suffering for yourself in the hereafter.

And then when you do finally go to paradise remember there will be differences in rank in paradise.

If a man likes the feeling of flying and throws himself off a building for a twenty second sense of flying and ends up with broken arms and legs, would you call this man intelligent? What about sacrificing millions and billions of years for 5 or ten years of worldly life?

We must take heed of the warnings and not squander our lives with fleeting bodily pleasures, rather, we must strive to overcome our bodily tendencies and habits.

We will only be fooling ourselves if we don't strive and put in effort in this cause.

He who says this is an unnecessary effort is delusional; he is deluding himself. It is his composition that makes him live like this!

He lacks knowledge, he is ignorant, he does not know the events of the future!

While we have access to true knowledge if we follow the guidance of such people we will also be deluding ourselves and creating our own demise and suffering.

> **"Indeed if you follow their desires** (ideas and wants formed by their conditionings) **after what has come to you of knowledge, indeed, you would surely be among the wrongdoers."**[75]

It is popular to quote the words of Sufis like Yunus Emre, while we continue to eat, drink, indulge in pleasures. Just because we fast in Ramadan and pray every now and then we think we are Sufis and start quoting things like,

> *The place they call Paradise*
> *is but a few palaces and beautiful women*
> *Let them have it all...*

---

[75] Quran 2:145

All I want is YOU!

I wonder if there is an alternative place to go to on the other side, other than heaven and hell?

If you don't end up in one, you're going to end up in the other!

Its' as simple as that my friend.

It does not matter who you are, what your rank is, how wealthy you are, you will either go to one or the other, there is no other alternative!

The Rasul of Allah (saw) will be in heaven, if you don't like that and you prefer something else, well I have nothing to say…

But know that there will be significant differences in the ranks and lifestyles of those in heaven.

If you say I want to be among those who live the best of lives, I want to be as close to the life of the Rasul of Allah (saw) as I can be, I want to know Allah as those who knew him best and live like them in heaven, then I salute you.

But to naively claim "I don't want heaven I just want Allah" is nothing other than an illusion and ignorance.

Because this spawns the dualistic illusion that there is heaven, there is hell, and there is also Allah, far and beyond these!

86

DO WE UNDERSTAND THE MECHANICS OF EXISTENCE...

How will this cognition affect our outlook and perspective on others and ourselves? How will it affect our actions?

By others, I mean, whether a human, an animal or a plant, we must view everyone and everything as the meanings of the divine names, rather than their apparent 'label' or their seeming 'persona'!

If everyone and everything is a manifestation of a specific composition of divine names it is only logical that we view them and their actions as the result of those names. When you witness an action remember that this action is the output of the meanings of those names. Or don't analyze the action at all, just say, "this is how the meanings of these names manifest".

As for how we should see ourselves...

We must know that the being referenced with the word "I" or "me" is nothing other than the meanings of the names of the One. Nevertheless, when these meanings come together in the form of a composition, they form this body, and hence all bodily habits, desires, cravings etc.

If you can overcome these then the One comprising your essence may be revealed and observed! You must observe the One within, you must observe yourself as the One, such that duality is dissolved altogether, and only Oneness remains.

Only when you realize that you are the One in essence, and that you are only in this body temporarily, you may actually begin to abandon your bodily habits and recognize your reality!

What you should do in order to experience your reality:

1.   Always speak and advise the truth.
2.   Always advise patience against the hardship of complying with the divine laws.
3.   Either talk positive and beneficial things or remain silent.
4.   Either listen as a student, teach as a teacher, or remain as a listener between the two.
5.   When you hear something that goes against the Truth either refuse it and correct it or leave that place!

Let us now explore these a little further:

ADVISE THE TRUTH: When you talk with someone, advise the truth from one level higher than their level of understanding and perception. One's level is revealed by their actions, when you see this, advise them to abandon their ego and bodily tendencies and encourage them to comply with the divine laws in a way that they understand. If they chose not to take any heed then leave that place.

ADVISE PATIENCE: When the application of the divine laws become too burdensome on one's ego, remind them that this is expected, and that overcoming the composition is not easy as it forces one out of his comfort zone and habitual make-up, and that one must be patient in this process. For without patience, one may not reap any benefit from his striving. Everyone prepares his end with his own hands.

If he doesn't listen there's nothing you can do anyway!

SPEAK GOOD OR REMAIN SILENT: Explain the importance of the infinite journey ahead of us. Answer their questions if they have any. If you can bring them into a state in which they are open to receiving, explain the reality in a way that they understand. But if you see that they are not open to receiving than do not compliment him as this will only cause harm to him rather than helping him.

TEACH, LEARN, OR LISTEN: Either talk to teach or listen to learn. Make sure your speech is positively contributing to the process of life after death, for example teaching a useful information, encouraging them to do something good or refrain from a harmful act, or abandon a habit, etc... If you hear them say something that goes against the Truth, stop them, correct them or leave that place.

Remember the warning,

"When you hear Satan talk, leave!"

Or speak the truth!

If you can, if you have the opportunity to, then speak the truth, but if you don't have the opportunity to, then leave.

If you can't do either, ask yourself, why? What is stopping you from this? The answer is within you.

All of these are the recommendations and advices of the Rasul of Allah (saw).

If we are of those who speak the Truth, advice the Truth, and seek the Truth we will be of those who live in falsity and defend the falsity in which they are living.

When the Truth comes, falsity dissolves and disappears!

Where there is truth falsity cannot remain!

What is falsity?

All acts that are spawned from and promote the compositional make-up which veils one from the Reality!

87

ON FAITH AND ITS REQUISITES

Islam and faith...

An ongoing debate for many years!

In fact, a very well-known Imam of a madhap once said,

"Having faith in Allah, His Rasul and his teachings is sufficient" and recorded this in one of his books.

In response to this Abdulqadir al-Jilani noted in his "*Al Ghaniyyah*" this Imam and his madhap as one of the deviant madhaps that don't lead to salvation.

In "*Al Ghaniyyah*" Gaws al-Azam Abdulqadir al-Jilani mentions the hadith:

"My ummah will divide into 73 groups, and only one group will reach salvation. The rest will remain in darkness and loss."

In reference to those who remain in loss and who don't reach salvation, Abdulqadir al-Jilani says, "*the Qadariyyah group is one of them*" and adds:

"*This person asserts that faith is simply to believe in Allah and His Rasul without having to practice their recommendations. Based on what Barhuni says this is an incorrect belief.*"

What Gaws al-Azam asserts is:

If someone believes in Allah and His Rasul (saw) and accepts the practices and recommendations but does not comply with them, then he has deviated from the path of faith and is thus considered faithless!

Is this the case?

Let us explore this a little further...

What is faith and in what do we place our faith?

I discussed this topic in detail in *"Intellect and Faith"* but based on its importance I shall also discuss it here.

What do you have faith in? In the religion of Islam!

To have faith in Allah and His Rasul is one of the prerequisites of the religion of Islam. It is one of the laws.

To have faith in Allah and His Rasul (saw), is a requisite of the religion of Islam.

Now when you have faith in something, you automatically accept its conditions. When you have faith in the religion of Islam you are by definition accepting to comply with its recommendations and practices.

When you have faith that a heater can burn your hand, you won't touch it. If you know you can drown where you don't know how to swim, you won't go in there.

Actions are the natural by-products of having faith in something.

What do you have faith in? In the religion of Islam! Since You have faith in the religion of Islam this means you accept its requirements, which need to be fulfilled. If they are not being fulfilled, then "faith" is not yet established.

In other words, faith = actions.

Actions aligned with the requirements of Islam.

If you claim to have faith in the religion of Islam you must fulfill its requisites and recommended practices.

The five pillars of Islam:

- Word of Unity, and its natural results
- Salat
- Fasting
- Pilgrimage
- Giving alms.

These are the first recommendations!

So, if someone claims to have faith but does not perform salat, does not fast, go to pilgrimage, or give alms, his faith is questionable and may only be known by Allah!

Abu Bakr (ra) as one who has fully understood this principle, sent an army to slay those who refused to pay alms after the Rasul of Allah (saw) passed away. For they had left faith, only those who leave faith may be slayed.

If one does not pay alms he is refusing one of the pillars of Islam which means he has lost his faith. Losing your faith in that practice means he has turned away from religion, which means he can be slayed.

This makes it evident that faith and its recommended practices are one and whole. One without the other is not possible.

Consider this: One claims to have faith but does not fulfill the requirements of his faith. What will the cost of this be?

As I explained earlier these recommendations are preparatory precautions for the person, for the difficult times awaiting him.

Just like you feel the need to use tongs to hold something that you believe will burn your hands.

If you don't feel the need to take the necessary precautions for a potential danger it means you don't really have faith in its danger.

When one believes with conviction that there is danger ahead, he will take the necessary precautions.

If he doesn't have faith in the teachings, then he won't feel the need to comply with the recommendations.

The whole purpose of faith is so we take the necessary precautions, to learn about and prepare for the life awaiting us after death.

If the requisites of faith are not being fulfilled, then there is no faith! It's as simple as that!

If one chooses to live like those who don't have faith he must also put up with its consequences.

Since there is no compulsion in religion, everyone is left to his own.

Those who wish to believe may believe and fulfill the requisites of his belief and prepare for the life in which he has faith.

And those who wish not to believe may live however they like provided they know that they will inescapably live the consequences of their choice.

The most important point is to always be mindful of the verse:

> **And man will only accrue the results** (consequences) **of his own deeds** (what manifests through him; his thoughts and actions)![76]

For whatever one does he will inescapably face its consequence! Nothing happens without a reason or cause!

---

[76] Quran 53:39

88

THE PURPOSE OF RELIGIOUS PRACTICES

Now let's consider a different perspective…

We have already established that man is comprised of a composition of divine names.

The make-up of man, the formation we refer to as a human, is a point of manifestation of the divine names in the form of a composition.

Some names are stronger than others, which form the temperament of the person and drive him to output certain actions.

The composition forms the person's make-up, nature, temperament, conditioning, etc. Our habits, natural tendencies, character, are all the natural results of this composition.

When one lives completely subject to his composition, and outputs the actions that are automatically driven to be output by the composition, he will consequently go to hell.

This composition will create both his physical and psychological hell.

This being the case, what do you think the purpose of the recommendations of Islam, such as salat, fasting, pilgrimage, and paying alms is?

These practices drive you to do things that challenge your compositional make-up, for they comprise actions and behaviors that go against your programming!

Remember your composition creates your comfort zone, what serves your personal-bodily health, wealth and vested interests per se…

Salat, to begin with, is the biggest game changer. It directly forces you out of your comfort zone.

Just as you're sitting comfortably with a friend, sipping your tea while deeply immersed in a chat, you have to stop that program and run another program; salat.

This program, on the contrary, enables you to develop and accumulate spiritual power. The power to use your will against the tendencies of your bodily desires, amongst others.

Fasting, on the other hand, directly extinguishes the fire of your bodily temptations. It totally stops and forbids the programs of your nature, even if temporarily.

The bodily nature, food, sexual activity, sleeping, and all bodily comforts are cut off for a while forcing you to overcome your natural tendencies.

Challenge against bodily temptations is also driven by certain names in your composition. By suppressing the activity of certain names you are allowing the activity of other names to become stronger, hence creating balance and reducing the fire of your temptations.

Pilgrimage, needless to say, is a huge challenge on its own!

Giving alms, means you go and give what you've earned through hard work and effort to someone else without any gain or profit in return.

As can be seen, just these simple actions play a big role in reducing the fire of bodily temptations on a big scale, they force you out of the comfort zone of your "nature" and help you gain faith and eternal bliss in the hereafter.

So, without engaging in these practices, you can't make any changes in your composition. It's impossible!

In other words, whether we have insight to the perspective of certain scholars and saints in the past or not, by simply observing the functioning of our composition, we can clearly see that:

Faith without action and practice serves no purpose!

This is the absolute plain truth that is also certified by the intimates of the reality.

Another important topic to consider is... prohibitions!

We already talked about the recommendations, salat, fasting, pilgrimage, alms, etc...

But there are also the prohibitions.

Is it possible to comply with all the prohibitions at once and if not, how will this affect ones faith?

You have a certain composition, which drives you to engage in certain activity that include the things that are prohibited.

So you are not asked to eliminate all forbidden activity from your life at once, because this is not possible.

You already have a composition that is formed. The whole point of the recommendations is to overcome this compositional make-up, which automatically moves you away from forbidden activity.

Hence, we are told:

"Indeed, salat will prevent one from indulging in ego-identity based tendencies and prohibited actions."

Striving against your ego with salat will also ease the practice of other things, in time! It takes time to overcome and re-write the composition.

In other words, when one engages in prohibited sinful acts such as gambling, adultery or drinking alcohol, he does not become faithless, he is still considered a believer. He does not fall out of Islam.

He can repent!

Now on repentance...

One should repent as soon as he engages in a sinful activity, immediately after, with sincere remorse, he must admit that he was consumed by his ego, seek forgiveness and repent! Whatever the sin may be, one must regret what he has done and turn to Allah in repentance.

For when a servant commits a sin Allah waits for him to repent. If he doesn't repent within a day after he has committed the sin, it is recorded as a sin. If he repents, Allah will forgive him for He forgives the sins of those who repent.

"Why should I repent when it's an ongoing sinful activity that I can't seem to give up!?"

One should still repent, as Allah may accept his repentance and protect him from committing that sin again.

The important thing is that you turn to Allah with the conscience that you are guilty.

No matter the size of your sin, never refrain from turning to Allah! It will eventually open the way to salvation.

No matter what your conditions are, always find a way to turn to Allah and never let anything hold u back from doing so!

But if you really don't feel like turning to Allah, if you don't have the want to, then know that you are in serious danger.

Islam is all about challenging your ego-identity and overcoming your habitual, compositional make-up!

It is about uniting the divine names and becoming moralize with the morals of Allah! This is the fundamental meaning and purpose of Islam.

Islam has come to complete and perfect morals.

What does it mean to perfect ones morals? It is to become moralized with the morals of Allah, which means eradicating the body-nature based behaviors. And this doesn't happen instantly; it takes time.

Simply put, it is normal to fall short and make mistakes; this does not make you an unbeliever, but not fulfilling the requisites do!

Hence the Rasul of Allah (saw) says:

"If one has the means to go to pilgrimage but does not, and he dies within that year, he may die as a Jew or he may die as a Zoroastrian."

Why?

Because it does not matter! He is considered to be an unbeliever! Not fulfilling the requisites automatically brings about disbelief! To not comply with the prohibitions is a sin driven by your body-nature, which you must neutralize with a good deed. This is a very sensitive and important topic and must be understood well!

To reiterate, general inadequacies, shortcomings and sinful behavior does not result in faithlessness, it only means you are a sinner.

But any inadequacy regarding the five pillars will take one outside of Islam. One may repent after committing a great sin. But not fulfilling the recommended practices is an implicit way of denying them! The automatic result of denying faith and Islam is unbelief.

Unbelief or "*kufr*" means "to cover" the truth!

A *kafir* is one who covers the reality.

Hence those who cover the truth that Muhammad (saw) brought: **"There is no god, only Allah!"** and live as though there is a deity-god outside somewhere, are called the coverers of the truth, i.e. unbelievers...

89

STEPS THAT TAKE ONE TO ALLAH

Once somebody has established their faith in Islam and accepted Allah and His Rasul, the angels, the books, all of the Rasuls and Nabis, the judgment day, that he will give account and be resurrected... what are the steps he should be taking, how should he progress?

Some divide this process of spiritual evolution into seven, some into three, and some into four stages.

The seven stages are:

Nafs-i Ammarah – The Inciting Self.

Nafs-i Lawwama – The Self-Accusing Self.

Nafs-i Mulhima – The Inspired Self.

Nafs-i Mutmainna – The Peaceful Self.

Nafs-i Radhiya – The Pleased Self.

Nafs-i Mardhiya – The Pleasing Self.

Nafs-i Safiya – The Pure Self.

Those four stages include only:

Nafs-i Ammarah – The Inciting Self.

Nafs-i Lawwama – The Self-Accusing Self.

Nafs-i Mulhima – The Inspired Self.

Nafs-i Mutmainna – The Peaceful Self.

And the three stages include only:

Nafs-i Lawwama – The Self-Accusing Self.

Nafs-i Mulhima – The Inspired Self.

Nafs-i Mutmainna – The Peaceful Self.

The last group does not include the Inciting Self. The Inciting Self is the self that is constantly demanding. Who is demanding? The One behind the apparent 'self' which is the Rabb. Hence one who is at the level of the inciting self is subject to the demands of his Rabb, that is, his composition.

I have explained in previous chapters that the self is created from the level of *rububiyyah*, as it is comprised of the divine names. In this respect the demanding self exists within every being, whether it be a human or an animal. In this light some see it as the default stage and don't consider as a stage within the levels of spiritual evolution.

The next stage, the self-accusing, or 'loathing' self is named after the root word "*lawm*" which refers to the guilt and shame that is felt when one realizes his inadequacy as a servant in the sight of Allah. This is where one recognizes his faults and admits his shortcomings and accuses and loathes himself.

If this state prolongs, and the person begins to engage in certain practices and realizes certain realities, he may begin to receive inspirations. These inspirations will help him to realize that he does not have an independent separate existence, that he is comprised of the names of Allah and his existence is totally dependent on Allah. He will witness that essentially nothing exists other than Allah, including himself. This state is called the "The Inspired Self."

However, there is a very fine point here...

When one comes to this realization he may easily fall into the pit of thinking, "I don't exist, only Allah does and Allah does as He wills! He is not limited by anything. Therefore, I don't have to perform salat, or fast, I can do as I like and I will not be held accountable for it!" This thinking is the natural consequence of the Inspired Self.

It is generally those with an imitative faith that fall into this dangerous abyss!

If the person follows a master (*sheikh*) and accepts this as part of his master's teachings and recommendations, this acceptance is not 'recognition'. For when one really recognizes that the essence of all is only

Allah, he will no longer see a master to follow, if he does then he hasn't fully recognized Allah!

But he may recognize this and with this consciousness still follow his master, this is acceptable. But in the absolute sense, one cannot follow or be tied to 'another' when he becomes conscious of the oneness of Allah.

As a result of these inspirations if he goes into further research, he will see that the divine names that comprise him are in the form of a composition, that is, the reality that 'he is the One', is in respect to the fact that he is comprised of the names of the One, and these names bring about the meanings and actions that manifest through him.

However, the names are not in the form of a composition with Allah, they are present with Him in the absolute sense; unconstrained!

If he can observe this, Allah will have opened the way to the Peaceful Self.

Why?

When he sees his essence is composed of a composition of divine names, he will also see that he does not have the ability to use these names as he likes or when he likes, or in the way that he would like to. He will realize that he lacks the ability to manifest and administer the names, and that on the contrary, the names have control over him!

With this realization he will accept that even though in essence he is the One, he still needs to comply with the divine laws and orders. He must take heed of the teachings of the Rasul of Allah (saw) who has relayed the divine orders. In this light he will see that the level of *Uluhiyyah* encompasses both the names and the acts (the plane of manifestation) and hence only the One to whom these names belong has the absolute power to manifest them as He likes.

Whereas the names manifest through him, without his control. Hence, he will see that he is a composition of names - a program- and his disposition, character, temperament etc. are formed because of this composition.

He will see that only through complying with the divine laws and the teachings of the Rasul of Allah (saw) he may be able to overcome the limitations of his compositional make-up and unite with Allah.

After this he will totally commit himself to the recommendations of the Rasul (saw).

When he was under the command of his emotions and natural tendencies his guide was his Rabb, the names that comprise his make-up. But now his guide will become Allah!

This is the beginning of the process of becoming moralized with the morals of Allah!

When one begins to adopt the morals of Allah he reaches the state of the "Peaceful Self"; he becomes certain of the existence of Allah.

The following levels, Nafs-i Radhiya – The Pleased Self, Nafs-i Mardhiya – The Pleasing Self and Nafs-i Safiya – The Pure Self are attained because of this certainty, according to some scholars, they are not separate states.

The consciousness at the level of the Inciting self, is different to that at the level of the Inspired and Peaceful Self. But after the Pleasing Self, primarily there is no difference.

The self develops and gets to know Allah to the extent that it becomes moralized with the morals of Allah. Until then he knows his Rabb. After the Pleasing Self the way to knowing Allah opens through the names and he is free to advance as much as he can...

The Pleased Self (radhiya) is about overcoming the conditions of the names and finding oneself at the level of the names. The Pleasing self (mardhiya) is about finding oneself at the level of the attributes and observing his essential reality. Not from the point of Rabb but from the point of *Rahmaniyyah*!

The Pure Self cannot be described or talked about! It is the state of the Absolute Self (*dhat*)! It is the reflection of the Absolute Self (*dhat*)! One cannot talk about the Absolute Self; hence it is not possible to talk about the Pure Self.

So then essentially there are three levels to knowing oneself.

The Self-Accusing Self, the Inspired Self and the Peaceful Self.

Until the state of Peaceful Self, one knows only his Rabb. If at the state of the Inspired Self one receives *divine inspirations* among others (not all inspirations are divine), this will force him to move on to the state of the Peaceful Self.

At the level of the Inspired Self one has the opportunity to turn from Rabbani calls to Divine calls. If he can turn to the divine calls with absolute certainty he will reach the state of the Peaceful Self and his guide (*wali*) will become Allah (*waliyyullah*). He will begin to adopt the morals of Allah and embarks on a path to becoming an intimate of Allah.

Let us underline an important point here:

Sainthood (*wilayah*) is to know Allah. The only way to know Allah is by understanding the secret of Unity (*wahdah*). Being grateful, being pleased, acknowledging one's poverty and impotence, and experiencing love are only steps that take one to unity.

If these steps are followed properly and one reaches unity then the door of sainthood will open! One who has not reached the secret of unity cannot become a saint!

Sufism is based entirely on the mystery of unity. For without foregoing your person, your individual notion of a self, and dive into the ocean of unity, you cannot know Allah! And one who does not know Allah cannot be an intimate of Allah (*wali* - saint).

It's easy for people to look at one's deeds, behavior and speech and label as them a saint, especially if they see someone to be above themselves!

Whereas in reality for one to be a saint he must know Allah; he must have reached and experienced the secret of unity and he must have adopted the morals of Allah.

This process begins at the level of the Inspired Self. When he reaches the Peaceful Self he experiences oneness. **But only at the level of the Pleasing Self does oneness turn into unity…**

90

THE MEN (SAINTS) OF THE UNKNOWN (RIJAL AL-GHAIB)

The spiritually tasked men known as the "The Men of the Unknown" are of two groups:

A. The administrators

B. The executers

The administrators are also known as The Council (*Diwan*) or The High Council (*Diwan al-Kabir*).

They conduct two types of meetings:

1. Monthly meetings, which occur on the 14th night adjoining the 15th of every lunar month, at various places.

2. Annual meetings, conducted at the Mount Hira, where the Rasul of Allah (saw) retreated before he was assigned as a Rasul.

Most of the members of the High Council are the great saints who have already made their transition to the life after death, while a third of them comprise the high degreed saints who are presently in servitude on Earth.

The High Council consists of 66 members. Amongst these are the *Ghawth*, his two assistants, *Qutb al-Irshad*, and *Qutb al-Aqtab*, and 4 other *Qutbs*, who administer 4 elements, all of the 7's, and 11 others besides the administrative chamber of the *Ghawth* known as the '*Mufarridoon*'.

This council makes decisions regarding the necessary precautions that need to be taken on behalf of existence based on divine knowledge. These decisions are then passed on to the Executers.

The general president of the High Council is the Rasul of Allah (saw). If he doesn't attend a meeting then the Perfect Man (*Insan al-kamil*) of that time attends in his place.

The rank of the Perfect Man is the highest rank and only one person every few centuries is given this rank on earth.

The Reviver comes every century. His duty is to revive the religion according to the current understanding of the century. He is also a member of the Council. The final Reviver is known as the Mahdi. The Mahdi is also the Perfect Man.

The *Ghawth* is both the chairman, when the Rasul (saw) isn't present, and the Chief of Executers.

The *Qutb al-Irshad* works in the area of astrology and manifesting the effects of various stars and planetary constellations upon the people and the jinn.

The *Qutb al-Aqtab* relays the decisions of the *Ghawth* to those of concern. Even the saint of the jinn who attends the Council receives orders from the *Qutb al-Aqtab*.

The executers are like an army. They are responsible for executing the decisions made by the Council. Their commander in chief is the *Ghawth* of that time. The *Qutb al-Aqtab* is like a Chief of Defense.

Then comes the 4's, then the 7's who have some degree of administrative function, then the 12's, the 40's and then the 300's, who are actually 313 in number. After them, the 1200's and after them the local *Qutbs* take charge.

Only a few of these saints in the Council and the Executers have reached the station of Self Conquest (*fath*), while some of them have reached the station of Unveiling (*kashf*). The rest fulfill their function without knowing.

Abdulqadir al-Jilani is known as the The Great Ghawth (*Ghawth al-Azam*) because he was not only the *Ghawth* of his time but also the Perfect Man.

The second Perfect Man is Abdulkareem al-Jili. He has written many books on the Reality and *Marifatullah* (gnosis), the most popular one being 'The Perfect Man'.

The people of Self-Conquest are aware of everything that transpires on Earth. The knowledge of the people of unveiling on the other hand is limited to their field of duty.

Every saint on duty knows others on his level and the one below him. The higher group is known only to the head of the lower group. Other than of course, those who can attend the Council – who obviously know who their superiors are by means of the Council meetings. Among them are Indonesians, Arabs, Pakistanis, Afghans, Turks and saints from other races.

This is all I can discuss on this topic here!

I thought it was important to share this information to highlight the importance of such sacred duties and the existence of those who are charged with them.

91

COMMON MISPERCEPTIONS

Here I want to touch on some of the most frequent misperceptions formed due to lack of knowledge of Allah and the divine laws in effect in the universe:

1- After recognizing and accepting the unity of existence, not feeling the need to comply with the divine orders; not fulfilling the recommended physical practices due to the realization that one is not his 'body'.

2- Only engaging in the physical practices without thought and contemplation and regarding everyone who does not fit into a particular "shape" to be unbelievers who will be cast to hell.

3- Creating a deity-god in one's mind and calling this god "Allah" and then construing and judging the behavior of others based on this made-up god.

4- Denying the Jinn and the Angels, who are discussed in length in the Quran, and as a result of being captive within the prison of the five-sense delusion, regarding them merely as 'evil thoughts and/or bacteria.'

5- Disregarding the words of the Rasul (saw) such as "If knowledge is in China, go and acquire it!" and "Wisdom is the lost asset of the believer, seek it and take it wherever you find it!" and instead wasting their lives by only taking heed of a single source.

6- Not doing thorough research on religion and confusing it with concepts such as necromancy, evoking the spirits of the dead, or alien encounters, and becoming deprived of the teachings of the Rasul of Allah (saw) regarding the life after death, hence creating their own eternal suffering.

7- Waiting for the great arrival of "the Mahdi" on a white horse with a sword in his hand!

8- Confusing religion with politics and trying to change governmental regimes based on religious teachings and hence missing the point of religion.

9- Thinking religion is only something needed in the life after death and indulging in the worldly life, unaware of the life awaiting him after death.

10- Assuming Allah to be on a throne far beyond somewhere and the Rasul (saw) as a soldier appointed by Allah to ensure the peace of the people living on Earth.

92

"THE MOST COMMON MISTAKE OF AN ASPIRING SUFI"

The Quran and countless enlightened scholars and saints, from Hadhrat Ali (ra) to Abdulqadir al-Jilani, Muhyiddin Ibn Arabi and the Perfect Man, Abdulkareem al-Jili, disclosed and proved the truth that the essence of existence is Allah and that nothing exists besides Allah.

In our present modern world, science teaches the importance of the unity underlying existence and the fact that existence is essentially a "unified field" as early as high school. This knowledge is no secret. The tendency to want to hide this as some super-secret stems from being stuck in an imaginary world of the past centuries.

However... there is a very important point to take heed of...

The fundamental laws of existence will never change. The common laws, regulations, the system and order that governs existence are not alterable. These laws that were in effect in the past, are still in effect today, and will continue to be in the future. Remember the verse:

You will not find an alteration in Our Sunnah.[77]

Despite the fact that your being is the One in essence, your body cannot function optimally when you stop eating and drinking. Similarly, your after-life body will also be subject to certain laws to which you must comply.

---

[77] Quran 17:77

If you don't engage in the obligatory practices, commonly referred to as worship, no matter who you are and what your status is, you will inescapably be subject to the conditions of the domain of life that you go to.

As much as the internal aspect of the UNITY of existence is true and valid, so is the external aspect entailing the laws and regulations...!

No matter what degree you feel yourself to be at, just as you are living inside a body today, you will also continue your life after death with a body.

Just as water drowns and fire burns you in this world, so too in the hereafter they will have the same effect. This is unavoidable!

Just as the Rasul of Allah (saw) has warned us regarding the precautions we must take regarding the health of our body in this world, he has also made recommendations under the label "worship" as precautions for the life awaiting us after death.

And just like someone who claims to be the "ONE" but doesn't take heed of these precautions was to be thrown into fire in this world, he will inevitably burn, in the same way he will helplessly burn and suffer in the fire of the hereafter. His knowledge will be of no avail to him!

As for the verse:

> **And serve your Rabb** (engage in the practices of prayer and servitude to your Rabb – the Names comprising your essential reality – while your ego self still exists) **until there comes to you the certainty** (until you realize the inexistence of your ego self, which is the realization of the reality of death; the experience of the *Wahid'ul Qahhar*. After this certainty, servitude to one's Rabb will continue as the natural outcome of this process).[78]

It means continue to worship and perform the obligatory practices until you reach the state of "certainty" and the experience of the reality!

But it does not, in anyway suggest that you can abandon these practices once you reach certainty!

It simply means, one must continue to engage in these practices until they reach the state of certainty, and after that, they must continue to engage

---

[78] Quran 15:99

in these practices, not as the "person" but as one who has annihilated his 'self' i.e. as the manifestation of the acts of Allah taking place!

Enlightened beings in the past referred to this as "*Ubudiyyah*" (servitude).

In Sufism, there are two important concepts, *fanabillah* and *baqabillah*.

In the first, one reaches the essence of existence, in the second, he begins to observe existence from the point of that essence.

The first observation is "internal" observation (*batin*) and the latter is external (*zahir*).

Most Sufi aspirants can't go further than this second observation. Thus, they remain in the first station of unity and become deprived of experiencing and giving the due of many, much higher states of reality. If they could move on to the next phase and realize that just as the inner realities are the One so are the external realities, their actions would be different.

Unity is a reality that is observed and experienced at the level of consciousness. Its external aspect manifests within the parameters of certain laws. Hence just as we are subject to certain laws of nature in regards to our bodily life we are also inevitably subject to the laws of the life after, and must therefore be prepared for it. Those who don't perform the obligatory practices will inescapably suffer its consequence.

93

THE GREAT MISUNDERSTANDING OF THE BIASED

As for the common mistake of the second group...

Some call themselves people of '*shariah*' and some people of this or that '*tariqah*'...

But the truth is they have neither rightly comprehended *shariah* nor *tariqah*...

Generally, their 'leader' knows nothing about Sufism!

They gather pure hearted people with good intentions and spend their days relating stories from the past to them, in the name of giving morality lessons (!) in fact some are even possessed by the jinn! Not to mention, anyone that refuses or questions their ideas is directly labelled an "unbeliever"!

"He who calls one with faith an 'unbeliever' kills him." (Tirmidhi)

Hence, they continually fall into faithlessness without even being aware of it because of their ignorance.

Such people neglect spirituality and contemplation, and only focus on appearance, falling into a great loss.

For them belief equals a scarf, a cap, a robe, and a beard!

The ignorant who believe them, devoid of true religious knowledge, view everything from a very flawed lens, and live in a world far from the reality.

No matter how big their mistakes may be, someone who declares the word of unity, performs their daily salat, fasts, goes to pilgrimage, and gives alms, cannot be called a nonbeliever! Nobody can know whether this person will go to heaven or hell.

None has the discretion to make claims about whether one will go to heaven or hell. But based on their actions, one may deduce that this action will cause suffering or may take him to hell, but nobody can make an absolute claim about it.

One who makes such claims proves he knows nothing about religion and reduces himself to a pitiful situation in the sight of the learned ones.

The religious requirements are clear.

Women, according to the Quran, should cover their ornaments. If they accept that this is the law of Allah yet admit their inability to comply by it, Allah may or may not forgive them. But this, in no way, means they are non-believers, should they fail to comply with this law.

To refuse and deny a single verse in the Quran is equivalent to denying the whole of religion, because it is package, it is either accepted wholly, or denied altogether.

So, what is the whole package that we need to accept?

The Quran and the hadith of the Rasul of Allah (saw)!

Refusing the interpretations of those who came later does not make one a non-believer!

If someone says "I accept the laws in the Quran and the teachings of the Rasul of Allah (saw) but I am unable to follow them" this also does not take one out of religion.

But to say, "These laws and teachings are inapplicable today, they are invalid and irrelevant to our time" takes one out of religion, as this goes into denial!

My intent is to show that religion is an integral system of laws (entirely based on physics, chemistry, and electromagnetic laws) aimed at enabling man to know himself, his origin, his essential reality, rather than a collection of imaginary rules and regulations for the purpose of uniformity.

I'm open to debating this both from the perspective of Sufism and modern science. Everyone is free to write a book and disclose their proof, should they be inclined to believe I am mistaken.

In today's world everything is debatable. Every religious law and regulation is scientifically explicable.

This being the case, to remain trapped within the inadequacy of the past centuries and instilling fear into people serves no benefit to mankind.

To sum up, one who accepts all of the laws of the Quran and the Rasul of Allah (saw) but fails to comply with them, commits a sin (i.e. becomes loaded with negative charge). However, religion shows ways to neutralize this negative charge and turn it into a positive one. In no way does he become an unbeliever for not complying with the laws. He who claims otherwise admits his ignorance.

Religion is not about a cap, a robe, and a beard! Nowhere among the pillars of faith can you see the requirement of a beard! To claim one without beard in not a Muslim is nothing other than blind ignorance. To duly evaluate this one needs an intellect!

You can record the Quran and the entire collection of hadith on your computer today and make it play over and over again.

To carry and relay information that was also carried and relayed to him does not make one a scholar of religion.

One must comprehend that knowledge, and explain it according to the time he is living in.

One who cannot explain in modern terms the purpose of religion, why it offers what it does and what the consequences of not complying with it are, is not a religious scholar but a *carrier*!

The judgment is up to the listener!

The duty of religious figures is not to copy and paste information in the format of the past but to update this knowledge according to the needs and the language of the present day to enable others to understand the benefits of complying with it and the cost of not complying with it.

People have gained immunity to the expressions used in the past, such as, "If you do this you will go to heaven, if you don't do this you will go to hell" Such wording is extremely outdated and ineffective!

Also, I feel it's important that we understand that the principle point of Sufism is the reality of "Unity"!

Tariqah is a path that takes one to the Reality (*haqiqah*).

A path that does not lead one to the reality is either an institution of good morals or a conference on the external laws of religion.

A path that does not illuminate your essential reality to you can only be a group that is involved in the surface values concerned only about avoiding certain dangers.

To go and submit yourself to some guru without knowing the external laws of religion and a certain level of Sufi culture, is a great risk, for there is no compensation for years spent in vain.

Moreover, to correct the incorrect beliefs and cleanse yourself from the damage it gave you requires a long time and strenuous effort.

You can check the level of your knowledge by comparing everything you've learnt until today, to what you take away from this book, in addition to answering the questions below:

What is you relation to the meaning of the name "Allah?"

Which of your actions belong to you and which pertain to Allah?

Who is the being you refer to as "I" and what qualities does it have?

How will life after death be?

How is the life of the grave, where is it, and how many types of it are there?

Is it possible to come back to this world?

Does resurrecting into a new body mean coming back to this world with a different body or to a domain of life after the entire human race is wiped out after doomsday?

Is man responsible for what he does in this world? Or can he get away with it?

Where and how will one give account?

Can one save himself from certain dangers awaiting him in the future? If so, how?

Are the recommendations of the Rasul of Allah (saw) "restrictions" put by Allah out of amusement, or are they requirements based on a certain system and order?

What is punishment?

What does the punishment of Allah mean?

What is heaven and hell? Why are they eternal? Are they physical, psychological, or both?

What are the 8 heavens (Absolute Essence, Attributes, Names, Acts and their two aspects) where are they and how can they be reached?

What does it mean to unite with Allah? Can it be experienced here? Or is it something that pertains to the life after death? How can something free of space and location be reached?

Is there progress and development in the afterlife? Can one attain something they were not able to attain in this world, in the afterlife? What can be gained in the afterlife?

Where is the life after death?

What is death and how many types of life are there after death?

What is a test? Are we being tested? Who is testing us and why?

What is servitude, who is a servant? How many types of servitude are there?

Is man a body, a spirit, something beyond these, or all of these?

If everything I have shared until today does not answer these questions, you have no time to waste!

For if you haven't duly comprehended the importance of the future that is awaiting you then indeed you are also not giving the due of your present moment!

If you insist on amusing yourself with illusory thoughts such as "Whatever Allah wills that will happen, so and so master has my back anyway, he will save me" then go ahead and stay in your delusion! But if it is too late when you realize that nobody can be of any avail when you don't actually put the effort in and fulfill the requisites of your servitude, what will you do?

The following verse refers to everyone who dies without having duly prepared for the afterlife:

When death comes to one of them, he says, "My Rabb, send me back (to the worldly life)."[79]

---

[79] Quran 23:99

It is evident through this verse that the preparation for the afterlife is only possible in this world, and those who die without preparing will forever be remorseful and helpless.

94

THE DIFFERENCE BETWEEN GOD AND ALLAH

To create a god in your head based on your own logic and conditioning and then calling that god "Allah" and judging everyone by this made-up god in your head...

The vast majority of the people today deify and worship a god of their own imagination and creation. They assume there is a god somewhere, a "great" god, who sometimes intervenes with human affairs and sometimes watches from afar... a god who calls to account, sometimes rewards and sometime punishes... A god who allows tyranny to take place on earth, and have millions of people suffer... Sometimes this god is Jewish, sometimes Christian... sometimes none... When things get tough they turn to this god and ask for help, and expect it to come in a particular format, which almost never happens, which is then tied to some 'reason'!

This god is expected to act according to our wants and needs, otherwise his godhood is questioned.

Everyone uses their own god to threaten others, "If you don't do this god will punish you" and everyone goes into some form of expectation from this god, they expect that he showers his bounties upon them, regardless of how they act.

Whereas...

If only we could put aside this man-made "god" and try and understand the "Rabb of the worlds" that Islam refers to with the name "Allah"!

If only we could see that the god we imagine into existence has nothing to do with the reality...

If only we could focus more on deciphering the codes of the universe and the immutable laws of the miracle of nature that govern life.

If only we could understand the laws, the order and system of the One denoted with the name Allah and the 'what-why-how's of the creation of Allah, most certainly our perspective will shift, and we will have a much better understanding of everything!

Otherwise...

If we refuse to leave our secure little cocoon and stubbornly close our eyes to see the reality, we will inevitably have to open our eyes into deep suffering and pain!

No excuses will be valid when it is too late!

Making claims about how something should or shouldn't be without basing it on the Quran or hadith, or making claims about what Allah will or will not do in the future are generally based on the 'god' in our heads. We will most probably experience great remorse for this.

Thus, we must put out aside the god in our heads aside and learn about Allah, the Rabb of the worlds! There is no way of conceiving or comprehending the damage our ignorance can cause us in the hereafter!

Whatever the case may be, let us not make any judgment about anyone, and simply say, "He or she will face the consequence of his /her actions, the judgment is up to Allah" and leave our personal opinions aside.

We are not here to judge anyone, we are here to get to know Allah, the universe He created, the laws and the system that govern us, and to fulfill their requisites to prepare for the life after death.

Remember every game has its own set of rules which must be observed if you want to play that game. You can't just add or take out rules as you wish, you can't kick a ball if you're playing basketball or dribble the ball if you're playing football!

The Rasul of Allah (saw) has clarified the rules of the religion of Islam.

The choice to comply with them or not bounds only the individual - just as their consequences!

But this is for certain:

Nobody has the discretion to modify the laws of religion as they like!

You are free to make an interpretation.

You are free to have an opinion.

You are free to act.

But you do not have the freedom or the right to change the laws!

For the Rasul of Allah (saw) has notified us that no other Nabi will come after him. Since only a Nabi can change the laws of religion, it is clear that this path is closed to humanity for as long as we shall live.

This being the case, everyone is free to accept or reject the teachings of the Rasul (saw) provided they are ready to face its consequence!

Let us not make up religious laws based on the made-up god in our heads!

Let us not create a world based on this imaginary god, for these delusions will only drive us into great suffering.

What is the reality?

This should be our primary concern.

How sad for us if this is not what we are thinking of, studying and researching about…

How said for us if we are not using out brain for this purpose.

95

THE IGNORANCE OF DENYING THE JINN AND THE ANGELS

The Quran openly and extensively talks about the existence of the jinn and the angels.

Yet, those who are confined within the limits of their sensory perceptions, or who are inadvertently possessed by the jinn misconstrue the meaning of these beings and deviate from the truth.

What does the Rasul of Allah (saw) say in regard to the jinn who are always with us and affect us?

He says there are two beings that are always present with us, one of them is a jinn and the other is an angel. They constantly send specific frequencies to the persons brain based on their own make up and meaning.

The jinn[80] predominantly propel the person towards the material, the bodily life, and all the transitory fleeting things that will be left behind, and hence prevent him from taking life after death seriously. If and when the person remembers the jinn immediately try to channel the person away from this remembrance, and if the person's make-up is permitting, they will be easily drawn to this energy!

This is how people inadvertently become possessed by or affected by the jinn.

The only tool to save one from this force is "knowledge"! Through knowledge one can correctly identify the force at play and take the necessary precautions to protect himself.

---

[80] More information on the jinn can be found in *"Spirit, Man, Jinn"*

The dhikr that creates a protective magnetic shield around the person against the jinn is:

"La hawla wala kuwwatah illa billah"

"Rabbi inni massaniyyash shaytanu Bi noosbin wa adhab; Rabbi audhu Bika min hamazatish shayateen wa audhu bika Rabbi an yahduroon. Wa hifzan min qulli shaytanin mareed."[81]

If a person is disturbed by the jinn during their sleep in the form of nightmares, they can recite these protective prayers a few hundred times and they will see that the pressure is lifted immediately.

Contrary to common knowledge, the Satan known as "Iblis" is a jinn, not an angel. The following verse makes this clear.

"And when We said to the angels, 'Prostrate to Adam,' and all but Iblis prostrated. He was of the jinn..."[82]

The jinn that are of the same category of Iblis generally propel humans away from experiencing their reality, constantly pushing them towards bodily desires.

The following sahih muslim hadith explains how there is a jinn assigned to every person:

Narrated by Abdullah Ibn Masud (ra):

The Rasul of Allah (saw) said:

– *Assigned to every single one of you, with no exception, is a jinn.*

The followers asked:

– Oh Rasul of Allah! Is there one assigned to you too?

– *Yes there is! However, Allah has helped me by making it a Muslim, so that it advises nothing but good to me.*

Another hadith openly says:

---

[81] Quran 38:41 – 23:97-98 – 37:7
[82] Quran 18:50

"Assigned to man are two beings, one is a jinn and the other is an angel."

One drives man away from the truth while the other encourages towards the truth! They constantly generate thoughts in the person according to their own nature.

If the jinn overpowers the person inadvertently becomes ruled by it, as explained in the following verse:

"O community of jinn, you have truly possessed (misled from reality) **the vast majority of mankind."** [83]

As I explained in detail in *"Spirit, Man, Jinn"* the biggest entertainment of the jinn is to compete with one another on how many people they were able to trick and delude. As the following hadith explains:

Jabir (ra) narrates from the Rasul of Allah (saw):

"The Satan sends his army in units and they create provocation and disorder among the people. Among them the one with the highest rank is the one that causes the greatest provocation."

Hence, we are constantly subject to countless provocative thoughts throughout our day that delude us and drive us to make mistakes.

Whereas...

1400 years ago, the human body was described as "earth", denoting the minerals and water that comprise its basic make-up. Similarly, the jinn are made of radiation and were hence described as "toxic smokeless fire that penetrates into the cells."

The Quran describes "Satan" as a "jinn" and stresses the supremacy of consciousness over bodily greatness.

I have provided a lot of detail on the topic of the jinn in *"Spirit Man Jinn"* which I wrote in 1972, hence there is no need to go into further detail here.

The truth is, the Quran clearly states that the majority of the people are under the ruling of the jinn.

---

[83] Quran 6:128

It explains how the jinn divert and digress the people from the truth and drive them away from fulfilling the requisites of the reality. It also highlights the importance of not becoming seduced by them by reminding us of the realities awaiting us in the afterlife.

Despite the warnings of the Rasul of Allah (saw) if one chooses to believe in the jinn in the guise of "psychics" and/or "spirits", then clearly they are creating their own downfall, and no amount of regret and remorse will be of no any benefit to them when they face the reality.

As for the angels…

As opposed to the radiation-based make-up of the jinn, the angels are made of photon like light.

In fact, when we examine the different beams and rays of light, we are in effect examining the angels, albeit unconsciously!

Think of it like examining a human under a gigantic electron microscope. You see the intricate details of the cells; you identify the DNA, and all the inter-molecular structures, but you are totally unaware that this is a human.

Similarly, science today is examining many such structures without knowing what the actual object or being is!

The angels are just as real and widespread as the jinn, and they compose the very raw material of the universe!

To deny the existence of this elementary material that has an enormous effect on the brain and the jinn, is pure ignorance and bigotry!

If instead we try to comprehend these beings and force our brains to ascend to a higher level…

We may perhaps begin to understand and identify these countless conscious beings who rule our brain, sometimes via physical means and sometimes through their metaphysical cosmic makeups.

These beings are comprised of pure force, like the pure Spirit.

Due to our primitive ignorance we deprive ourselves from knowing and understanding them!

Man is created for knowledge; to learn, to research, and to grow…. how sad for him to imprison himself within the cell of ignorance!

At some point or another, science will advance enough to develop the necessary technology to identify these beings called the jinn and make contact with them.

But the angels will never be detected and identified via material tools, because to perceive the angels the brain must work at extremely high levels and it is impossible for man to invent a tool of equal capacity to himself.

When one denies the existence of the angels he unconsciously and ignorantly denies the countless qualities within himself. This loss is inexplicable! It is impossible to explain to the ignorant one how great a loss he incurs by confining himself to the limits of the five senses.

96

DENYING OF KNOWLEDGE AND WISDOM

The greatest miracle of the final Rasul, Muhammad (saw) in comparison to the prior Nabis and Rasuls is "KNOWLEDGE".

He has shared such invaluable knowledge in regard to the creation and make-up of humans, to life after death, and has pointed to such paramount realities through the metaphors and allegories he was forced to use due to the limitations of his time, that the likes of this has not occurred in the history of humans.

When the Rasul of Allah (saw) said, *"The earth is on the horns of a bull"* he was symbolically describing the relation between earth and the constellation Taurus, the bull. And when he said the earth is on the back of a fish, again, he was pointing to the era of Pisces that the earth is in. How much more openly could he have said it?

Moreover, he pointed to a reality, 1400 years ago, that we have only come to discover in the last fifty years:

"THE SUN WILL GROW SO MUCH THAT IT WILL ONLY BE A 'MIL' AWAY FROM EARTH."

The person who narrated this asks the Rasul (saw), "Does the word "mil" mean a "mile" as in the unit of distance, or the mile we use as an eye liner?"

Let's consider…

During the 1950's scientists calculated and predicted that the flames of the Sun will engulf Mercury, Venus and the Earth in the future; devouring the entire earth into its "center" which is 6500 centigrade degrees…

1400 years ago, a man comes forward and says the Sun will engulf the earth and the earth will evaporate like a drop of water within hell!

Thus, he warns people and reminds them to take precaution and prepare themselves for the future!!!

If our brains do not work enough to evaluate this knowledge, there is nothing further to say!

This man, yes this man, has reminded us, over and over again, of the importance of "knowledge"!

He said, "Only with knowledge can you attain the goods of both this world and the afterlife. If you want the worldly life, turn to knowledge. If you want the afterlife, turn to knowledge. If you want both, again turn to knowledge!"

He said:

"If knowledge is in China, then go to China."

"Wisdom (the knowledge of the why and how of things) is the lost jewel of a believer, acquire it wherever you find it."

He told us a true guide is one who is open to all knowledge. He presents knowledge according to the level of the people whom he addresses. He encourages to mix with and talk to everyone, to learn new things, and to teach what you learn…

A true guide is one who has enough knowledge to correct the wrong information the people may have been given previously. He does not feel the need to restrict people from interacting with others.

Knowledge is not reading a few books that were written from a few different scholars "on the same path" and then narrating this to others. This is nothing other than pulling people back into the past.

Hadhrat Ali (ra) says, **"Raise your children not according to your current time but the times in which they will live."**

This tells us we must be equipped with not only the knowledge of our current times but the knowledge pertaining to the future.

This being the case, how sad that most people are still regurgitating the knowledge and information of past centuries!

Many intellectuals have spoken out against the dogmatic approach and the outdated information of religion, showing the current advancements of science as proof.

Incapable of handling these intellectuals, the "narrators" of religion helplessly tell them to stay away from such knowledge.

The solution is not in fleeing and hiding from the truth, but to confront it and deal with it!

It is not to close your eyes but to open them even wider to determine inadequacies and shortcomings, if any, and replace them with the correct information, to protect the people and prepare them properly for the future.

It is to become one who has duly comprehended religion rather than simply narrating past information, and to be able to answer the questions that can lead to provocation, in accordance to the time and place of the event.

In short, a true guide should take his power from the truth and have a level of knowledge that can enable those who are stuck within their conditioned worlds to overcome the boundaries of matter and discern the realities of the metaphysical life.

For all of this there is only one prerequisite...

KNOWLEDGE!

97

DELUSIONS OF MAKING CONTACT WITH THE SPIRITS AND ALIENS

As for those who, without any proper research on religion, devote themselves to the "realm of the spirits" and receive information from them for the "good" of humanity...

When they see the reality after death:

> **"When death comes to one of them, he says, "My Rabb, send me back** (to the worldly life). **So that I might do righteousness in that which I left behind** (i.e. a faithful life that I did not heed or give importance to; the potential that I did not utilize and activate)." **No!** (It is impossible to go back!) **His words are invalid!** (His request is unrecognized in the system)..." [84]

Despite the frequent reminders in the Quran that there is absolutely no return to the worldly life after death, some people still assert the idea of reincarnation, a belief of Indian origin, that has nothing to do with Islam.

The biggest pitfall of the spiritualists, or shall I say, the point through which the jinn most commonly deceive them, is through this concept of reincarnation.

In "*Spirit Man Jinn*" I explained in detail why reincarnation is unacceptable. I also touched on it in this book, where I explained how through death the brain stops functioning and hence is unable to upload new data to the spirit.

---

[84] Quran 23: 99-100

No matter who the deceased may be, even if they are a martyr, there is no way for them to come back to this world with a new body. Here is a Hadith to validate this:

Jabir Bin Abdullah (ra) narrates:

Rawi Jabir's father was martyred during the battle of Uhud. The Rasul of Allah (saw) asked,

"O Jabir, why are you so sad?"

Jabir replied "O Rasul of Allah. My father has been martyred, and he has left behind children and debts!"

The Rasul of Allah (saw) said, "O Jabir, shall I then give you the glad tidings of how your father was greeted by Allah?"

– Yes O Rasul!

– Allah has never spoken to anyone without a veil. Despite this, Allah spoke to your father without a veil, and asked him:

– O my servant, ask of me that I may give..?

Your father said:

– O my Rabb, reincarnate me (send me back to the world), so that I may be martyred again on your way!

Upon this Allah said:

– IT HAS BEEN PREDETERMINED BY ME THAT THE PEOPLE WILL NEVER RETURN TO THE WORLD.

Then your father said:

– O Rabb, then inform those whom I left behind of my situation.

The Rasul of Allah (saw) said:

– Upon this Allah revealed the verse:

"And never think of those who have been killed in the way of Allah as dead. On the contrary, they are alive with their Rabb receiving provision (from the forces pertaining to their innermost essential reality)."[85]

---

[85] Quran 3:169

As can be seen, even the martyrs, who are free to roam around after death, cannot return to the worldly life with a new body.

I presume I have made it clear enough that those who accept reincarnation, are openly denying the teaching of the Rasul of Allah (saw).

The spiritualists have become so used to being under the effects of the jinn that they are unable to objectively evaluate these warnings.

The jinn have created such a fantasy world…

There are aliens!!! They come from such and such star!!! They want to govern humanity but they are keeping themselves hidden to avoid chaos. They have godly powers. But they don't use it to not intervene in the affairs of humanity. They are super benevolent, but they do nothing about the millions who are killing each other!!!

They don't influence the thoughts of presidents to stop the wars and save the lives of thousands… even though they can…but one glorious day, with a magic wand, the "Golden Age" is going to magically begin, and everything is going to be perfect!!!

These aliens, who delude humans into thinking they are from outer space, are going to openly reveal themselves to humans in the future!

The people of knowledge can easily recognize this as the play of the 'jinn' mentioned in the Quran.

The biggest deception of the jinn in this century is to present themselves as aliens; and seize control of many people via the channel of the psychics they interact with.

In the past they presented themselves as 'spirits' of people who lived in the past, then they claimed to be the spirits of important saints such as "Abdulqadir Jilani" or "Rumi". Today they most commonly claim to be "aliens" and promise the coming of a "golden age" to people.

The most common assertions of the jinn who present themselves as aliens are:

"Moses (pbuh), Jesus (pbuh) and Muhammad (saw) along with Bayti Dost, Qadri Dost and Mustafa Molla are appointed and delegated by the aliens, and they are of the jinn; they are not human.

Islam and the Quran are no longer valid, heaven and hell don't exist, jinn and the Satan are not real.

People are reincarnated and sent back to this world after they die, many times over. The "Book of Knowledge" has replaced the previous sacred books and it is the current source which will be valid until year 3000.

Aliens make contact with humans for the purpose of saving them. They are pure servants of Allah. There are many powers greater than Allah.

Allah has taken form and lives among the people within a system called Beta Gurz. Mankind will become more powerful than Allah in the future.... Etc etc etc...."

The biggest protection against these jinn who easily deceive people with inadequate knowledge of Islam and Sufism, via hallucinations and illusions, is to recite the following verses between 100-500 times every day:

"Rabbi inni massaniyyash shaytanu Bi noosbin wa adhab; Rabbi audhu Bika min hamazatish shayateen wa audhu bika Rabbi an yahduroon. Wa hifzan min qulli shaytanin mareed."[86]

I have provided great detail on the illogical aspects of the "Book of Knowledge" in *Spirit, Man, Jinn*, for those who are interested.

In the past they used to appear as saints, especially in graveyards, to trick people and entertain themselves. Now they've changed their costume and style and have become the savior aliens!

They make no contribution to the growth and development of humans, they bring no invention, and camouflage this as "non-intervention" thereby diverting mankind from the truths of the afterlife.

The jinn, described as "fire" i.e. whose make-up is radiation, and who have existed on earth since when the earth was a ball of flame, are not intellectually greater than mankind, and hence can't discern the realities regarding the afterlife very easily.

Due to this, they spend their lives in pursuit of power and control and manipulating mankind.

---

[86] Quran 38:41 – 23:97-98 – 37:7

They can access data of the past and with this knowledge they pretend to be the spirits of people who lived in the past, but also present past philosophies as new.

Many who are captivated by them are devoid of religious knowledge on this topic.

The West are deceived easily as Christianity does not give any knowledge regarding the jinn.

As for the East, despite the comprehensive knowledge shared by Muhammad (saw) they fail to duly evaluate this information and hence easily accept incorrect information.

As a result:

The philosophy being established by the jinn today is a mixture of past and new philosophies:

Man is born, he grows, does good and bad, then dies, realizes his mistakes and suffers, then high level noble spirits reincarnate him and send him back to the world with a new body, over and over again, until he reaches enlightenment... As for the evil spirits who are unable to leave earth, they constantly disturb the weak spirits and possess them!

While all of this taking place, god, who is named Allah, sits somewhere far in space and observes it all!

Those who don't know about the realities of the afterlife, who are deprived of religious culture and philosophy are easily deceived by such absurd notions.

In short:

Life after death continues in two ways until Doomsday. The first is the life of the grave, and the second is an unrestrained life where the spirit is free to roam around as it likes. Every person that dies moves onto either one of these lifestyles.

The life of the grave is for those who reject and refuse the teachings of the Rasul of Allah (saw) and the general population of Muslims.

The second level, the unrestrained life, is for those who fought in the way of Allah and reached the mystery of "dying before death" and the station of divine closeness. These people have died to themselves, their identity, before the death of their physical bodies. They overcame their bodily desires and the conditionings of the bodily life and hence when they physically experienced death, they became free of the restraints of the body, and able to live freely until doomsday.

They can interact with one another, and even intervene in worldly affairs, if necessary, such as taking part in various combats.

This is a very comprehensive topic, enough to be a book on its own.

To sum up, the word jinn, which means "creatures that are not perceivable by the five senses of humans" have, in every century, found various ways to deceive humans and take them under their control. They are also known as the Satan.

The only way to protect oneself against their deception is through KNOWLEDGE!

98

THE "MAHDI"

Albeit for centuries certain hadiths regarding the "mahdi" (messiah) were construed incorrectly, unfortunately in modern times, they are still being misinterpreted as though we are awaiting *a messiah on a white horse with a sword in his hand* to descend from the heavens and miraculously change the governmental regimes, make the poor rich, and establish ultimate peace on earth.

Can such a powerful person really exist? If so, how can he take down Israel, who is supported by the USA, the hub of space technology? Can his magic sword really change the existing systems? Can he make Islam the ultimate regime on earth?

I'm not sure…!

Can such powers, which were not given to Muhammad (saw) the most beloved person to have ever come to Earth, be given to him?

I'm not sure…!

While the great majority of the societies hold worldly values higher than the values of the afterlife, don't really understand the realities of the afterlife and only engage in certain practices out of 'custom' and societal conditioning, I highly doubt the coming of *a mahdi on a white horse*!

Countless highly regarded saints and scholars in the past century have prophesized the coming of the Mahdi in the beginning of the century ahead of them, yet none of these prophecies have been fulfilled.

As a matter of fact, there are tell signs signaling it is not yet time, but somehow these are being overlooked.

The most common hadith regarding the Mahdi says while the Mahdi is on duty on Earth, Jesus (pbuh) will descend to the Earth. They will live together for some time. Meanwhile the Antichrist will appear and Jesus will kill him.

The hadith says, Jesus (pbuh) will return "While an imam *that is of you* is your leader…"

This suggests that at this time the majority will have accepted the religion of Islam and will be fulfilling its requisites.

Whereas there isn't such a population on Earth today in favor of an Islamic regime where the principles of Islam are practiced, hence a leader from amongst such a population cannot arrive.

The Rasul of Allah (saw) spent his life in pursuit of enabling the discernment of the truths and aiding people to prepare for and save their afterlives.

What is incumbent on us is to warn the people around us about life after death, to encourage them to take the necessary precautions, and share our knowledge in a way they understand.

I presume when the Mahdi arrives – and he *will* arrive, based on hadiths – his mission will be to warn the people against the dangers awaiting ahead. Since he will be created with an advanced capacity, he will be successful in his mission. During a pilgrimage season, they will want him to reveal himself, after which an army will be sent from the Middle East to remove him but the army will be plunged under the earth. This is what the hadiths tell us!

The laws of Allah will never change! Thus, there will be no supernatural activity that will bring chaos to the masses! Until this noble person arrives (whether from Indonesia, Pakistan, Arabia or some other country) to explain and clarify the principles and purpose of the religion of Islam, we have certain responsibilities!

If we die before the Mahdi arrives surely we can't say, "I was waiting for the Mahdi that's why I couldn't prepare"!

When his time comes the Mahdi will appear, accomplish his mission, and die!

But we are already here! And we don't know when we will die! Perhaps very soon!

So, let us ask ourselves:

Do I know the realities of the afterlife and am I ready for them?

If our answer is 'no' then our priority should not be to wait for the Mahdi but to prepare ourselves for our afterlife!

99

RELIGION IS NOT POLITICS

Misusing potential power to provoke the youth for the purpose of bringing down the governmental regimes and establishing an Islamic government...

Religion was not sent so that the people can establish sovereignty on Earth!

There is neither a government in the afterlife nor is there a place for governmental regimes!

Nobody will be called to account regarding the governmental regimes in the grave!!!

Religion is for the individual, not for a government!

And just because the governmental regime is not Islamic, one who dies with faith in Allah and His Rasul (saw) will not go to hell.

Islamic regime came to an end with after the four caliphates after which the regimes of the sovereignties began.

There is no room for dictatorship or sovereignty in the name of Islam!

The principles of Islam do not agree with civil-martial dictatorship!

Amongst the pillars of Islam there is no rule such as "If you don't change the governmental regimes and make them Islamic you will die as an unbeliever."

If one's faith was based on a governmental regime, there would have been no Muslims left on Earth after the four caliphates and no saints would have been raised since!

It is not governments that need to take precaution for the afterlife but the individuals!

It is those who have not grasped the real purpose of religion or who have been wrongly conditioned, that invest their energy into governments instead of focusing on the 'individual' who needs to be saved and fulfilling the necessary practices in this way.

If we had truly understood the purpose of Islam our attitudes would have been entirely different today. So then let us put our focus into understanding this purpose and align our behaviors accordingly.

And let us not forget there are hundreds of millions of Muslims living under countless different governmental regimes who will go to heaven regardless, provided they live according to the pillars of Islam and fulfill its requisites.

100

RELIGION IS FOR THE HERE AND NOW!

As for those who claim, "Religion is a matter of the afterlife, we'll deal with it once we get there" ...

My purpose in writing this book is to illustrate precisely how the whole point of religion is for *this worldly life.*

After death, there is absolutely **nothing** more one can do.

One who experiences death, and is no longer able to use his body, has lost all available options! He can no longer do anything that can provide any form of benefit to his future. He is forever stuck with whatever power, spiritual strength, etc. he was able accumulate until that point!

So, let's assume someone claims:

"I believe in Allah. I also believe in the Rasul of Allah. What they say is the truth. But let me work for my worldly life now, and after I die, I'll work for my life there. Everything has its place, the world for the world, and the afterlife for the afterlife. One needs a shelter in this world, and faith in the afterlife."

This person has neither a religion, nor faith! Nor has he accepted the Rasul of Allah (saw)!

For he has not understood a single word from the teachings of the Rasul!

Faith is necessary in **this world** so that one can accept it and follow the recommendations of the Rasul of Allah (saw).

You don't need faith in the afterlife! At that point everything is out in the open anyway! There is nothing to "believe" in, everything is exposed and openly seen!

Doubtless, if one has faith in the Rasul of Allah (saw) his behavior will inevitably change!

If someone you trust tells you, "If you keep going down this route you will encounter such and such dangers and eventually fall off a cliff, but if you take these precautions, you can save yourself from the dangerous abyss ahead" will it make any sense to say, *"I believe you but I'll follow your recommendations after I fall off the cliff"!!??*

Let me repeat:

The Rasul of Allah (saw) has seen the dangers awaiting us in the future with the permission of Allah, and has warned us to take certain precautions in order to be safe!

You either believe him and take his advice to protect yourself, or you take no heed and face the consequences!

In any case, there is nothing you can do after you die! This is why the Quran repeatedly and frequently reminds us:

> **'Oh, if only we can go back** (to our biological life on earth; as biological life is required to activate the forces within the brain) **and not deny the signs of our Rabb** (our intrinsic divine qualities and potential deriving from the Names that comprise our essential reality) **and be among the believers'.**[87]

But this is not possible!

You must take heed, understand the message of religion and follow its recommendations while in *this world*. Whether you do or not, the consequence is yours to face!

You will leave behind everything you own, your home, your savings, all your possessions, even your body, and start life anew…

Who wouldn't want to be prepared for this? Who would want to wake up to this new life with no preparation and in eternal remorse and suffering?

---

[87] Quran 6:27

To recap, the most primary message of the Rasul of Allah (saw) is, "Make the most of your current moment and prepare in the most optimum way with these recommendations, otherwise you will forever burn in regret!"

You can either choose to prepare for your afterlife while you are still here in this world, or be ready to suffer indefinitely!

The choice is yours…

> **"And Allah did not cause them to suffer, but it was they** (their constructed self, ego- identity) **who caused their own suffering."**[88]

101

ISLAM IS NOT OUTDATED; IT IS TIMELESS...

Another common misconception...

To think of religion as a set of rules put by the Rasul of Allah (saw) for the sole purpose of establishing peace and order among the people...

To think of religion as a social order!!!

Allah exists but He is a universal force. He is the infinite force that created the universe and everything within it. Nothing on earth is His concern. It means nothing to Him whether people go to hell or heaven. He does not talk to anyone.

The Nabis and Rasuls are geniuses who have come to bring peace and order to the people. They've established principles and laws based on the times to which they came. These laws address the primitive people of that age. Ablution, for example, came to the people who lived in the desert, so that they may keep clean among all the dust and dirt, and salat came to encourage them to move and to do gymnastics, while fasting came to prevent gluttonous and unhealthy lifestyle!

In short, yes Allah exists, but He has not sent any religion. Prophets brought about certain beneficial practices but none of these are valid today after 1400 years. Modern and civilized man can determine these for himself now...

And many other similar absurdities...

This picture is the sad outcome of being deprived of foresight, science, the ability to observe things from a wide lens and not knowing the reality of man.

They are those described as:

"They have brains; yet they do not think (contemplate)!"

The hardest thing in life is to force such primitive brains to think and cognize the truth!

These people must first become aware of the make-up of the universe.

Then, they must learn about the make-up of man, and its mechanics. Then the Earth, and its end. Then the outcome of a person who is addicted to the world. Then the formation of man's spirit, and the conditions of life without a body. After all of this, they must learn about the practices they must adopt to save their spirit.

Then they must understand the scientific background of the messages of the Rasul of Allah (saw) and finally how these truths are explained in the Quran though metaphors.

<u>To be able to explain all of this you must first learn it for yourself!</u>

I have tried, to the best of my ability, to outline the main topics in this book without going into too much detail. Surely there is so much more than what I have covered here. In the past, most of these truths were revealed through self-discovery and spiritual unveiling and explained with metaphors, due to the limitation of their time. With the grace and blessing of Allah I have been shown many realities, some of which there is no possibility for me to share as the level of knowledge and science is still very inadequate!

Allah willing, with scientific advancements in the future I may be able to explain them…

102

CONCLUSION

I started this book with the words "I have penned this book for brains that can think"...

I don't know if I was able to encourage you to think and contemplate throughout this book... But I'm sure you may have found some of the topics I shared controversial or contrary to your previous knowledge. Perhaps you are still denying or refusing to accept some of the things you've read here.

Put aside your denial just for a moment and think...

Put aside your conditioning and objectively evaluate the things you've read.

Contemplate!

If you were born and raised near The Ganges were you going to dive into and sanctify this river that is severely threatened by pollution and sewage in the name of the goddess Ganga? Or if you were born into an Algonquian group would you be dancing around a totem with an axe in your hand and leaves around your waste glorifying the Sacred Spirit of Manitou?

Good thing you're here today!

I have tried to explain the entire system of man in this book. The scope of this topic far surpasses the limits of a book, however, even this much I know, is going to weigh heavy on brains that are tired, foggy, and not accustomed to thinking outside its box.

In the past the enlightened ones said, "the entire world is just a dream"! The pantheistic thought based on the dark materialist approach of the 19th century is now beginning to disappear.

In the sight of a brain that contemplates, the universe has literally and scientifically shown itself to be an illusion. Yet such a dream that those stuck inside it are forever going to experience it as though it is real.

Religion, through Sufism has addressed all issues. Yet the masses who don't know what Sufism is about are deprived of this blessing! Some Western philosophers have taken bits and crumbs of these realities and have enthroned them, while sadly the Muslims are not even aware of the treasure they are sitting on!

Initially this book was going to be named 'Man and Sufism' however without knowledge on the world and the relationship between man and the world I did not find it appropriate to delve into the depths of Sufism. Rather, in this book I focused on the formation of man, the effects that influence him, and the future that is awaiting him. I aimed at emphasizing on the importance of the brain and tried to elucidate the importance of conceiving the religious laws not as arbitrary but as obligatory practices comprising the mechanism of the function of life!

If I have been able to show the difference between the concept of an external god beyond and 'Allah that is within your very existence', even to some extent, I would be sincerely grateful.

If I've been a cause for people to consider, research, debate about these topics and uplift them from the stale state of their simple daily activities to a higher level of contemplation and consciousness then I would consider myself blessed.

Ahmed Hulusi
17. 10. 1986
Istanbul

ABOUT THE AUTHOR

Ahmed Hulusi (Born January 21, 1945, Istanbul, Turkey) contemporary Islamic philosopher. From 1965 to this day he has written close to 30 books. His books are written based on Sufi wisdom and explain Islam through scientific principles. His established belief that the knowledge of Allah can only be properly shared without any expectation of return has led him to offer all of his works which include books, articles, and videos free of charge via his web-site. In 1970 he started examining the art of spirit evocation and linked these subjects parallel references in the Quran (smokeless flames and flames instilling pores). He found that these references were in fact pointing to luminous energy which led him to write *Spirit, Man, Jinn* while working as a journalist for the Aksam newspaper in Turkey. Published in 1985, his work called *The Human Enigma (Insan ve Sirlari)* was Hulusi's first foray into decoding the messages of the Quran filled with metaphors and examples through a scientific backdrop. In 1991 he published *The Power of Prayer (Dua and Zikir)* where he explains how the repetition of certain prayers and words can lead to the realization of the divine attributes inherent within our essence through increased brain capacity. In 2009 he completed his final work, '*Decoding the Quran, A Unique Sufi Interpretation*' which encompasses the understanding of leading Sufi scholars such as Abdulkarim al Jili, Abdul-Qadir Jilani, Muhyiddin Ibn al-Arabi, Imam Rabbani, Ahmed ar-Rifai, Imam Ghazali, and Razi, and which approached the messages of the Quran through the secret Key of the letter 'B'.

NOTES

Printed in Great Britain
by Amazon

83021392R00222